Coffee Culture, Destinations and Tourism

D1345383

TOURISM AND CULTURAL CHANGE
Series Editors: Professor Mike Robinson, *Centre for Tourism and Cultural Change, Leeds Metropolitan University, Leeds, UK* and Dr Alison Phipps, *University of Glasgow, Scotland, UK*

Understanding tourism's relationships with culture(s) and vice versa, is of ever-increasing significance in a globalising world. This series will critically examine the dynamic inter-relationships between tourism and culture(s). Theoretical explorations, research-informed analyses, and detailed historical reviews from a variety of disciplinary perspectives are invited to consider such relationships.

Full details of all the books in this series and of all our other publications can be found on http://www.channelviewpublications.com, or by writing to Channel View Publications, St Nicholas House, 31-34 High Street, Bristol BS1 2AW, UK.

TOURISM AND CULTURAL CHANGE
Series Editors: Professor Mike Robinson, *Centre for Tourism and Cultural Change, Leeds Metropolitan University, Leeds, UK* and Dr Alison Phipps, *University of Glasgow, Scotland, UK*

Coffee Culture, Destinations and Tourism

Edited by
Lee Jolliffe

CHANNEL VIEW PUBLICATIONS
Bristol • Buffalo • Toronto

Library of Congress Cataloging in Publication Data
A catalog record for this book is available from the Library of Congress.
Coffee Culture, Destinations and Tourism/Edited by Lee Jolliffe.
Tourism and Cultural Change.
Includes bibliographical references and index.
1. Coffee–Social aspects. 2. Coffee industry–Social aspects. 3. Coffee industry–Economic aspects. 4. Culture and tourism. 5. Heritage tourism. I. Jolliffe, Lee. II. Title. III. Series.
GT2918.C64 2010
306.4'819–dc22 2010005008

British Library Cataloguing in Publication Data
A catalogue entry for this book is available from the British Library.

ISBN-13: 978-1-84541-143-5 (hbk)
ISBN-13: 978-1-84541-142-8 (pbk)

Channel View Publications
UK: St Nicholas House, 31-34 High Street, Bristol BS1 2AW, UK.
USA: UTP, 2250 Military Road, Tonawanda, NY 14150, USA.
Canada: UTP, 5201 Dufferin Street, North York, Ontario M3H 5T8, Canada.

The policy of Multilingual Matters/Channel View Publications is to use papers that are natural, renewable and recyclable products, made from wood grown in sustainable forests. In the manufacturing process of our books, and to further support our policy, preference is given to printers that have FSC and PEFC Chain of Custody certification. The FSC and/or PEFC logos will appear on those books where full certification has been granted to the printer concerned.

Typeset by Datapage International Ltd.
Printed and bound in Great Britain by Short Run Press Ltd.

Contents

Acknowledgments

This book has been compiled as a companion to my edited book, *Tea and Tourism, Tourists, Traditions and Transformations* (2007). After researching tea and tourism, a logical step was to diversify into examining coffee in relation to tourism. As with the 'tea book', this is a book written by researchers who are interested in culture, heritage and tourism related to a popularly consumed beverage, in this case coffee, from both an academic and practitioner perspective. I hope that this book will open up possibilities for both theoretical and applied research on the various aspects of coffee in relation to culture, hospitality, tourism and development.

I would like to acknowledge the individuals and organizations that made this book possible. On a personal level, I am grateful for the continued support of my family. During my 2007 sabbatical, I had a welcome home at Hanoi University where my Vietnamese colleague, Huong Thanh Bui (now at Griffith University, Australia), actively participated in my coffee tourism research in Vietnam. Also at Hanoi University, Hang Nuygen, Giang Khong Yen and Huong Do assisted in surveying international tourists in Hanoi. In New Brunswick, Karen Kwan (now at Hong Kong Polytechnic University, China) analyzed the survey data collected in Vietnam. Funding for field work in Vietnam was provided by the University of New Brunswick. My son, Christian Tschirhart, hosted me during visits to Leipzig, Germany, introducing me to the historic Coffee Baum and many other fine cafés in both Leipzig and Berlin. TTRA Canada Chapter conferences and the Second International Conference on Hospitality and Tourism (Universita Utari and National Heritage Department) in Malaysia (2007) provided friendly venues for the presentation of some early thoughts on the subject of coffee and tourism through papers on the possibilities of coffee tourism in Vietnam (TTRA Canada 2004 and 2008) and on proposing a research agenda for coffee tourism (Malaysia 2007).

I am grateful to Channel View Publications; Mike Robinson, Series Editor, and staff members Sarah Williams and Elinor Robertson, who welcomed the idea of a book on coffee and tourism. I appreciate the participation of colleagues around the world who have taken up the cause of investigating, reporting and analyzing the various aspects of the relationship of coffee to tourism, making this an international investigation of the relationship of our daily cup of coffee to culture, travel and tourism experiences as well as to the lives of the farmers who produce our coffee. A very special note of thanks goes to consultants Harro Boekhold, Contour Projects Ltd., Tanzania, and Bob Harvey and Diane Kelsay, Egret Communications, USA, for their willingness to participate in an academic book, making this a more complete investigation of the potential for coffee tourism projects to improve the livelihoods of coffee farmers.

Contributors

Harro Boekhold, Contour Projects Ltd., Tanzania

Nancy Chesworth, Mount Saint Vincent University, Canada

Evi Eftychiou, University of Nicosia, Cyprus

Warwick Frost, La Trobe University, Australia

Harold Goodwin, Leeds Metropolitan University, England

C. Michael Hall, University of Canterbury, New Zealand

Bob Harvey, Egret Communications, USA

Charles Johnston, Auckland University of Technology, New Zealand

Giang Khong Yen, Hanoi University, Vietnam

Karen Kwan, Hong Kong Polytechnic University, China

Lee Jolliffe, University of New Brunswick, Canada

Diane Kelsay, Egret Communications, USA

Jennifer Laing, Monash University, Australia

Nicos Philippou, University of Nicosia, Cyprus

Rochelle Reddy, University of Canterbury, New Zealand

Keir Reeves, University of Melbourne, Australia

Karina Rowling, University of Canterbury, New Zealand

Wendy S. Shaw, University of New South Wales, Australia

Janna Tipler, University of Canterbury, New Zealand

Adam Weaver, Victoria University of Wellington, New Zealand

Fiona Wheeler, Monash University, Australia

Leanne White, Victoria University, Australia

Part 1

Introduction

Chapter 1
Common Grounds of Coffee and Tourism

LEE JOLLIFFE

As we live, work and travel around the world, it is obvious that coffee is inextricably connected with our everyday lives. If we are coffee drinkers, we grind beans on waking for a ceremonial cup to welcome the day, pick up a coffee enroute to work and later meet friends for coffee at a café. According to Boé (2000), coffee is drunk for pleasure, for cultural reasons or out of habit. Even if we are not coffee drinkers, it is difficult not to be embraced by the social space of the café (Boniface, 2003) as we consume other beverages, be it at an independent café or at a city center or airport Starbucks (Clark, 2007). During travel, we may serendipitously come into contact with coffee culture, such as the pioneering café culture of Seattle in the USA, the historical café culture of Leipzig, Germany, or café trends in Hanoi, Vietnam. Many travelers seek out the café as a social place to relax and socialize while enjoying coffee. Other travelers visit locations where coffee is produced and participate in the coffee harvest (Ewing, 2006).

Coffee has a long history. Originating in Ethiopia in the Horn of Africa, the cultivation of the wild plant 'coffea Arabica' may have begun as early as the 6th century. While there are many myths about coffee discovery, according to Tannahill (1988) the first written reference is attributed to a 10th-century Arab physician. The first coffee house was established in Constantinople in 1534 (Tannahill, 1988). However, it was not until the 17th and 18th centuries that coffee moved from a novel to a popular drink (Cowan, 2005). In both London and Paris, coffee houses became centers for coffee consumption and discussion (Shapira et al., 1975). Civitello (2005) refers to the emergence of these coffee houses as public meeting places changing social and political habits. While the coffee house in England did not endure because of the rise of tea, these establishments are nonetheless seen as reflective of the rise of a more democratic and modern society (Cowan, 2005).

Plate 1.1 Coffee Baum, Leipzig, Germany (Source: Lee Jolliffe)

In the 18th century in Leipzig, Germany, close ties between the coffee houses, the mercantile class and trade fairs encouraged the creation of music and the exchange of ideas (Schwalbach, n.d.). Between 1731 and 1734, Bach wrote his Coffee Cantano, a comic opera about addiction to coffee, at the Coffee Baum (Plate 1.1). During Bach's time in Leipzig (1725–1750), patrons enjoyed coffee and played games and live music at Richter's outdoor coffee garden. In Vienna, café culture is acknowledged as having played a critical part in a vibrant intellectual and artistic activity at the beginning of the 20th century. In Paris, such café culture is acknowledged to have contributed to modernity (Habermas, 1989).

As the drinking of coffee became popular, countries formed their own rituals around coffee, each region's coffee taste acknowledged as being related to its history, work habits and style (Calvert & Stacey, 1994). In the USA, the boycott of tea resulting from the revolt against the tea tax imposed by the British (the Boston Tea Party of 1773) established coffee as the traditional distinctive drink of the country (Perry, 2001). Countries adopted coffee as part of their national identity, as with the coffee-producing country of Colombia that has marketed itself as a producer of

Figure 1.1 Logo of The National Federation of Coffee Growers, Colombia (Source: The National Federation of Coffee Growers of Columbia)

fine coffee (Kummer, 1997) with their logo showing Juan Valdez and his mule climbing the mountain. The National Federation of Coffee Growers logo is now used by distributors around the world to certify that the coffee is 100% Colombian (Figure 1.1).

Coffee as part of food and beverage tourism is a cultural experience (Boniface, 2003). Different coffee traditions lend themselves to culinary tourism, and locations with unique forms of coffee production and heritage may use this in destination branding. Coffee is experienced through travel and besides collecting coffee experiences, travelers may collect objects related to coffee as souvenirs (Timothy, 2005) or may purchase coffee beans as a souvenir (Berger, 2005).

Defining Coffee

Coffee begins as the seeds of the berry or fruit of the coffee tree, a tropical shrub of the genus *Coffea* (Canadian Oxford Dictionary, 2004).

Coffee as a drink is made from the roasted and ground seeds. Coffee cultivation requires a frost-free climate with moderate rainfall and adequate sunshine; the tropical regions where coffee grows are known as 'origin regions' (Knox & Huffaker, 1997). Most coffee is grown within a broad geographic band bordered by the Tropic of Cancer to the north and the Tropic of Capricorn to the south (Calvert & Stacey, 1994). There are two main species, *Coffea arabica*, known as Arabica coffee and *Coffea canephora*, known as Robusta coffee. Robusta is grown at lower altitudes than Arabica. Robusta is generally used for blending instant coffee as it is of lower quality than Arabica, which is used for specialty coffee (Castle, 1991).

Some of the major producing countries are listed in Table 1.1. Each country produces coffee of different types, utilizing different farming systems that range from farmers with smallholdings to large corporate plantations.

In many countries, coffee berries are collected for processing from small farmers by cooperatives or associations. According to Davids (2001), coffee is processed by versions of either a dry or wet method. In the dry method, the oldest of the processing methods, coffee is picked and left out in the sun to dry. Periodically raked, it can take from ten days to three weeks to dry. In the wet method, the fruit covering the bean is stripped, the fruit is then fermented and washed and then further fermented (by a wet or dry method). After this step, the coffee is washed and dried, either by the sun or by mechanical means. After processing, coffee is often shipped off as green beans to be roasted in the importing country.

Coffee was traditionally sold at coffee auctions, a system gradually replaced by commodities markets, in which coffee is purchased before it is grown. Consequently, coffee as a commodity has an associated industry behind it that includes farmers, cooperatives, processors, brokers and coffee industry associations. The farmers who cultivate coffee around the world are only the first to be involved in the long journey of coffee from the bean to the cup.

Coffee and Hospitality

Coffee is directly connected to hospitality, in home and commercial hospitality settings. At home, like tea (Jolliffe, 2004), coffee may be offered as a sign of hospitality. Likewise in commercial settings, coffee is on the menu as an accompaniment to a restaurant meal, or in café settings coffee is viewed as the main attraction. Coffee culture inspires the design of café settings (Bellamy, 1997). Coffee is associated with

Table 1.1 Sample of coffee-growing countries by region

Region	Country	Profile
The Americas	Brazil	Arabica (80%) and Robusta (20%) grown mostly on small coffee farms
	Columbia	Arabica coffee grown on modern plantations or small traditionally run farms
	Costa Rica	Arabica coffee grown on family-owned farms where many export directly
	Guatemala	Fine quality Arabica beans grown by small producers and marketed by coffee cooperatives
	Hawai'i	Arabica grown on small family-operated coffee farms
Africa and Middle East	Ethiopia	Arabica grown by all forms of cultivation – from wild trees to partially developed plots to smallholders to plantations
	Kenya	Arabica grown by smallholders and/or large plantations
	Yemen	Arabica grown on very small family-run farms
The Pacific	Java	Robusta produced mostly by small farmers and cooperatives
	Papua New Guinea	Much of the Arabica grown by smallholders on native farms
Asia	Indonesia	Most Robusta (90%) produced on small plantations
	Vietnam	Robusta produced on small farms with some state large plantations. Limited Arabica grown

Source: http://www.coffeeresearch.org/; Perry (2001); Thorn (2006)

various forms of food service outlets, such as coffee houses, coffee shops, coffee bars and cafés. Each of these types of establishments has differing levels of informality (Boniface, 2003) in settings where coffee and food are served.

For hospitality operators, coffee may represent a profitable aspect of their business. Coffee has become an industry trend with operators adopting particular blends of coffee beans that act as a signature for their operations. Companies such as the global company Starbucks (Clark, 2007) have transformed both coffee and traditional café culture by branding distinctive café ambience and coffee experiences.

A recent boom in coffee drinking is acknowledged to have led to an increased number of franchised coffee houses, such as Starbucks, Costa Coffee and Caffè Nero (Laurier *et al.*, 2001). The former researchers investigated the social life of the café, in profiling the Flaming Cup Café as a place of informality and social equality as patrons share tables and, if they wish, interact in an adult setting.

Going for coffee involves more than just consuming the beverage itself, it is a small social event as part of everyday life. Informal gatherings focusing on drinking coffee as common ground for interaction include coffee hours, coffee mornings and the coffee klatch, the latter combining coffee with conversation. In Canada, the vernacular includes a coffee row, a regular gathering of people at a café for coffee and conversation, especially in rural areas (Canadian Oxford Dictionary, 2004). The Canadian coffee and donut chain, Tim Hortons, encouraged the institutionalization of the coffee break, a social break from work accompanied by coffee (Penfold, 2008). In the UK, the colloquial speech includes a coffee morning, defined as a morning gathering at which coffee is served, often in aid of charity (Oxford English Reference Dictionary, 2002).

Around the world, cafés have thus evolved as social meeting places with a distinctive ambience, or third places for meeting away from home and work (Boniface, 2003). They are seen as a place to relax, discuss, socialize and study (Davids, 2001). Coffee is referred to as 'the drink of the present' by Walker (2004) and as a 'hip' beverage by Thorn (2006), indicating that a background of history and modern marketing makes it an attractive product for modern consumers.

Coffee and Tourism Experiences

Coffee and tourism collide where coffee consumption becomes a hospitality product and where tourism activities relate to experiencing aspects of the history and production of coffee. Coffee tourism can thus be part of cultural and culinary tourism initiatives. If seen as a niche area of tourism (Novelli, 2005), it would be a very small sector, appealing to 'coffee enthusiasts'. However, viewed as part of the overall tourism experience, coffee can be an integral part of the travel journey and can form a routine or special part of the experience once at the destination.

Coffee tourism is defined as being related to the consumption of the coffee, history, traditions, products and culture of a destination (Jolliffe & Bui, 2006).

Interest in coffee can be peaked by artifacts representing the inquiry, such as the souvenir jute shopping bag from Costa Rica's Doka Estate that proclaims (in Spanish) 'three generations of coffee' and 'fabulous French roasted Costa Rica Coffee', and the shopping bag from Maine's Carpe Diem Coffee Roasting Company with the quote 'Coffee should be black as Hell, strong as death, and sweet as love', attributed to a Turkish proverb. Shopping adds value to the tourism experience (Westwood, 2006) and single origin specialty coffee beans can be a souvenir.

Since coffee experiences are a familiar part of everyday life, as with culinary experiences described by Long (1994), these encounters are not usually perceived of as being exotic or out of the ordinary. However, when we travel, out of habit seeking out a local café may be an introduction to the local culture and its coffee traditions. We thus come into contact with a beverage that is familiar, yet through its different cultural and hospitality contexts provides a distinctive experience. In these encounters, we are participants in culinary tourism, described by Molz (2007) as the intersection between food and travel. For example, the coffee and donut chain, Tim Hortons, noted as a ubiquitous part of the Canadian foodscape (Penfold, 2008), provides a familiar experience for Canadians and a unique experience for visitors. However, culinary tourism as branded in Canada is not noted to include coffee (Hashimoto & Telfer, 2006). Evolving coffee traditions around the world are subject to change as part of globalization, for example the international coffee company Starbucks has influenced global coffee culture (Clark, 2007) and many cafés around the world compete, as in this picture of café signage from Daegu, South Korea (Plate 1.2).

Coffee rituals are reflected in the coffee paraphernalia that Davids (2001) describes as being used to transport coffee from the pot to the palate. This includes a variety of cups, pots and coffee-making machines. The history and material culture associated with coffee can be experienced at coffee museums around the world. In Leipzig, Germany, besides a lively contemporary café culture, the city houses the historic Coffee Baum, a restaurant, café and museum complex, known as one of the oldest coffee houses in the world. Some coffee companies have established their own museums, such as Café Chicco D'Oro's 'World of Coffee Museum' in Switzerland, established to tell the history of the produce, to illustrate its economic importance and to document

Plate 1.2 Coffee chain signage, Daegu, South Korea (Source: Lee Jolliffe)

the value of this well-loved beverage (http://www.chiccodoro.ch). In Zurich, the Johan Jacobs Museum documents aspects of coffee in terms of art, commerce and culture of the beverage through its collection of paintings and print, silver and ceramics. The collection includes 2000 historical postcards of Viennese cafés in various European cities. Another cultural aspect to be considered is the 'art of coffee'. Just as the preparation of food in the form of gastronomy is proposed as a fine art, so too can coffee be expressed through coffee preparation, as with latte art and barista competitions around the world, e.g. the Barista cup title in the USA (Bellamy, 1997).

Coffee as a contemporary product is inextricably linked to place and consumers are able to drink coffee from individual countries of origin whose properties can be distinguished by taste, although blended coffee had been the norm (Thorn, 2006). Specialty coffee from single estates or regions has become popular; as Molz (2007) remarks, food acts as a transportable system of place and identity. With the rise in popularity of specialty coffees exposing consumers to more interesting brews, Thorn (2006) observes that with roasting and blending styles varying around the world, tasting coffee at home or as we travel can be a culinary experience.

Table 1.2 Types of coffee destinations

Type 1	Coffee-producing destination
Type 2	Coffee culture destination
Type 3	Coffee history destination

Three basic types of coffee destinations can be identified (Table 1.2). First, coffee-producing countries have distinct locations that could be considered as 'coffee-producing destinations', e.g. Colombia, where 'coffee finca tourism', opening up coffee farms to visitors is acknowledged to have been around since the 1990s (Ewing, 2006). Second, locations where significant café cultures have emerged could be 'coffee culture destinations', e.g. the café district of Seattle where Starbucks established their first café. Third, particular locales associated with the history of the production, sale and consumption of coffee can be considered 'coffee history destinations'. London, UK, the location of the early coffee auctions, is an example of a coffee history destination, evidenced by the exhibits housed at the Bramah Tea and Coffee Museum in London.

As destinations look for ways to differentiate themselves from others, culinary aspects are highlighted, with food and drink being seen as a significant attraction (Boniface, 2003; Hjalager & Richards, 2002). This also applies to coffee-producing destinations, as studied in the case of Buon Ma Thuot, Vietnam (Jolliffe & Bui, 2009). At many destinations, coffee is associated with the café as a meeting point for arts and discussion; when cafés are clustered, café districts have evolved and some locations have introduced coffee festivals as a means to promote their coffee production or consumption.

Gradually, the idea of branding a coffee destination is emerging as is evidenced by field work in the Central Highlands of Vietnam (Jolliffe *et al.*, 2009). Coffee farm tours, trails and routes are emerging as the foci of tourism activities in a number of the countries where coffee is produced, such as in Costa Rica where producer Café Brit diversified their income from coffee by developing a farm tour with associated visitor services (Brennes *et al.*, 1997). At Café Brit, tourism was employed to open up export markets for the company.

The Attraction of Coffee Tourism

Traveling to coffee-producing countries provides opportunities to experience coffee at its origins by visiting coffee farms, coffee-processing facilities and even cafés overlooking coffee plantations, or exploring the origins of coffee through organized coffee tours or trails (Batten, 2007). Coffee prepared at its origin may not taste the same as that consumed at home, but the experience of observing the harvesting and production can be a highlight for many visitors. This can involve staying in coffee-related accommodations, e.g. hotels overlooking coffee plantations. In these settings, coffee is often incorporated into the menu. For example, an article in a UK newspaper, *The Independent* (2007), notes that on the island of Mauritius,

> Guests of the five-star Beau Rivage hotel can tour the plantation and then head back to the hotel to try its special coffee-tasting menu.

The article lists a number of other locations (Table 1.3) where travelers can experience various aspects of coffee.

Examples of other resources for coffee tourism are listed in Table 1.4. These include operating coffee farms around the world, established coffee attractions and historic coffee houses and cafés are still in operation and can be visited by tourists. Globally, the number of contemporary café outlets is increasing. The Specialty Coffee Association predicted that by 2000 more than 2500 coffee cafés and espresso bars would have opened across the USA (Bellamy, 1997). New forms of attractions incorporating coffee are emerging. Coffee bars or cafés are being combined with other types of retail outlets. In Toronto, Canada, The Bloc Garden Centre, Floral Studio and Art Market opened in the Art and Design District in 2009. The complex includes The Garden Café serving organic fair trade coffee and occasional events include 'Fair Trade Coffee Tastings'.

Table 1.3 Coffee experience settings

Location	*Establishment*	*Experience*
Moreeba, North Queensland, Australia	Australian Coffee Centre	Interpretive center on a farm
Jamaica	Old Tavern Estate	Coffee farm tours
Central Java, Indonesia	Losari Coffee Plantation Resort and Spa	Resort in plantation setting with tours
Arusha, Tanzania	Arusha Coffee Lodge	Hotel on a working coffee plantation with tours of functioning plantation

Source: Batten (2007)

Table 1.4 Examples of resources for coffee tourism

Resource	Example
Coffee farms	In Hawai'i, 11 regions on five islands house 830 farms state wide (Steinner, 2009)
Coffee attractions	In Hawai'i, the Kona Coffee Living History Farm, operated by the Kona Historical Society is exhibiting 'The Kona Coffee Story: Along the Hawai'i Belt Road' (http://www.konahistorical.org)
Coffee parks	In Colombia, Paqu Naccionale Café, a coffee theme park, is dedicated to the coffee culture of its region
Historic coffee houses and cafés	Le Procope, Paris (1686) Coffee Baum, Leipzig, Germany (1694) Floria, Venice, Italy (1720) Café Landtmann, Vienna, Austria (1873) Les Deaux Magots, Paris, France (1914)
Coffee tour routes	Columbia's 'Rutas Cafeteras' where visitors can stay at haciendas in an area where coffee is grown (Mesalles, 2000)
Coffee festivals	Kona Coffee Cultural Festival is Hawai'i's oldest food festival (http://www.konacoffeefest.com/)

Resources for developing coffee tourism and the emerging products noted give some idea of the possible extent of such tourism. With coffee produced in over 60 countries around the world and consumed world-wide, the potential is enormous.

Coffee Tourism and Sustainable Tourism Development

Who produces the coffee is an important factor, for the return on coffee farming does not always provide an adequate living for the producer. The International Coffee Organization (2008) notes the global importance of coffee as a livelihood for producers:

Coffee is one of the world's largest traded commodities produced in more than 60 countries, providing a livelihood for some 25,000,000 coffee farming families around the world. Many of these countries are heavily dependent on coffee, which can account for over 75% of their total export earnings.

Historically, a number of countries (such as Brazil, Colombia and Costa Rica) have relied on coffee as their single export crop, as Tannahill (1988) observes, with a profound effect on social and political conditions as well as on local land, labor and capital. Bacon *et al.* (2008) discuss the implications of the global coffee crisis on small-scale coffee producers in Mexico and Central America due to severely depressed coffee markets since 1999. This crisis has threatened the livelihood of these producers and differentiated coffee markets (Jaffe, 2007) are one option for improving livelihoods. Another option is tourism initiatives that can address some of the issues generated by the crisis, especially for farmers in third world countries.

Through drinking coffee, we are linked to the cycle of coffee production in faraway lands, as well as to its marketing and consumption. Some long-producing countries are easily identified with coffee (such as Brazil and Columbia), while others who are relative newcomers (such as Vietnam) are not so easily identified. The cheaper Robusta from some countries (such as Indonesia) is typically blended with Arabica from other countries (such as Brazil), to achieve a balanced taste and reduce the price of the blend. In his article on the latte revolution, Ponte (2002) notes the contradiction between the rise of specialty coffee and the remuneration paid to producers. This reflects a growing awareness of the situation of disadvantaged coffee farmers around the world who produce coffee, often for little financial return.

Addressing inequalities in the remuneration to coffee growers are a growing number of fair trade and pro-poor and community tourism initiatives aimed at improving the lives and livelihoods of coffee farmers in producing countries. The exploitation of the coffee farmers who are often smallholders is part of the dark side of coffee history and business (Wild, 2005) and these projects address some of the historical and contemporary inequalities. In developing countries where coffee is produced, coffee-related tourism clearly has potential as an instrument of social change in the form of sustainable development projects.

Research Framework

Gradually, as these many threads and thoughts about the linkages between coffee and tourism have been woven together, the idea for a book that links coffee and tourism emerged and evolved into the present volume. Other tourism researchers and practitioners, all of whom are experiencing and researching coffee and tourism from diversely different personal and academic perspectives than my own have joined in contributing to the volume. The pursuit is interdisciplinary, drawing on approaches from various academic areas including tourism, fair trade, material culture studies, culinary history, geography, anthropology and sociology.

Existing studies of coffee range from investigations into health benefits, to studies of cultivation, production and marketing, to studies of the habits of coffee drinkers. The history of coffee provides a background for the enquiry, drawing for example from Ukers (1948) classic work, *The Romance of Coffee*. Shapira *et al.* (1975) note that coffee is a commodity and it can thus be studied in terms of trade. Information on the commerce and marketing of coffee, e.g. from The International Coffee Association, is relevant. A well-studied area is that of the culture of coffee houses (see, e.g. Cowan, 2005). Travel has contributed to coffee culture dissemination, spreading coffee-related traditions. Coffee as a beverage is a part of many tourism trips, consumed, experienced, appreciated and, in some cases, studied, as with visits to coffee museums and interpretative centers. However, there have been few studies of coffee in relation to travel and tourism, and this book aims to fill this literature gap.

Researching coffee, contributors drew on existing documentary information, but also used participant observation, taking notes on their own experiences in a variety of situations. This research may have been carried out on home ground or by traveling to coffee-producing locations. The inquiry draws on the editor's previous experience researching the relationship of coffee and tourism (Jolliffe & Bui, 2006; Jolliffe, 2007; Jolliffe *et al.*, 2009; Jolliffe & Kwan, 2008), exploring the nature of coffee tourism, coffee festival and destination development and interests in coffee-related tourism.

There are practical limitations to this investigation, as coffee is grown in over 60 countries around the world we only investigate coffee experiences in a limited number of countries, e.g. from Africa (Tanzania), Central America (Costa Rica), Asia (Vietnam) and the Pacific Rim (Vietnam, Papua New Guinea, Australia, New Zealand). As every country has its own café culture, we only investigate this culture in a limited number of locations, including New Zealand, Australia and Cyprus. Development projects linking coffee and tourism are emerging around the world and we profile several initiatives linking tourists from Canada, the USA and Europe with projects in Mexico, Costa Rica and Tanzania. Therefore, the book does not claim to be inclusive on the subject of coffee culture, destinations and tourism, but rather it purports to be a beginning with scope for research and enquiry beyond this volume.

Organization of the Book

The common grounds of the book, woven through the chapters, are found in the places where coffee is produced and consumed. In the first section, this introductory chapter provides a framework for what follows, defining coffee and coffee tourism, examining the relationship of coffee to hospitality, discussing the experience of coffee at its origins and identifying the association of coffee to development.

The second section, Coffee Culture and Tourism Contexts, explores and illustrates café environments as social places where coffee is consumed, providing insights into understanding these places and their role in coffee-related hospitality and tourism. The first two chapters examine the development of café culture in New Zealand. In Chapter 2, Hall, Tipler, Reddy and Rowling explore the design of café culture in New Zealand, focusing on 19 cafés in Christchurch. The study found that the café type had an impact on how customers judged the café and its service, and that table layout was significant as it enables social interaction. Regardless of the differences between the cafés studied, it is concluded that the physical design of the environment, referred to as servicescapes, is integral to the coffee experience. The authors further postulate that the extent to which the café will maintain its traditional third-space role will depend on design elements being matched with the coffee consumer. In Chapter 3, Weaver examines the café culture of Wellington, New Zealand, in relation to urban experiences. In this city, cafés have become a central component of destination image. Findings indicate that the emergence of café culture here is consistent with urban development and gentrification and that beyond coffee the central activity of cafés is talk and sociability. It is observed that cafés here act as locations for tourists to exchange experiences. White, in Chapter 4, examines coffee as an event, using semiotics – the philosophical theory of signs and symbols – to explore events ranging from the informal get-together at a local café, such as those profiled by Hall *et al.* in Chapter 2 and Weaver in Chapter 3, to the large coffee events sponsored by The International Coffee Organization. White also investigates the material culture of coffee-making paraphernalia that accompanies the home coffee event ritual. In Chapter 5, Eftychiou and Philippou trace the evolution of the *kafeneion* (traditional Cypriot coffee house) and its current embodiment as traditionalized coffee houses developed to evoke traditional and rurality for tourism purposes. This chapter demonstrates how contemporary political and social forces influence commodification of the coffee-house form, a trend worthy of study in other countries, as with the *kapitiam*, the Malaysian traditional coffee house.

The third part of the book, Coffee Destination Experiences, concentrates on destination experience and development. Jolliffe, Kwan and Yen, in Chapter 6, report on international tourist experiences of coffee in Vietnam. In this major coffee-producing country, coffee-related tourism is emerging and international tourists surveyed in Hanoi are interested in potential coffee tourism products, such as café culture tours of Hanoi's historic Old Quarter. In Chapter 7, Frost, Laing, Wheeler and Reeves examine the coffee culture and heritage relationship to destination image in Melbourne, Australia, profiling the strength of the independent and diverse café culture here. Johnston, in Chapter 8, traces the development of Kona, Hawai'i, one of the world's top coffee-producing locations, outlining the historical and contemporary relationship of coffee and tourism here. The author notes that Kona will never be a coffee destination, but that coffee tourism has offered a value-added diversification for coffee growers, positioned as lending a helping hand to the coffee farmers as they strive to survive in a niche coffee market. In Chapter 9, Shaw takes an anthropological view to narrating serendipitous coffee experiences of researchers working the coffee-growing highlands of Papua New Guinea. The priority here is not dedicated coffee tourism in the normal sense, the author sees less formal forms of coffee tourism prevailing in the short term, but if coffee production expands, related coffee business tourism may develop to some extent. All these chapters reveal the experiences of coffee-related destinations from the differing perspectives of visitors and researchers, tourism related to coffee being positioned differently in each destination.

The fourth part of the book, Responsible Coffee Tourism and Cultural Change, outlines coffee tourism projects in producing countries as forms of pro-poor or community tourism with poverty alleviation objectives, demonstrating how coffee tourism can be an agent of cultural change. Responsible coffee tourism approaches are examined within a number of chapters. In Chapter 10, Hall introduces the blending of coffee and fair trade hospitality in cafés in New Zealand and outlines how fair trade coffee has been mainstreamed through café activities. Notably, according to Hall, this is one of the first studies to examine the reasons that cafés have adopted the fair trade product. In Chapter 11, Chesworth reports on the evolution of Canada's first fair trade coffee cooperative, from importing and retailing to a number of social justice activities, including the beginnings of small-scale coffee tourism, linking Canadian customers with coffee-producing cooperatives in Central America. Goodwin and

Boekhold, in Chapter 12, further develop and illustrate the responsible coffee tourism theme with their detailed report on how coffee tourism has been implemented to improve the livelihoods of farmers producing coffee in the foothills of Mount Kilimanjaro, Tanzania. As a case study, this illustrative chapter could be the model for such development elsewhere. In Chapter 13, Harvey and Kelsay document the impact of the global coffee crisis on farming communities in Central America and outline the response in the form of the La Ruta Del Café Sustainable Community Tourism Project, demonstrating the power of coffee communities working together, within and beyond national borders. This chapter has a regional reach in Latin America, spanning coffee-growing regions from Mexico to Panama. The La Ruta del Café project is evolving and with the authors participating as development consultants, a coffee lodge project is being implemented in Costa Rica as a demonstration tourism project aimed at diversifying coffee revenues and improving the livelihood of coffee farmers affected by the global coffee crisis.

The fifth and final part of the book consists of a final chapter by Jolliffe that discusses coffee-related tourism, drawing lessons from the preceding chapters and discussing areas for further research.

References

Bacon, C.M., Mendez, V.E., Gliessman, S.R., Goodman, D. and Fox, J.A. (2008) *Confronting the Coffee Crisis: Fair Trade, Sustainable Livelihoods and Ecosystems in Mexico and Central America*. Cambridge, MA: MIT Press.

Batten, R. (2007) *The Complete Guide To: The Coffee Trail. The Independent*, 17 February.

Bellamy, B. (1997) Coffee time. *Restaurant Hospitality*, February, 112–113.

Berger, A.A. (2005) *Vietnam Tourism*. New York: Haworth Press.

Boé, P. (2001) *Coffee*. London: Cassell and Company.

Boniface, P. (2003) *Tasting Tourism: Travelling for Food and Drink*. Aldershot: Ashgate.

Brennes, E.R., Bola, I., Burciaga, R., Jimeno, M. and Salas, F. (1997) Café Brit S.A. *Journal of Business Research* 38 (1), 23–33.

Calvert, C. and Stacey, J. (1994) *Coffee, the Essential Guide to the Essential Bean*. New York: Smallwood and Stewart Inc.

Canadian Oxford Dictionary (2004) Don Mills, Ontario: Oxford University Press Canada.

Castle, T.J. (1991) *The Perfect Cup: A Coffee-Lover's Guide to Buying, Brewing, and Tasting*. Reading, MA: Aris Books.

Clark, T. (2007) *Starbucked: A Double Tall Tale of Caffeine, Commerce and Culture*. New York: Little Brown and Company.

Coffee Research.org. On WWW at http://www.coffeeresearch.org/. Accessed July 16.7.09.

Cowan, B.W. (2005) *Social Life of Coffee: The Emergence of the British Coffeehouse.* New Haven, CT: Yale University Press.

Davids, K. (1979) *Coffee: A Guide to Brewing and Enjoying Coffee.* San Francisco, CA: 101 Productions.

English Reference Dictionary (2002) Oxford: Oxford University Press.

Ewing, E. (2006) Café Culture. *The Guardian,* London, 3 October.

Habermas, J. (1989) *The Structural Transformation of Public Space: An Enquiry into a Category of Bourgeois Society.* Oxford: Polity Press.

Hashimoto, A. and Telfer, D. (2006) Selling Canadian culinary tourism: Branding the global and local product. *Tourism Geographies* 8 (1), 31–55.

Hjalager, A. and Richards, G. (eds) (2002) *Tourism and Gastronomy.* London: Routledge.

International Coffee Organization (2008) On WWW at http://www.ico.org. Accessed 30.6.08.

Jaffe, D. (2007) *Brewing Justice: Fair Trade Coffee, Sustainability and Survival.* Berkley, CA: University of California Press.

Jolliffe, L. (2007) Coffee and tourism: A research framework. Presented at the Second International Conference on Tourism and Hospitality, Universiti Utara Malaysia and The Department of National Heritage, Ministry of Culture, Arts and Heritage Malaysia, Putrajaya, Malaysia.

Jolliffe, L. and Bui, T.H. (2006) Coffee and tourism in Vietnam: A niche tourism product? Presented at the Travel and Tourism Research Association – Canada Chapter Conference, Montebello, Quebec.

Jolliffe, L., Bui, H.T. and Nuygen, H. (2009) The Buon Ma Thuot coffee festival, Vietnam: Opportunity for tourism? In J. Ali-Knight, M. Robertson, A. Fyall and A. Ladkin (eds) *International Perspectives of Festivals and Events* (pp. 125–136). London: Elsevier.

Jolliffe, L. and Kwan, K. (2008) Blending coffee and international tourist experiences in Vietnam. TTRA Canada Conference Victoria, BC.

Knox, K. and Huffaker, J.S. (1997) *Coffee Basics: A Quick and Easy Guide.* New York: John Wiley.

Kummer, C. (1997) *The Joy of Coffee.* Boston, MA: Houghton Mifflin Company.

Laurier, E., Whyte, A. and Buchner, K. (2001) An ethnography of a neighborhood café, informality, table arrangements and background noise. *Journal of Mundane Behavior* 2 (2), 195–232.

Long, L. (2004) *Culinary Tourism.* Lexington, KY: The University Press of Kentucky.

Mesalles, L. (2000) Coffee. In J. Jafar (ed.) *Encyclopedia of Tourism* (p. 89). London: Routledge.

Moltz, J.G. (2007) Eating difference: The cosmopolitan mobilities of culinary tourism. *Space and Culture* 10 (1), 77–93.

Novelli, M. (2005) *Niche Tourism: Contemporary Issues, Trends and Cases.* London: Butterworth-Heinneman.

Oxford Canadian Dictionary (2004) Don Mills, Ontario: Oxford University Press.

Penfold, S. (2008) *The Donut: A Canadian History.* Toronto: University of Toronto Press.

Perry, S. (2001) *The New Complete Coffee Book.* San Francisco, CA: Chronicle Books.

Ponte (2002) The 'Latte' revolution? Regulations, markets and consumption in the global coffee chain. *World Development* 30 (7), 1099–1112.

Schwalbach, B. (n.d.) On WWW at http://www.bachnetwork.co.uk/. Accessed 15.6.09.

Shapria, J., Shapira, D. and Shapira, K. (1975) *The Book of Coffee and Tea*. New York: St. Martin's Press.

Steinman, S. (2009) Coffee cornucopia: Hawai'i serves as paradise for those with refined affections for bean varieties. *Star Bulletin*, Honolulu, Hawai'i, 22 July 22.

Tannahill, R. (1973) *Food in History*. New York: Crown Trade Paperbacks.

The Viennese Café and Fin-de-siècle Culture – Research Project. On WWW at http://viennacafe.rca.ac.uk/index.html. Accessed 21.7.09.

Thorn, J. (2006) *The Coffee Companion: A Connoisseur's Guide*. London: Quintet.

Ukers, W. (1948) *The Romance of Coffee*. New York: The Tea and Coffee Trade Journal Co.

Walker, J. (2004) *Introduction to Hospitality Management*. Upper Saddle River, NJ: Prentice Hall.

Westwood, S. (2006) Shopping in sanitized and un-sanitized places: Adding value to tourist experience. *Journal of Retail and Leisure Property* 5 (4), 281–291.

Wild, A. (2005) *Coffee: A Dark History*. New York: W.W. Norton.

Part 2

Coffee Culture and Tourism Contexts

Chapter 2
Coffee Servicescapes: The Design of Café Culture in New Zealand

C. MICHAEL HALL, JANNA TIPLER, ROCHELLE REDDY and
KARINA ROWLING

Cafés have become an integral part of dining out in New Zealand, even featuring in New Zealand's tourism promotion. However, it is only relatively recently that New Zealand has begun to develop a café society. Until the mid-1990s, draconian licensing laws and food regulations all but ruled out side-walk cafes and eating and drinking outdoors (Beckett, 1998). Although New Zealand may be a late-comer to the café scene prevalent throughout Europe, America and Australia for decades, café and al fresco dining is now common in even the most remote parts of New Zealand. In the main centres of Auckland, Wellington and Christchurch, this has developed into a wide range of sophisticated cafés offering everything from Thai cuisine to Italian-style espresso bars, or a unique blend of contemporary New Zealand cuisine and pop culture. The increase in eating out and the development of a café culture has also seen the food service sector become the third largest retail sector in New Zealand (Hall & Mitchell, 2000, 2002).

It is possible to suggest three (largely circumstantial) reasons for the rapid development of New Zealand café society. As New Zealanders have been exposed to overseas café culture (through international travel and media), they have becoming increasingly educated and discerning with respect to the coffee and drink they consume. Increasing numbers of travellers of varying nationalities, too, are creating demand for café-style dining in New Zealand, particularly as dining is the number one activity of international visitors to New Zealand (Hall & Mitchell, 2002). Conversely, local chefs and entrepreneurs have, as a result of their own exposure to other café cultures, developed innovative and experimental café products. It is possible to debate the relative influence of both supply and demand factors. Regardless though, travel and tourism have had a crucial role in changing New Zealand cuisine and lifestyle

(Hall & Mitchell, 2000, 2002). Another reason for the recent development of café society is the way in which coffee has become a symbol of cosmopolitanism as tastes in food and drink have become glocalised as a result not only of travel, but also the mobility of media and food and lifestyle shows and magazines in particular (see Kjeldgaard & Ostberg, 2007, for a discussion of this in the Norwegian context).

One element of New Zealand café culture that has not received any significant degree of study is the role of the servicescape, the physical evidence of service that provides the physical surroundings in which the café experience occurs. This chapter focuses on research conducted on the servicescapes of 13 cafés in Christchurch, New Zealand. The chapter compares and contrasts different servicescapes to determine relationships to particular café types. However, before discussing the analysis of servicescapes, the chapter will first review the potential role of servicescapes and how they may affect the position and success of cafés.

Servicescapes

Servicescapes provide tangible and intangible aspects of a service on which perceptions, expectations and overall evaluations are based and which are of increasing interest because of the extent to which they can affect the consumer experience (e.g. Bitner, 1990, 1992; Wakefield & Blodgett, 1996; Pérez-Rivera, 1998; Robson, 2002; Ward *et al.*, 2003; Tombs & McColl-Kennedy, 2003; Newman, 2007; Edwards & Gustafsson, 2008). The servicescape encompasses the entire surroundings in which a service is delivered, including three core aspects identified by Bitner as ambient conditions, spatial layout and functionality, signs, symbols and artefacts, and social interaction (Bitner, 1992; Lovelock *et al.*, 1998). These core attributes are discussed below.

Ambient conditions, spatial layout and functionality

Atmospheric dimensions are discovered through the five senses (Edwards & Gustafsson, 2008) and are experienced through: visual (i.e. colour and brightness), aural (i.e. volume and pitch), olfactory (i.e. scent and freshness) and tactile dimensions (i.e. softness, smoothness and temperature). These areas of the servicescape make up a category that Bitner (1992) terms ambient conditions and are designed to enhance individual perceptions of the service and its physical environment. They include aspects such as temperature, noise, air quality and lighting.

Temperature in a servicescape is important in terms of customer comfort (Bitner, 1992). Noise is important in terms of creating a certain type of atmosphere within the environment, but also in terms of disguising any operational background noises that may be distracting (Edwards & Gustafsson, 2008). In the case of a café, this may include aspects such as the coffee machine, other conversations and music. Studies show that the more a customer enjoys the music, the more they enjoy the overall experience in terms of the positive effect it can have on their perceptions (Edwards & Gustafsson, 2008). Music can also be used to make waiting times appear shorter. If perceived time is smaller than actual time, it can result in people spending more, especially on unplanned purchases (Oakes, 2000).

Air quality is most effective when it is linked with other aspects of the servicescape that add to the atmosphere, such as music. It is the most subtle way to influence customers because if it is done within broad parameters it goes unnoticed but has an effect in terms of branding (Edwards & Gustafsson, 2008). Scent, including the smell of coffee, is not only used to entice customers into a place, but also to energise workers within the servicescape (Mattila & Wirtz, 2001; Ward *et al.*, 2003). Similarly, lighting is also used to enhance or deteriorate the way employees and customers perceive the servicescape (Bitner, 1992).

Spatial layout and functionality is defined as 'the way in which equipment and furnishings are arranged, and the ability of those items to facilitate consumer's enjoyment' (Wakefield & Blodgett, 1996: 47). It has an influence on atmosphere in terms of being indicative of status, personal space, privacy and interaction (Robson, 2002). If tables and chairs are cluttered or too close together, personal space and privacy decreases. This could annoy customers in terms of creating discomfort. Layout can also affect the quality of service delivery as it hinders employee's ability to move freely within the physical environment, thus creating a slower service overall. On the other hand, facilities should not be so sparse that the space appears bare, as this can give an impersonal and/or unfriendly impression (Newman, 2007).

The ability of equipment within the servicescape to perform to a high standard is an indication of overall functionality (Bitner, 1992). This aspect of the servicescape is important as it may or may not be in the total control of the provider. If a piece of equipment is faulty, it could be due to a manufacturing issue. However, the negative perception that is likely to be created by the customer or the employee would be placed on the service provider. This can be viewed as an issue as it highlights that there are certain areas of the servicescape that have the potential to damage the providers' reputation, even if it is not directly caused by them. An area of equipment that is often manipulated by the service provider is the type of seating used. If it is hard and/or uncomfortable, it can discourage customers from spending long periods of time there, thus allowing faster and larger customer turnover (Bitner, 1992). Cleanliness is another aspect of functionality, but differs from equipment in a way that, depending on the values of each individual, could have the potential to cause equipment to malfunction. For example, to some customers, if a table is not clean, it may be viewed as an inappropriate place to sit down and have a coffee on, and thus the equipment malfunctions.

Signs, symbols and artefacts

Signs, symbols and artefacts are the 'signage and décor used to communicate and enhance a certain image or mood, or to direct customers to desire destinations' (Wakefield & Blodgett, 1996: 47). Pérez-Rivera (1998) divides this area of the servicescape into explicit (clear and open) and implicit (implied and unspoken) communicators. This aspect of the servicescape can also be used to communicate to those within it to facilitate individual behaviour such as crowding and ways to behave (Zeithaml *et al.*, 2006). They are important as they are often the primary aspect a customer notices when entering a servicescape and are therefore used to form first impressions. These indicators include aspects such as artwork, certificates and photographs on walls. They are relevant to the servicescape in terms of what they communicate to consumers and employees, such as the overall mood of the café and the expected quality or type of service provided (Perez-Rivera, 1998; Aubert-Gamet & Cova, 1999).

Signs are an example of explicit communicators within the servicescape as they are directly suggesting a piece of information. They inform those within the environment of different labels (such as place name), where different aspects are (such as the bathroom or the exit) and how to behave (such as not to smoke in certain areas or not to sit at tables that have been reserved) (Bitner, 1992).

The exterior of any café is a particularly important part of the servicescape because it is often what initially attracts a customer to a provider (Newman, 2007) and therefore helps to determine a customer's first impressions, expectations and final perceptions of the servicescape and its provider. The exterior design of a building or shop is the primary aspect of the facility exterior that is seen and should capture the attention of the customer and then communicate the type and quality expected of that particular service provider (Ward *et al.*, 2003).

The availability of car parks and their proximity to a café is a part of the servicescape that has not been explored in depth. However, the available research shows that this can have a large affect on the mood of the consumer, which can then be transferred onto the service provider (Bitner, 1990). The overall streetscape or mallscape is another area of the facility exterior that has the ability to affect the consumer experience (Clarke & Schmidt, 1995; Hall, 2008). The addition of design elements such as containers, plants and sculpture can affect the servicescape experience and can increase the activity within a streetscape (Bitner, 1992). The surrounding environment of a café (such as other buildings in the area) therefore contributes to the overall impressions that consumers may have about service, especially for first time customers. These formed impressions are transferred to other areas of the servicescape and thus have the ability to determine whether a customer will enter or not (Bitner, 1992; Hall, 2008).

Social interaction

Social interactions or exchanges in the service encounter are critical within the servicescape at customer to customer, customer to employee, and employee to employee levels. The customer and the employee have a mutually beneficial relationship as their presence within the service environment is imperative. The way the servicescape is designed either supports or does not support these interactions (Bitner, 1992; Bonnim, 2006). This includes aspects such as the way tables are set out, how much room there is to manouever about or between them, the process of ordering (i.e. if you order at the counter or table), the friendliness or approachability of the staff members and the desire of the customer to interact with others.

According to some commentators, the social interactions between customer and employee may be more important than the actual physical experience (Tombs & McColl-Kennedy, 2003; Lin, 2004). It is possible that the underlying reason is experience differentiation, which is becoming increasingly significant with more competitors entering the market. This is supported by evidence presented in a study carried out by Nickson *et al.* (2005), who suggests that to employers, the way an employee looks and sounds is more important than their technical skills. The result of this is employers tend to hire people that are positively appealing to visual and audio senses, although in the case of a product such as coffee the skills of a barista to make a good cup of coffee will also be important. However, for some service providers, differentiation is not a focus. This is relevant to those cafés who are part of a franchise or chain, as they face the difficulty of ensuring homogeneous service quality in terms of the organisation they are representing (Nickson *et al.*, 2005). The outcome of this is that customers may have even higher expectations of consistency in all areas of the servicescape (or brandscape) and it may be even more difficult for providers to meet this requirement.

Service evaluation

Customers and employees evaluate services according to their perceived expectations and the result they feel they received. The servicescape plays three important roles; attention creating, message creating and effect creating. When these three roles are successful, the expectations of the service experience are likely to be higher. This is because the physical environment communicates the quality of the service via symbolic cues that heighten the consumers' appetite for the service (Lovelock *et al.*, 1998). However, because expectations have been set, if any area of the service or servicescape fail (e.g. the coffee is cold, the table is dirty or the music is too loud), the customer perception of the actual service may decrease in quality (Zeithaml *et al.*, 2006). Indeed, Mattila and Wirtz (2005) suggest that a pleasant servicescape may not actually be enough to ensure a satisfying experience. More importantly, it is how it can create a match between target arousal and arousal congruency levels. Target arousal refers to the level of stimulation a consumer looks forward to in a service before they actually experience it. Arousal congruency is when the actual arousal level matches the level of the target arousal. Thus, it is important for service providers to attract the right target group who has stimulation expectations that are similar to the firms' service positioning. They then need to match their service delivery to the stimulation level held by the group in order for a satisfying experience to occur (Reimer & Kuehn, 2005).

Case Study

Cafés are a form of 'interpersonal service' with interaction between both customer and employee. In situations such as this, '...the servicescape must be planned to attract, satisfy and facilitate the activities of both customers and employees simultaneously' (Zeithaml *et al.*, 2006: 322). They are also recognised as 'elaborated environments', an environment in which servicescapes 'are very complicated, with many elements and many forms' (Zeithaml *et al.*, 2006: 322).

The following section discusses a study of 13 different cafés based in the Riccarton area of Christchurch, New Zealand. The research compares and contrasts different servicescapes within two distinct settings; cafés that are part of a streetscape and cafés within a mall, which are, in turn, divided into open- and closed-plan cafes. Therefore, the café settings studied are similar to those encountered in most towns and cities in the developed world.

The primary research objective was to identify the different elements of servicescapes and how they can affect a consumer's perception and overall satisfaction of a service encounter. A servicescape evaluation criteria form was designed and developed based on the relevant literature. The dimensions of the servicescapes focusing on tangible cues of a service were included in the evaluation: ambient conditions, spatial layout and functionality, signs, symbols and artefacts, facility exterior and social interaction (Table 2.1). Each category was then divided into smaller, relevant evaluation sections. Ambient conditions was divided into temperature, air quality, noise, smell and lighting. Spatial layout and functionality was separated into layout, equipment, furnishings and interior design. Signs, symbols and artefacts were divided into signage (interior and exterior), personal artefacts and style of décor. Exterior facility was divided into exterior design, parking, landscape and surrounding environment. These five elements formed the criteria for evaluation and from this, four of the five main senses, sight, smell, taste and sound, could be analysed.

The café servicescape evaluation framework utilised a range of features including Likert scales, a yes or no rating system, numerical analysis and the use of open-ended questions. The opportunity was also provided for additional qualitative comments to be made on each individually examined element on the basis of personal observations. Thus, the evaluation criteria utilised both quantitative and qualitative elements. The evaluation framework was utilised in a series of repeat solo and group visits by three field researchers. It was necessary to thoroughly examine the physical evidence of each café over time by multiple researchers because 'the physical evidence of the service will influence the flow of the experience, the meaning customers attach to it, their satisfaction, and their emotional connections with the company delivering the experience' (Zeithaml *et al.*, 2006: 320). The three field researchers jointly evaluated each café in order to avoid any discrepancies and inconsistencies in comparing the different components in each individual establishment. The researchers were required to purchase items from each café in order to experience the servicescape and to observe the impact of the surroundings on consumers. This also meant that the researchers spent substantial time in each café. Field results were also independently cross-checked by the research supervisor. The

Table 2.1 Components of servicescape analysis

Element	Component
Ambient conditions	Indoor temperature. Air quality. Background noise. Music volume. Music tempo. Type of music played. Does music match style of café? Patron noise. Traffic noise. Quality of natural light. Quality of lighting. Type of lighting. Does lighting match style of café?
Spatial layout and functionality – layout	No. of tables and chairs match space? Does style of furniture match clientele? Does style of furniture match overall styles and feel? Is restroom clearly visible and accessible? How many toilets available? Did you have to queue for bathroom? Is restroom spacious enough to allow reasonable movement? Does restroom offer hooks to hang coats/handbags? Handwash provided? Facilities to dry hands with? Can staff see when you need assistance? How available are extra condiments?
Spatial layout and functionality – furnishings	Type of furniture used? Colour of furniture? Style of furniture. Do pictures/paintings match style and feel? Type of pictures/paintings used?
Spatial layout and functionality – equipment, cleanliness and interior design	Style of cups used? Colour of cups? Aesthetically pleasing? Do they match colour scheme used throughout café?

Table 2.1 (*Continued*)

Element	Component
	Any branding present on the cups, plates or cutlery? Overall cleanliness of internal area? Overall cleanliness of restroom area? Does interior design reflect mood/image café is trying to portray?
Signs, symbols and artefacts – interior and exterior signage	Clarity of cash register? Prices for food and beverage clearly displayed? Opening hours clearly visible? Restrooms clearly marked? Wheelchair access to both interior area and restroom? Easy to locate the facility?
Facility exterior – exterior design, parking, landscape and surrounding environment	Exterior aesthetically pleasing in terms of design and maintenance of building? Safe and secure parking readily accessible? Is parking within close proximity to café? Approximate walking distance from parking space to café. If landscaping present, is it aesthetically pleasing and well maintained? Does surrounding area fit the image of the café?
Social interaction	Manner of staff. Efficiency of staff. Effect on perception that presentation of staff plays? Effect on perception that interaction between staff and customer play? Did the presence of other patrons add to atmosphere of café? Were you greeted on arrival? Were you acknowledged/thanked when leaving? Degree of interaction that actually occurred between the customer and employee.
Service evaluation	When evaluating the service encounter, were expectations met, not met or exceeded?

approach, therefore, primarily utilises a combination of research elements used in content analysis as well as in field ethnography. Thirteen cafés were examined in depth; however, for reasons of privacy, they are not named in the present chapter.

Results and Discussion

The results from analysis of the cafés demonstrated that certain aspects of servicescapes hold greater importance and have influencing effects on the overall success of service encounters. Furthermore, they showed that the four different elements within the physical environment (ambient conditions, spatial layout and function, signs, symbols and artefacts and facility exterior) have various weightings of importance on consumer satisfaction and perceived level of quality associated with the service. In the interest of this analysis, the findings have been summarised into the three categories: streetscape, open-plan inside mall and closed-plan inside mall (Table 2.2).

Ambient conditions

For a positive service encounter, the temperature and air quality within the servicescape should not be at extremes and the music and traffic noise should blend into the background. This is in line with what Bitner (1992) suggested when discussing ambient conditions of a servicescape. In terms of interaction, patron noise must be kept to a minimum depending on the time of day.

Spatial layout and functionality

Table layout had a high effect on social interaction. This reflects Robson's (2002) observations of the role of spatial layout in influencing atmosphere in terms of privacy. The comfort of the chairs differed between the categories of the cafés, depending on the experience individual cafés were trying to create. Cafés that want to encourage a more relaxing, social environment are more likely to have comfortable seating that accommodates those customers who stay for extended time periods. Whereas, cafés that have less comfortable seating are more likely to be encouraging a higher customer turnover and discouraging long-staying patrons. Independent street cafés created a more social atmosphere through comfortable seating compared to the open-plan cafés inside the mall (see also Bitner, 1992). In terms of restroom facilities, it was found that they should be easy to locate, have adequate room and the number of cubicles should match the café's seating capacity. The

Table 2.2 Summary table of results of servicescape analysis

Café type	Ambient conditions	Spatial layout and functionality – layout and furnishings	Spatial layout and functionality – equipment, cleanliness and interior design	Signs, symbols and artefacts – interior signage and exterior signage	Facility exterior – exterior design, parking, landscape and surrounding environment	Social interaction	Service evaluation
Street cafés	Temperature and air quality did not appear to have a great impact on the service encounter unless they were extreme. Music and traffic noise did not appear to play vital roles in shaping consumer experiences as they blended into the background, however patron noise did prove to have detrimental effects.	Few of the factors appeared to be very important when evaluating the servicescapes of street cafés. However, they did indirectly influence consumer perception. Seating was comfortable and suited for long stays. Artwork and the colour and style of furniture also had similar effects. The restrooms played a vital role in making the service encounter a negative or successful one.	The style, size, branding and colour of equipment did not have a strong effect on forming perceptions, but did help shape the consumer experience in minor ways, such as making the environment aesthetically pleasing and helping to reflect the mood and image the cafés were trying to portray. What did draw attention however, were	The size, clarity and particularly the shape of interior signage made for easy execution of service delivery. Patrons did not have to search very hard to find the bathroom facilities as these were clearly labeled by male and female clothing signs, all food items were clearly visible in a readable font size, and the specials were clearly marked and	Building and design maintenance in all cafés examined were modern, clean and comfortable, while landscaping had been used to develop the attractiveness of the cafés. The most significant issue for street cafés was parking access, which was observed to create frustration and	If staff proved capable in the areas of promptness and efficiency, the researchers found that this made allowances for the manner, degree of interaction and presentation of staff, unless these areas were exceedingly bad. The level of interaction between staff and customers	Those elements that had extreme negative scores were noticed more in the service evaluation in areas such as music volume, background noise and spatial layout of the tables.

Table 2.2 (Continued)

Café type	Ambient conditions	Spatial layout and functionality – layout and furnishings	Spatial layout and functionality – equipment, cleanliness and interior design	Signs, symbols and artefacts – interior signage and exterior signage	Facility exterior – exterior design, parking, landscape and surrounding environment	Social interaction	Service evaluation
	on the service. Some patron noise levels were at such high levels that it prevented ease of interaction between customers, creating negative connotations toward the café. The aid of natural light assisted already existing lighting structures, creating a balanced effect in all cafés examined.	It was found that if toilet facilities were not clearly visible and accessible with adequate room and equipment, this could harm the service encounter.	the levels of cleanliness of the equipment (i.e. cutlery), internal area (i.e. kitchen area visible to patrons) and restroom facilities. Cleanliness levels were found to be a very important factor in shaping good consumer experiences and perceptions when not up to standard.	distinguishable by being written in white chalk on a blackboard. Other interior signs were immediately identifiable to customers, including red emergency exit signs and opening hours. All these factors contributed to successful and comfortable service encounters.	annoyance for customers in a number of cases.	shown in this category of cafés was generally low, leaving patrons more time to socialise among themselves when visiting in groups.	

Table 2.2 *(Continued)*

Café type	*Ambient conditions*	*Spatial layout and functionality – layout and furnishings*	*Spatial layout and functionality – equipment, cleanliness and interior design*	*Signs, symbols and artefacts – interior signage and exterior signage*	*Facility exterior – exterior design, parking, landscape and surrounding environment*	*Social interaction*	*Service evaluation*
Open-plan cafés inside mall	Findings revealed that all elements within ambient conditions (i.e. air quality, background noise, music, lighting, patron noise, traffic noise) were at a consistent level. The standard of air quality had an even mixture of freshness with moderate to warm temperatures, lighting was balanced between natural and artificial,	The elements of spatial layout and functionality were consistent with standard modern mall design providing for a similarity of layout and functionality, although one café had poor wheelchair access. Artwork, colour, style of furnishings and bathroom facilities were consistent with mall standards. These factors did not appear to be very important when evaluating the servicescapes of the	These factors did not appear to have a large impact on servicescape evaluation.	The most important factors under this heading that contributed were the clear price labeling in relation to the range of hot beverages and food. The visibility of opening hours, clear markings of restrooms and location of the facility were consistent to mall standards.	The exterior of the café and environment in which it was situated was determined by mall standards.	Staff promptness, friendliness and efficiency appeared strongly influenced by pre-existing levels of expectations of mall service. The design of the coffees was found to discourage social interaction between staff and customers in term of friendly interaction, but was high in	The cafés in this category showed a range of evaluations. However, one café that exceeded expectations was found to be extremely aesthetically pleasing in a manner that differentiated itself internally from the external mall environment. This was an interesting result as

Table 2.2 (*Continued*)

Café type	Ambient conditions	Spatial layout and functionality – layout and furnishings	Spatial layout and functionality – equipment, cleanliness and interior design	Signs, symbols and artefacts – interior signage and exterior signage	Facility exterior – exterior design, parking, landscape and surrounding environment	Social interaction	Service evaluation
	and music was moderately low volume and tempo with a modern 'classic hits' genre. It is important to note, however, that patron and background noise was dependent on the time and day, when weekends and lunch times had considerably higher noise levels compared to weekdays.	open-plan cafés, except for one café that utilised shared food court seating rather than dedicated seating, which created distance between customer and service provider. Furniture was not designed for customers to stay for long periods of time. As malls have high foot traffic, the seats were generally not overly comfortable so as to discourage staying, in order to have a higher patron turnover.				delivering and concluding the service. There was limited table service because the ordering was done at the counter and then brought over. Therefore, the social interaction that naturally occurs when ordering from each individual table was lost.	compared to all other cafes in the framework, which were otherwise highly standardised in terms of aesthetics.

café's overall cleanliness should be to a high standard, including the parts of the kitchen that can be seen and the restrooms. It is also important that the interior design matches the mood and image the café is trying to portray.

Signs, symbols and artefacts

The café must have clear signs showing the available beverage and food options, along with prices. The bathroom location and opening hours must be clearly visible from most areas within the servicescape. As suggested by Zeithaml *et al.* (2006), signs are used to communicate with patrons as indicators of behaviour and need to be clear and comprehensive. Another important aspect is the siting of staff in terms of allowing patrons to get staff attention from where they are sitting.

Facility exterior

If landscape is present in the servicescape, maintenance is critical in terms of facilitating the formation of positive perceptions, as is the exterior of the building. This is confirmed by Newman (2007) and Bitner (1990) as the facility exterior of a service experience is often what is used by customers to form first impressions and therefore needs to be attractive. The exteriors of mall cafés were clearly influenced by general mall policies and décor.

Social interaction

In some servicescape designs, the aim of the environment is to facilitate social exchanges between customer and customer, employee and employee and customer and employee. This is at times only applicable to the cafés that are trying to portray their service as a café experience. Tombs and McColl-Kennedy (2003) stress this very same point when they noted that in some cases, social interactions between customers and employees are more important than the experience itself. Street cafés were designed to facilitate low customer and employee interaction, but encourage customer interaction. The outcome of this was that it created a relaxed, more free-flowing environment. However, this environment type caters for those who are seeking high levels of social experiences, but may not be as well received by those customers who do not fall into this category.

The levels of social interaction between customer and employees were observed to be relatively high in both the closed- and open-plan cafés inside the mall. This was indicated in terms of delivering and concluding service encounters, but not in terms of general social interactions during the service experience. A possible reason for this is that malls have a high level of foot traffic; therefore, rapid service delivery results in a higher turnover, which is in line with mall culture. It is also possible that no interaction is actually expected by the customer (which could be influenced by pre-purchase expectations) in terms of open-plan cafés inside the mall. Closed-plan cafés tended to have more groups using them and a slightly longer length of stay.

Conclusions

A range of factors influence perceptions when evaluating services-capes. These perceptions are formed before, during and after the encounter and all can have an impact on how the café and its services are judged. It was found that type of café (street, open-plan inside the mall and closed-plan inside the mall) had a large affect on such perceptions. This was shown through the associations made between those cafés inside the mall and the mall itself. This meant that many aspects of these cafés were standardised, thereby making it harder to differentiate the servicescapes between them beyond that provided by standard branding practices. Interestingly, local café chains (e.g. Coffee Culture) provided for more individual servicescapes when compared to other cafés of the chain in other locations in comparison with interna-tional chain stores (e.g. McDonald's and Starbucks) that have highly standardised servicescapes (see also Thompson & Arsel, 2004).

Table layout was found to have a very significant effect on the café experience as it served to enable or disable social interaction. Although this may be more relevant to some market segments than others, this observation does reinforce recognition of the long-standing social function of coffee houses, which is retained even in some modern mall environments. In some cases, the nature of a service is seen purely as a social event and if table layout does not aid this, customers may experience dissatisfaction. This can then lead to a negative evaluation of the café servicescape and its provider as a whole. Servicescapes play an important part when evaluating a service experience and it is therefore extremely important for cafés to be aware of this and adapt their environments to create an overall flow from inside to out.

Street cafés show the greatest variety of servicescape. By contrast, open-plan cafés inside a mall have the highest degree of standardisation, where the temperature, type of music and lighting, aesthetic quality, opening hours visibility and landscape are all very generic and homogeneous. The closed-plan café's category operates in a middle ground with standardisation present in some areas but not in others. However, also of significance is the extent to which the café servicescape must be understood as being contextualised by the streetscape or mallscape in which they are situated (Hall, 2008). The street cafés clearly possess greater individuality. Indeed, this seemed to be related to the distance from shopping malls. Nevertheless, mall cafés and the highly standardised coffee chain stores that dominate them continue to maintain a strong position in the coffee marketplace.

In the same way that not all cups of coffee are the same, neither is the design of coffee shops. Cafés clearly serve a range of functions ranging from quick and immediate service of food and drink, to providing a space for social interaction for which coffee is only a side element of the reasons for selecting a particular shop. Nevertheless, regardless of their business model, the physical design of the environment – the servicescape – is integral to the coffee experience. The extent to which cafés maintain their traditional roles of meeting places, third spaces and even locations of opposition will therefore depend on the extent to which the design elements are successfully matched with the coffee consumer.

References

Aubert-Gamet, V. and Cova, B.C. (1999) Servicescapes: From modern places to postmodern common places. *Journal of Business Research* 44 (1), 37–45.

Beckett, F. (1998) More than mutton. *Decanter* 23, 56–59.

Bitner, M.J. (1990) Evaluating service encounters: The effects of physical surroundings and employee responses. *Journal of Marketing* 52 (2), 69–82.

Bitner, M.J. (1992) Servicescapes: The impact of physical surroundings on customers and employees. *Journal of Marketing* 56 (2), 57–71.

Bonnim, G. (2006) Physical environment and service experience: An appropriation-based model. *Journal of Services Research* 6, 21–50.

Clarke, I. and Schmidt, R.A. (1995) Beyond the servicescape: The experience of place. *Journal of Retailing and Consumer Services* 2 (3), 149–162.

Edwards, J.S.A. and Gustafsson, I.B. (2008) The room and atmosphere as aspects of the meal: A review. *Journal of Foodservice* 19, 22–34.

Hall, C.M. (2008) Servicescapes, designscapes, branding and the creation of place-identity: South of Litchfield, Christchurch. *Journal of Travel and Tourism Marketing* 25 (3/4), 233–250.

Hall, C.M. and Mitchell, R. (2000) We are, what we eat: Food, tourism and globalization. *Tourism, Culture and Communication* 2 (1), 29–37.

Hall, C.M. and Mitchell, R. (2002) The changing nature of the relationship between cuisine and tourism in Australia and New Zealand: From fusion cuisine to food networks. In A. Hjalager and G. Richards (eds) *Tourism and Gastronomy* (pp. 186–206). London: Routledge.

Kjeldgaard, D. and Ostberg, J. (2007) Coffee grounds and the global cup: Glocal consumer culture in Scandinavia. *Consumptions, Market and Culture* 10 (2), 175–187.

Lin, I.Y. (2004) Evaluating a servicescape: The effect of cognition and emotion. *International Journal of Hospitality Management* 23, 163–178.

Lovelock, C., Patterson, P.G. and Walker, R.H. (1998) *Services Marketing: Australia and New Zealand*. Sydney: Prentice Hall.

Mattila, A.S. and Wirtz, J. (2001) Congruency of scent and music as a driver of in-store evaluations and behaviour. *Journal of Retailing* 77, 273–289.

Mattila, A.S. and Wirtz, J. (2005) Arousal expectations and service evaluations. *International Journal of Service Industry Management* 17 (3), 229–244.

Newman, A.J. (2007) Undiscovering dimensionality in the servicescape: Towards legibility. *The Services Industry Journal* 27 (1), 15–28.

Nickson, D., Warhurst, C. and Dutton, E. (2005) The importance of attitude and appearance in the service encounter in retail and hospitality. *Managing Service Quality* 15 (2), 195–208.

Oakes, S. (2000) The influence of the musicscape within service environments. *The Journal of Services Marketing* 14 (7), 539–559.

Perez-Rivera, M.M. (1998) Effects of attribute quality information on consumers' perception in servicescapes: An exploratory study. *American Marketing Association Conference Proceedings* 9, 306–311.

Reimer, A. and Kuehn, R. (2005) The impact of servicescape on quality perception. *European Journal of Marketing* 39 (7/8), 785–808.

Robson, S.K.A. (2002) A review of psychology and cultural effects on seating behaviour and application to foodservice settings. *Journal of Foodservice Business Research* 59 (2), 89–107.

Thompson, C.J. and Arsel, Z. (2004) The Starbucks brandscape and consumers' (anticorporate) experiences of glocalization. *Journal of Consumer Research* 31 (3), 631–642.

Tombs, A. and McColl-Kennedy, J.R. (2003) Social-servicescape conceptual model. *Marketing Theory* 3, 447–475.

Wakefield, K.L. and Blodgett, J.G. (1999) Consumer response to intangible and tangible service factors. *Psychology and Marketing* 16 (1), 51–68.

Ward, P., Davis, B.J. and Kooijman, D. (2003) Ambient smell and the retail environment: Relating olfaction research to consumer behaviour. *Journal of Business and Management* 9 (3), 289–302.

Zeithaml, V.A., Bitner, M.J. and Gremler, D.D. (2006) *Services Marketing: Integrating Customer Focus across the Firm* (4th edn). Boston, MA: McGraw-Hill/Irwin.

Chapter 3

Café Culture and Conversation: Tourism and Urban(e) Experiences in Wellington, New Zealand

ADAM WEAVER

Cities have typically been viewed as sites of cultural expression and sophistication. Cultural facilities represent an important element of the infrastructure thought to make urban areas more appealing. In many cities, the integration of culture and economic activity has been at the forefront of growth and development initiatives (Harvey, 1989; Lloyd, 2006). As Zukin (1995: 2) has observed, 'culture is more and more the business of cities'. Arts-based institutions and special events – associated with good taste, higher purpose and community pride – have become symbolic assets for city marketers. Developing a thriving cultural industry is seen as crucial to projecting the city as a desirable place to reside, invest and visit (Speake, 2007). The importance of culture has arguably increased as cities are drawn into inter-urban competition with the rise of globalization (Kearns & Philo, 1993).

Research that examines urban tourism often focuses on highly visible, flagship projects and hallmark events (Judd & Fainstein, 1999). Large-scale museums, performing arts complexes, art galleries and convention centers are seen as monumental evidence of mayoral and city council achievement. However, should the study of urban tourism simply address prominent tourist attractions or events? This chapter addresses the contributions that a particular type of small-scale establishment, the café, makes to urban tourism as well as the way in which cafés facilitate the exchange of tourism-related experiences. The café scene in Wellington, New Zealand, is used as a case study. Cafés are rarely tourist attractions unto themselves, but they may be a vital component of a distinctive and memorable urban ambience, as discussed by Hall *et al.* in Chapter 2. They have a growing presence in a number of cities around the world and may be seen as amenities that support the deployment of

41

culture and the arts as a means to attract tourists. Furthermore, café culture is often associated with discussion and sociability; cafés are places where people meet, either accidentally or deliberately, and are able to pass the time together and converse. Talk, as this chapter suggests, is important to tourism.

Through its aesthetic tastes and consumption patterns, a 'new middle class' (Ley, 1996) has been fundamental to the emergence of a café culture in many cities. The rise and evolution of the modern-day tourism industry also reflects the growth of this middle class. For some commentators, tourism enables these consumers to fulfill their bourgeois cultural aspirations (Mowforth & Munt, 2003). Many destinations seek to attract international tourists who are cosmopolitan and relatively affluent. Tourism New Zealand, the organization that markets New Zealand as a destination overseas, has identified the Interactive Traveler as its target market (Prior, 2004). This market possesses attributes one would associate with the new middle class. It consists of individuals who are well traveled, well read, frequent users of the internet, tolerant of other cultures, supportive of socially responsible business practices and connoisseurs of high-quality food and wine (Allen, 2005; Johnson, 2003). Tourism New Zealand also notes that Interactive Travelers seek opportunities to socialize (Allen, 2005). Cafés may therefore serve as dynamic social spaces that perform a seminal role in fostering human interaction and the sharing of experiences. Wellington's café culture, it could be argued, is well suited to promoting conviviality.

Data for this chapter were obtained from a variety of sources. Travel guidebooks produced by Lonely Planet, Rough Guides, Fodor's and Footprint were consulted. New Zealand guidebooks typically feature a chapter devoted to Wellington. With the proliferation of cafés in Wellington and elsewhere in the country, magazines targeting both café operators and patrons are being published. These periodicals can be found among other reading material in some of Wellington's cafés. *Café Culture* is a magazine that specifically addresses the Wellington café scene. A magazine distributed nationwide, *Café*, also contains articles that describe Wellington's cafés and café culture. Both publications feature retailer profiles, photographs and advertising designed to appeal to both coffee drinkers and the industry. The aim of these magazines is to expand the specialty coffee market and promote the use of quality coffee in existing hospitality enterprises.

A number of newspaper articles provided important information about cafés and café culture in Wellington. Moreover, major newspapers in New Zealand have published both short and extended pieces about the country's tourism industry that have been useful. Participant observation was a crucial dimension of this research. Casual visits were made to a number of Wellington cafés in order to experience their ambience and hospitality at first hand. These cafés, literally and figuratively, provided food for thought.

Café Culture in Wellington

Cafés have become a central component of Wellington's destination image. A number of travel guidebooks make reference to Wellington's café culture. One guidebook indicates that there are more cafés per person in Wellington than there are in New York City (Rawlings-Way *et al.*, 2008). The number of cafés in Wellington has become a measure of urban sophistication. This sophistication is also conveyed through references to prominent cities (Simply Paris Café and NYC Café) and names that are intended to evoke a sense of 'European-ness' (Caffé Italiano, Emporio Coffee, Scopa and Mon Ami) and 'urban-ness' (Gotham Café). One downtown café, The Loft, promotes itself through magazine advertisements as a place that has 'a New York loft feel'. This direct and oblique place referencing is intended to make cafés more appealing through associations with locales that are seen as having style and refinement.

Images of coffee are blended into the promotion of Wellington as a tourist destination. A three-minute video produced by Positively Wellington Tourism, the organization responsible for promoting travel to Wellington, features an opening sequence where images depicting the preparation of a caffé latte serve as an introduction to a succession of images that showcase the city. At the conclusion of the video, finishing touches are made to the cup of caffé latte. The message is clear: caffé latte and the city are ready and waiting to be consumed.

In Wellington, café culture is promoted as a must-see – and must-experience – dimension of the city. Cuba Street has achieved notoriety for its bohemian café scene and is mentioned in most travel guidebooks that profile New Zealand. One café in the Wellington suburb of Seatoun, the now defunct Chocolate Fish Café, became renowned because it was frequented by *Lord of the Rings* cast members during the making of the three films based on J.R.R. Tolkien's books (Mussen, 2008). The café was also near the home of the films' director, Peter Jackson.

In recent years, cafés and boutique coffee have become emblematic of urban refinement and sophistication (Scott, 2006). The spread of 'yuppie coffees' in the 1980s and 1990s has been portrayed as indicative of a desire by certain sections of the middle class to differentiate themselves from the banality of mass culture by consuming exotically 'traditional' products that evoke other, presumably more intriguing, places and times (Roseberry, 1996). Products such as 'yuppie coffee' increasingly allow consumers to portray themselves as they wish to be seen and to announce something about themselves. Starbucks, the international café chain, is typically associated with the popularization of distinctive designer coffee and cafés that have a warm, comfortable ambience (Clark, 2007; Schultz & Yang, 1997). The company is renowned for the iconic cultural status of its brand (Holt, 2004), the expressive names for its beverages and the modern décor of its cafés (Schultz & Yang, 1997). Cafés use atmosphere, layout, certain types of furniture, and employees to create a particular identity and image for the business. However, not all cafés are owned by, or resemble, Starbucks. Cafés are hardly homogenous.

In Wellington, there are cafés that are independently operated establishments as well as ones affiliated with international chains, such as Gloria Jean's Coffees, Esquires Coffee Houses, The Coffee Club and Starbucks. The décor of cafés varies: some feature sofas and cushioned chairs, while others have wooden chairs and tables. Menus also vary: some cafés function as coffeehouses, even bakeries, and primarily serve coffee, muffins, pastries and prepared sandwiches. Others have a full kitchen and serve restaurant-style food as well as coffee. Still other cafés resemble bars in that they sell a wide selection of wine, beer and mixed cocktails in addition to food and coffee. One Wellington café, Photo Expresso, promises patrons a combination of 'quality photos' and 'quality coffee'. A magazine advertisement for the café invites customers to 'browse through [their own] photos in a friendly, relaxed atmosphere'. Digital photographs are printed for patrons in a matter of minutes.

Cafés owned by large chains tend to have an appearance that meets set specifications. Their servicescapes are consistent across different outlets and decoration often consists of black and white photographs, landscape paintings or colorful abstract works. The recorded music played in these cafés is often light jazz and beverages are served in standardized – often branded – mugs and cups that carry the company's trademarked emblem. Merchandizing has also become more common-place: crockery, travel mugs and packaged coffee beans that carry the company's name and logo are available for purchase. The café's brand can be taken home by the consumer. Recent debates in tourism and the social sciences have emphasized the serial reproduction of culture and the homogenizing effects of globalization (Augé, 1995; Harvey, 1989;

Richards & Wilson, 2006; Ritzer & Liska, 1997). Chain-store cafés, which are internationally ubiquitous, have been seen as contributing to these oft-criticized trends (Clark, 2007).

Some consumers display a preference for cafés that offer unique or alternative products. These cafés may seek to evoke a bohemian atmosphere. Countercultural expressions are characterized by politically motivated art, music produced by small, independent record companies and furnishings that resemble those found in a second-hand shop. Even the café's coffee mugs and cups may not match. Furniture and fixtures may be an eclectic mix, such as in the Wellington café named Offbeat Originals. The staff in bohemian cafés may proudly display distinctive tattoos, body piercings, hairstyles and clothing. Recorded music played in the café may be unconventional and possibly performed by New Zealand-based artists. Visiting cafés that are corporate-free bastions of stylistic diversity may provide a symbolic remedy for feelings of disenchantment that could result from the increasing presence of corporate influence in daily life. For tourists, these atmospherics are either a spectacle to be experienced or a manifestation of their social values. Three cafés in Wellington promote themselves through the use of images that make reference to political radicalism, dissidence and the Cuban Revolution: Fidel's, Ernesto and Cubita. Fidel's has a distinctive logo, a drawing of Fidel Castro smoking a cigar, emblazoned on café signage, menus and even T-shirts available for purchase. The café's interior is decorated with black and white photographs of Cuban workers rolling cigars, and Castro. Inside Ernesto, there are photographs and paintings of Ernesto 'Che' Guevara, the Argentine revolutionary who participated in the Cuban Revolution and whose image became immortalized by the iconic Alberto Korda photograph. Cubita features a sepia-toned wall mural of what could be Havana in the 1950s or 1960s. The café's tables are covered with colored tiles, some of which bear a resemblance to the Cuban flag. A portrait of Che Guevara welcomes patrons at the entrance to the café (Plate 3.1) and a smaller portrait of Guevara is propped up against the cash register.

Coffee is invested with meanings, partly because it is a specialty item, rather than a basic staple. In drinking cappuccino in a city café, individuals may feel more cosmopolitan (Blum, 2003). The theme of cosmopolitanism is enhanced in some cafés by references to exotic places. A sense of the wider world is conveyed through signifiers of the international coffee trade – such as maps depicting major coffee-growing regions, printed materials featuring the image of coffee farmers in other countries, and the course burlap sacks associated with the harvesting and

Plate 3.1 Chai latte or Che latte? Café culture and the iconography of the Cuban revolution (Source: Adam Weaver)

transport of coffee beans. These signifiers are particularly in evidence in cafés that are part of large chains. In some cafés, menus and signboards turn coffee consumption into a type of imaginative cultural tourism by inviting consumers to select coffees made with beans grown and harvested in distant places. For consumers who want to make informed choices about the coffee they consume, some cafés even distribute free pamphlets describing the origins of different coffee beans. Posters, signs and other paraphernalia reinforce this combination of exoticism and cosmopolitanism.

Cafés complement arts- and entertainment-oriented facilities in cities. The relationship between cultural attractions and the café scene is symbiotic. A dearth of amenities such as well-regarded cafés and restaurants would probably be disadvantageous to nearby cultural institutions. Many cafés have evolved into venues where cultural events and attractions are promoted. The walls of some cafés feature bulletin boards where small posters announcing upcoming exhibits, concerts and album release parties are placed. Cafés may also offer patrons access to a selection of newspapers and arts-oriented publications free of charge. These media connect patrons to community events as well as the wider world of art and culture. In addition, many cultural attractions – e.g. museums, art galleries and performing art centers – have their own on-site cafés. The St James Theatre is home to The Jimmy Café and Bar;

Te Papa Tongarewa, New Zealand's national museum, has an on-site café that, through its décor, makes playful references to New Zealand food. This café is compatible with, and extends, the museum's overall theme: the country's culture and heritage. A number of cafés in Wellington have even taken on the attributes of private art galleries; they have become places where, for example, neighborhood artists place their work on display and make it available for purchase.

Cafés, Consumption and Conversation

Cafés are places conducive to casual conversation for a variety of reasons. Whereas bars and nightclubs are dark, noisy and crowded, cafés – similar to restaurants – feature furniture, lighting and music that permit patrons to sit and converse comfortably in pairs or small groups. Café visits, which do not necessarily involve the consumption of a meal, can therefore be relatively inexpensive. In many cafés, a cup of coffee comes with the right to sit for an undefined stretch of time. Coffee has become friendship, shared camaraderie, comfort and a moment of pleasure (Clark, 2007; Schultz & Yang, 1997). Although coffee and cafés are social facilitators, the commercial nature of cafés is undeniable. The rise of a global coffee culture has been prompted by the spread of corporate café chains such as Starbucks (Plate 3.2). However, economic

Plate 3.2 Starbucks: Symbol of corporate hegemony and a place to socialize (Source: Adam Weaver)

exchanges have not eclipsed social interactions. Cafés instigate contact by bringing people together, even if that time together is fleeting.

Publications consulted for this study made repeated reference to the role of the café as a communicative space for patrons. For instance, specific cafés in Wellington are described as 'abuzz with banter and conversation' (Carr, 2008: 6) and said to be places conducive to socializing or meeting up after an evening at the theater or cinema (Rees, 2008). Across New Zealand, café patrons can access the internet through CaféNET, a wireless Internet provider. Magazine advertisements for CaféNET suggest the service is marketed to individuals for whom Wellington at-large serves as their office or lounge. Tourists may also use CaféNET to communicate with friends and family members overseas via email. Cafés may therefore support human interaction that occurs both face to face and across great distances.

Enjoying café culture does not mean that patrons must participate in conversations. At times, patrons may have a strong desire to be left alone, to feel comfortable in those spaces where they can sit in the presence of others while not having to give of themselves (Clark, 2007). Consumers may derive a sense of excitement by being among other people in a café. Within a café, consumers can act upon the paradoxical desire to be out in public and yet also maintain a detached anonymity. Patrons can bask in the social spectacle of the café crowd. They can see others – and be seen. The social buzz is derived from the feelings of invigoration that individuals gain from being in a dynamic public space that has a stimulating and interesting atmosphere.

The rise of contemporary café culture – in Wellington and elsewhere – can be situated in relation to wider societal change such as the advance of postindustrialization. New entertainment- and event-driven landscapes of consumption are seen to be characteristic of the postindustrial or postmodern city (Clark, 2004; Harvey, 1989). There has been an infusion of arts- and leisure-based consumption culture in the redevelopment of downtown spaces. For some commentators, the countercultural and progressive impulses described as characteristic of earlier decades have been co-opted, commodified and trivialized in the 'festive' central cities of today. Cities as 'places to play' (Fainstein & Judd, 1999: 261–272) are manifestly designed for the middle classes. The city, in other words, conforms to the expectations of the affluent consumers it wishes to attract. In Wellington, there has been keen interest in hosting events and overseas entertainment acts. Cafés have figured in this rise in culture and entertainment. They can function as informal gathering places; they are places for people to come together for collective reflection and introspection. For middle-class tourists, cafés may be familiar environments. They are places where these individuals may relax and socialize – and even use as a work space – when they are not on holiday. Contemporary café culture intersects with the rise of a knowledge-based and experience-oriented economy that valorizes communication, creativity and cosmopolitanism.

The new middle class has become more prevalent and important in understanding urban fortunes. A varied group of occupations said to be responsible for the emergence of the new middle class – jobs related to the arts, media, technology, finance, real estate, social services, education, and public and non-profit sectors – has certainly become larger, and there are undoubtedly new areas of specialization, reflecting the education explosion of the 1960s and 1970s in Western countries (Ley, 1996), as well as the rise of creative industries (Florida, 2002). The disposable income of professionals – both residents and visitors – directs the entertainment and amenity focus of many downtowns. Cafés are a manifestation of the lifestyle that is desired by middle-class consumers. They are urban spaces that allow individuals to reconnect and (re)build familiarity. A café is a place to talk, to have rapport. Conversation is central to their existence. For the purposes of marketing, Tourism New Zealand wants international visitors to take their stories home with them, and to converse with family, friends and work colleagues about their travels (Van Beynen, 2007). Talking is seen as integral to destination marketing as New Zealand is dependent upon word-of-mouth recommendations from visitors.

Cafés have emerged as resources for socializing. Historically, they have been connected to intellectual engagement and enrichment (Sherry, 1995). For Habermas (1989), English coffeehouses of the 18th century were a key setting for the rise of public discourse and modern notions of public space. The discussions and debates that took place in the coffeehouse constituted a site of political participation – a realm of public opinion – in which the newly emergent bourgeois sought to translate their economic power in political clout. Today's cafés support many types of conversations. The café may represent a place where experiences can be revisited and travelers' tales shared through discussion.

Exchanging ideas and opinions underpins many of the types of activities undertaken by the new middle class, including the trade of intellectual capital at work, and communication is perhaps the means by which the significance of noteworthy experiences can be fully realized. Many commentators argue that the desire for social distinction is intertwined with the vigorous consumption of both tangible goods and ephemeral services (Bourdieu, 1984). Distancing themselves from mass consumer society, members of the new middle class demonstrate their taste through consumption. They prefer expensive specialty coffees, gourmet bread and organic vegetables; they want educational toys and all-terrain baby strollers for their children, and furniture that appears old and rustic (Brooks, 2000). They order not a regular cup of coffee, but a latte macchiato or an espresso doppio. Consumption becomes status differentiation and identity formation, and experiences obtained through consumption acquire a cachet when they are discussed with others. Tourism New Zealand indicates that Interactive Travelers are seeking genuine life experiences, ones that are deemed to be unique and 'real' (Gray, 2004) and worthy of being shared.

Travel and leisure increasingly involve cultural enrichment: museum attendance, eco-vacations and physical activities such as mountain biking, hiking and mountain climbing (Brooks, 2000). These types of activities and experiences are increasingly perceived as crucial to self-knowledge and self-expression, and the reflection and self-examination they invite becomes the fodder for stories and tales that can be told to others. Cafés provide tourists with the opportunity, and a space within which, to engage with travel companions. The phrase 'chattering classes' was used in a derogatory way to describe urban intellectuals whose views departed from those of Margaret Thatcher's conservative government of the 1980s in the UK (Moran, 2005). However, chatter is the currency used to exchange extraordinary and profound experiences. Talk may be cheap to some, but occasions when it has value needs appropriate recognition.

Conclusion

Culture has become a linchpin rather than just a reflection of economic activity (Harvey, 1989; Lloyd, 2006; Zukin, 1995). The rise of culture as a commercial resource is tied to the organization of the city around consumption rather than production. This shift represents a change in the political economy of cities. The symbolic economy of culture and entertainment means that, for example, festivals and the arts are nurtured for their economic worth rather than for their intrinsic value. To date, much urban tourism research has been confined to the study of prominent initiatives and hallmark events that enhance public reputation. However, what cafés offer to tourists as amenities has not received much attention. These types of communicative environments perform an important function that has not been fully acknowledged.

The emergence of a café culture is consistent with the fashioning of downtown spaces to cater to professionals, conventioneers, tourists and other visitors who have significant disposable income. Urban gentrification and a growing tourist trade bring middle-class consumers onto the scene who sustain the profitability of bars, restaurants and cafés. A vibrant café scene is founded upon the aesthetic sensibilities and cultural credentials of this market. Beyond coffee, the central activity of cafés is talk and sociability. They are places where one can be excited by others: their knowledge, their experiences, their stories.

That people talk to each other, and how they talk to each other, is important for a healthy society (Tresman *et al.*, 2007). Relevant to tourism researchers is the notion that conversation enables tourists to swap accounts of their journeys. Through talking with others, experiences are relived and enlivened. Part of sustaining tourism may involve keeping conversations going. An exchange of ideas requires suitable places for such exchanges to occur.

References

Allen, S. (2005) Haere mai to a cultural tourism era. *The Dominion Post*, 17 September, C1.

Augé, M. (1995) *Non-Places: An Introduction to an Anthropology of Supermodernity* (J. Howe, trans.). London: Verso.

Blum, A. (2003) *The Imaginative Structure of the City*. Montreal: McGill-Queen's University Press.

Bourdieu, P. (1984) *Distinction: A Social Critique of the Judgment of Taste* (R. Nice, trans.). Cambridge, MA: Harvard University Press.

Brooks, D. (2000) *Bobos in Paradise: The New Upper Class and How They Got There*. New York: Simon & Schuster.

Carr, J. (2008) New talent on old corner. *Café Culture*, Autumn, 6–9.

Clark, T.N. (ed.) (2004) *The City as an Entertainment Machine*. Amsterdam: Elsevier/JAI Press.

Clark, T. (2007) *Starbucked: A Double Tall Tale of Caffeine, Commerce & Culture*. London: Hodder & Stoughton.

Fainstein, S. and Judd, D. (1999) Cities as places to play. In D. Judd and S. Fainstein (eds) *The Tourist City* (pp. 261–272). New Haven, CT: Yale University Press.

Florida, R. (2002) *The Rise of the Creative Class*. Basic Books: New York.

Gray, A. (2004) Tourism strategy – Pure thinking: The strategies for selling New Zealand. *Management*, December, 90–92.

Habermas, J. (1989) *The Structural Transformation of the Public Sphere: An Inquiry into a Category of Bourgeois Society* (T. Burger, trans.). Cambridge, MA: MIT Press.

Harvey, D. (1989) *The Condition of Postmodernity*. Oxford: Blackwell.

Holt, D. (2004) *How Brands Become Icons: The Principles of Cultural Branding*. Cambridge, MA: Harvard Business School.

Johnson, A-M. (2003) Get hip, tourism expert tells NZ. *The Dominion Post*, 11 September, A3.

Judd, D. and Fainstein, S. (eds) (1999) *The Tourist City*. New Haven, CT: Yale University Press.

Kearns, G. and Philo, C. (eds) (1993) *Selling Places: The City as Cultural Capital*. Oxford: Pergamon Press.

Ley, D. (1996) *The New Middle Class and the Remaking of the Central City*. Oxford: Oxford University Press.

Lloyd, R. (2006) *Neo-Bohemia: Art and Commerce in the Postindustrial City*. New York: Routledge.

Mussen, D. (2008) Death of an icon. *Sunday Star Times*, 10 August, C4.

Moran, J. (2005) New statesman essay: The myth of the chattering classes. *New Statesman*, 24 October, 34–35.

Mowforth, M. and Munt, I. (2003) *Tourism and Sustainability: Development and New Tourism in the Third World* (2nd edn). London: Routledge (first published in 1998).

Prior, L. (2004) NZ targets the big spenders. *Travel Trade Gazette*, 4 June, 14.

Rawlings-Way, C., Atkinson, B., Bennett, S., Dragicevich, P. and Hunt, E. (2008) *New Zealand*. London: The Lonely Planet.

Rees, A. (2008) Never say never. *Café Culture*, Spring, 22–24.

Richards, G. and Wilson, J. (2006) Developing creativity in tourist experiences: A solution to the serial reproduction of culture? *Tourism Management* 27 (6), 1209–1223.

Ritzer, G. and Liska, A. (1997) 'McDisneyization' and 'post-tourism': Complementary perspectives on contemporary tourism. In C. Rojek and J. Urry (eds) *Touring Cultures: Transformations of Travel and Theory* (pp. 96–109). London: Routledge.

Roseberry, W. (1996) The rise of yuppie coffees and the reimagination of class in the United States. *American Anthropologist* 98 (4), 762–775.

Schultz, H. and Yang, D.J. (1997) *Pour Your Heart into It: How Starbucks Built a Company One Cup at a Time*. New York: Hyperion.

Scott, B. (2006) Scottish café society: Contemporary consumption issues and lifestyle identities. *International Journal of Contemporary Hospitality Management* 18 (1), 60–68.

Sherry, J. (1995) Bottomless cup, plug-in drug: A telethnography of coffee. *Visual Anthropology* 7 (4), 351–370.

Speake, J. (2007) Sensational cities. *Geography* 92 (1), 3–12.

Tresman, M., Pásher, E. and Molinari, F. (2007) Conversing cities: The way forward. *Journal of Knowledge Management* 11 (5), 55–64.

Van Beynen, M. (2007) A kiwi experience. *The Press*, 31 March, D1.

Zukin, S. (1995) *The Cultures of Cities*. Oxford: Blackwell.

Chapter 4

From the World Coffee Conference to the Local Café: Coffee Events Large and Small

LEANNE WHITE

This chapter examines a number of large and small 'coffee events' around the world. The chapter ties in with the overarching themes of the book – the coffee experience in the contexts of destinations, tourism and culture.

As the world's most popular drug and second most valuable legal commodity (after oil), coffee is marketed and consumed in such a way that it does not try to compete with other beverage products. Phrases such as 'Let's catch-up for coffee' and 'Let's have coffee' are strongly embedded in the social vernacular of today. As Taylor Clarke argues,

> Without coffee, half of western civilization would be crippled by blinding headaches; morning commuters would wander around in a daze, mumbling to themselves and clutching empty travel mugs; the long haul trucking industry would simply cease to exist. (Clarke, 2007: 169)

Coffee berries or cherries that contain the coffee bean (also see Chapter 1) were first grown in Ethiopia in the 9th century. Caffeine, 'the world's most widely-consumed behaviour-modifying chemical' is present in coffee, tea and chocolate, and is also added to cola, energy drinks and some tablets/medicines (Australian Consumer Association, 2007). The coffee trade has come full circle and today the best coffee in the world is said to be grown in Ethiopia – where coffee was first grown 1000 years ago, and most consumers prefer the taste of the Arabica bean (Angelico, 2007).

The symbolism associated with coffee events is examined. Textual analysis, in particular semiotics (examining how signs generate meaning) and content analysis (studying what is actually evident on the page or screen), are useful methodologies for deconstructing mediated representations of coffee imagery and event branding.

A combination of primary and secondary research, semiotic analysis and content analysis is undertaken to closely analyse the way in which coffee events are imagined, created, replicated and relayed across the world. The images examined in this chapter will be explored through the theoretical frameworks of tourism, culture and marketing.

Methodology

As outlined above, this chapter is concerned with examining coffee events of various shapes and sizes. The chapter undertakes an analysis of the images by applying aspects of semiotics – a key qualitative research methodology for deconstructing mediated representations. The search for representations of what will be referred to as the 'coffee event' can be found through a close examination of large and small coffee events and their visual imagery, as well as examining the way coffee is marketed and promoted to consumers around the world.

Semiotics is the study of signs, codes and culture, and a methodology for reading 'soft data', such as visual representations of coffee events. The word 'semiotics' is derived from the Greek name for an interpreter of signs – 'semeiotikos' (Cobley & Jansz, 1999: 4). Semiotics is a useful tool for examining the sometimes multilayered images of culture. The area of study originated in the early 20th century. Essentially, it is the study of how signs operate in society or 'the study of the social production of meaning' (O'Sullivan et al., 1994: 281) generated from sign systems. Meaning in this context is the dynamic interaction between the 'reader' and the message. Meaning is influenced by the reader's socio-cultural experiences, and the reader undoubtedly plays a central role in any semiotic analysis. Semiotics is a useful methodology for deconstructing our daily experiences and attempts to capture those experiences more permanently – with tools such as still and moving cameras.

According to Leiss et al. (1990: 214), the real strength of semiotics is 'its capacity to dissect and examine closely a cultural code and its sensitivity to the nuances and oblique references in cultural systems'. Leiss et al. incorporated the notion of a cultural frame into their research. They argue that 'a cultural frame is the predominant set of images, values, and forms of communication in a particular period that arises out of the interplay between marketing and advertising strategies, the mass media, and popular culture' (Leiss et al., 1990: 62). This notion is important to the primary object of examination of this chapter – the 'cultural frame' of coffee that has been produced through numerous visual depictions of the 'coffee event'.

Both qualitative and quantitative research methodologies have particular strengths and using both methods strengthens the final research outcome. Content analysis is a research methodology that is concerned with the frequency of content contained in a particular data set. Berelson (1952: 15) defined content analysis as 'a research technique for the objective, systematic and quantitative description of manifest content of communications'. Researchers have employed content analysis for nearly a century, but it became a popular form of analysis in the 1950s and is used in a variety of academic disciplines, including media studies, journalism, literature, tourism, history and marketing. Some content analysis will be integrated into this chapter, as it is a useful tool for examining the larger picture.

Content analysis is effectively a counting strategy and is put forward as an objective method for counting content. It is a useful research tool for identifying, categorising and describing trends. At its most basic level, 'content analysis simply entails inspection of the data for recurrent instances of some kind' (Wilkinson, 2004: 184). An essential feature of content analysis is the use of categories. When classifying data into categories, the main aim is to reduce the material and detect systematic patterns and structures. An example might be counting the number of times in which an image of coffee beans or a coffee cup appears in a magazine advertisement for coffee. Therefore, content analysis is primarily concerned with studying what is actually evident on the page. Quantitative content analysis of this kind does not concern itself with questions of quality or interpretation, but can easily detect systematic patterns.

A combination of semiotics and content analysis will be undertaken to closely analyse the way in which images and perceptions of coffee events have been imagined, created, represented, replicated and relayed across Australia and beyond.

Marketing and Consuming Coffee

Coffee events spread across the world with the growing popularity of coffee consumption from its birthplace in Ethiopia, Arabia, Turkey, Italy, France, England and eventually, the rest of the world. The first coffee house in London was built in 1652, and within 50 years there were 2000 coffee houses in that city alone (Angelico, 2007). A typical contemporary coffee event on the streets of France is shown in Plate 4.1.

Plate 4.1 A 'coffee event' in France (Source: Leanne White)

By the 1900s, 'coffee-house culture' was firmly entrenched throughout Europe (Banks *et al.*, 1999: 45). As coffee houses could remain open as long as they had customers, they became popular places for writers, students and those seeking lively discussion and debate. Coffee houses became known as 'Penny Universities' because for the price of a cup of coffee, the customer could sit and work in the comfortable and warm surrounds of the coffee house. Reading material was also plentiful and free.

The coffee bar emerged in the 1950s and remained popular in the 1960s when many young clients happily selected songs from the jukeboxes. Since the 1990s, there has been something of a revival of the café with some outlets providing internet access for customers (cybercafés) and others focussing on educating their customers about the benefits of specialty coffee.

As discussed by Hall in Chapter 10, many coffee consumers are becoming increasingly aware that the price they pay for a cup of coffee can represent a day's wages for a coffee grower. An alliance known as 'Fairtrade' aims to provide coffee growers with a better price and leave out the middle man or intermediary. A total of 500,000 growers are involved in the Fairtrade Movement (Angelico, 2007).

The Fairtrade certification requires that a premium be paid for products displaying the label. This helps to ensure that coffee producers and workers, many in third world countries, receive a fairer price for the higher quality bean. Fairtrade cooperatives are organised by groups of farmers who decide how the extra funds will be put to use in their community. The Fairtrade initiative essentially aims to ensure a better lifestyle for the grower and their family with benefits such as better housing, improved health care and safer work practices.

The Fairtrade logo is brown, blue and light green and displays a man with his arm in the air, while the accompanying slogan states 'Guarantees a better deal for Third World Producers'. Importantly, the words 'better deal' are emphasised with bold lettering. In Australia, labels such as Bean Alliance, Coffex, Jasper and Republica sell a range of products that display the Fairtrade logo.

While Fairtrade coffee is being favoured by an increasing number of consumers around the world, some argue that 'fairly traded coffee' should be the priority. The Canadian coffee retail chain, 'The Second Cup', buys La Minita coffee that is grown in the mountains of Costa Rica. The operators of La Minita (which means small mine) argue that good coffee will always command a good price and that Fairtrade coffee amounts to little more than cultural imperialism. Apart from Fairtrade (and fairly traded) coffee, the benefits of organic coffee, shade-grown coffee and rainforest alliance beans are also heavily marketed to discerning coffee drinkers.

While baristas take pride in coffee art, such as a leaf or a heart presented on the foaming milk, a Boston-based company, OnLatte Inc., has invented a printer that will create any image or corporate logo in caramelised sugar on top of the latte or cappuccino. OnLatte founders, Josh Grob and Oleksiy Pikalo, explained that customers can even have an image of themselves printed on top of their latte or even on top of a creamy-headed beer such as Guinness (Moore, 2008).

Coffee art is also undertaken by artists such as Dirceu Veiga, who sells postcards, calendars, posters and mugs through his website Coffee on Paper. The Brazilian artist specialises in caricatures and in 2007 began using the technique, which simply involves using coffee and paper. Coffee artists Andrew Saur and Angel Sarkela-Saur from the USA also paint with coffee and display their works on the website Coffee Art. They sell limited edition prints and custom paintings for individuals and can work from a photograph, idea or concept provided by the client.

The emphasis on the gourmet coffee experience and the importance of the bean can be found in many coffee outlets. This can occasionally involve displaying many types of coffee bean or even something as

Plate 4.2 A 'coffee event' in Bali (Source: Leanne White)

straightforward as using the humble coffee bean as a table decoration (see Plate 4.2).

International Coffee Associations, Festivals and Events

In the 1950s, the Pan American Coffee Bureau undertook an intensive marketing campaign and successfully sold the American public the idea of the 'coffee break'. As Mark Pendergrast (1999: 242) explains, the bureau advertised the concept so successfully that by 1952, 80% of companies surveyed had instituted the 'coffee break' as a formal part of the work day. The trend eventually caught on and coffee consumption increased significantly from the breakfast beverage of choice to a product that was consumed many times during the day.

The key organisation involved in the promotion of coffee on a global scale is the International Coffee Organization (ICO). ICO effectively aims to influence the way in which coffee is marketed and consumed internationally. ICO worked towards an International Coffee Agreement in order to produce relative stability for countries that both produce and consume coffee.

While ICO was formed in London in 1963, the first World Coffee Conference organised by ICO took place as recently as 2001. The inaugural conference was held in London where players from the coffee industry discussed a wide range of topics including strategies to combat the current low market prices. At the second world conference held in Brazil in 2005, delegates focused on various ways to develop a sustainable coffee economy. ICO will stage the third World Coffee Conference in Guatemala in 2010.

ICO has developed a number of International Coffee Agreements (ICAs) since the 1960s. The 2007 ICA consists of a 43-page document containing 51 key topics or articles. In 2000, it was decided that a global research network would be formed to better disseminate important research findings to all stakeholders in the coffee industry. The network would both enhance the effectiveness of research spending and improve productivity (Clarke & Vitzthum, 2001: 239).

As Clarke (2007: 169) explains, ICO 'should be one of the most influential agencies on the planet' as they are the leading body for 25 million coffee farmers. The reality is that ICO consists of just 35 people working out of basic offices in London's West End.

ICO acts as a governing body of sorts for many coffee organisations and associations around the world. One significant group is the Speciality Coffee Association of America (SCAA), who held their 21st Symposium and Exhibition in Atlanta in April 2009. The event was billed as just that – 'the event' in the coffee industry as it is the world's largest gathering of coffee professionals. A highlight of the event was the World Barista Championships (WBC). Gwilym Davies (who operates a coffee cart in London) took the coveted first prize at the WBC. His win followed on from being named the top barista in the UK earlier in the year.

'Specialty' coffee is also emphasised by Europe's key coffee group – the Speciality Coffee Association of Europe (SCAE). In 2009, the event was held in the German city of Cologne with prizes awarded to individuals and industry for 'Coffee Excellence'. The Australasian Speciality Coffee Association (AASCA) see their role as promoting quality coffee 'rather than commodity based, mass produced rubbish' (Bar Nine, 2009).

An important coffee event that contributes to the branding of the Central Highlands of Vietnam as a true coffee destination is the Buon Ma Thuot Coffee Festival. As Vietnam is the world's second largest producer of Robusta coffee, the event plays a significant role in contributing to coffee tourism as a developing but important niche for the country (Jolliffe *et al.*, 2008: 125). The authors also point out that one of ICO's recommendations is to use coffee festivals as a way to further encourage coffee consumption (Jolliffe *et al.*, 2008: 127).

Tasting the Bean and Serious Coffee Events

Specialty coffee growers and judges gather for the more serious coffee event such as the 'Cup of Excellence'. The Cup of Excellence is essentially a competition that selects the best coffee produced in a given country each year. The countries that are currently involved in running the competition are: Brazil, Bolivia, Colombia, Costa Rica, El Salvador, Guatemala, Honduras, Nicaragua and Rwanda.

The coffee is tasted by a highly trained group of coffee experts known as 'cuppers'. At the event, cuppers evaluate the best coffee based on a range of sensory inputs such as aroma, flavour, sweetness, acidity, mouth feel, balance and after taste. Coffee farmers ultimately benefit by being able to obtain a higher price for their quality crop.

As also noted by the authors of Chapter 7, Melbourne is Australia's 'undisputed coffee capital' and 'takes its coffee short, strong and very seriously' (Munro, 2009: 3). When Melbourne's Lord Mayor Robert Doyle (a 10-cup-a-day tea drinker) claimed that the city's coffee was overrated, he experienced the wrath of the city's coffee connoisseurs.

In Melbourne, some coffee outlets have even taken it upon themselves to educate their customers about how to properly enjoy the drink by dictating exactly what they serve and how. Examples include: no milk served with espresso; no decaf, skinny or soy; and serving coffee tepid with a written warning on the menu, 'Our coffee is served tepid so the milk remains creamy and full flavoured, not caramelised. If you wish us to burn the milk and have a hot coffee, just ask' (Hudson, 2009: 21).

Multinationals Manipulate Coffee Events

Depending on where you live, some of the dominant names on the supermarket shelves include Swiss-owned Nescafé (Nestle), US-owned Maxwell House (Phillip Morris) and US-owned Folger's (Procter and Gamble). The famous Maxwell House slogan 'Good to the Last Drop' has been a long-standing success story for the brand. Equally, 'Mountain Grown' Folger's have claimed that 'the best part of waking up is Folger's in your cup'. Other significant names in the global coffee market are Sara Lee and Lavazza.

While Nescafé have cleverly marketed their '43 beans in every cup' slogan for decades, the current slogan is: 'Coffee, a natural source of antioxidants'. The Nescafé range of instant coffees includes: Blend 43, Gold, Espresso, Mild Roast, Short Black, Café Menu and Greenblend. The symbol displayed on Nescafé coffee jars looks deceptively similar to the Fairtrade logo for the less-informed consumer. The Nescafé logo is brown, orange and white and also displays a man with his arms in the air. The words circling the symbol are 'Natural Coffee Antioxidants'.

Nescafé is also attempting to promote a quality instant coffee product (although the actual idea seems oxymoronic) by making their Gold range from '100% Arabica beans'. In the case of Maxwell House, Folger's and Nescafe, it is the home coffee event that is being promoted by these multinational organisations. Plate 4.3 shows some of the products from the Nescafé instant coffee range.

Starbucks has become something of a global phenomenon in the coffee world. The Seattle-based coffee giant was launched in 1971 and originally just sold coffee beans and ground coffee for consumption in the home. However, it wasn't until the 1990s under the leadership of Howard Schultz that the company became the global giant it is today. Starbucks aim to be the McDonald's of coffee and operate around 12,000 outlets across the USA alone (Berg, 2008: 23).

However, the Starbucks strategy has not been successful in all markets. The company opened their first store in Australia in 2000. Eight years later, Starbucks announced they would close 61 of their 84 stores across the country (Cooke, 2008: 3). Chris Berg (2008: 23) argues that the failed Starbucks experiment in Australia shows that 'multinational corporations actually have to offer something better than the

Plate 4.3 An instant 'coffee event' (Source: Leanne White)

local alternatives if they want to succeed' and that it is not enough to just arrive in a country and set up a store, 'you have to be really good'.

McDonald's also became a competitor to retail coffee outlets with the opening of their McCafes. The point of difference at McDonald's is that they use 'Rainforest Alliance Certified' coffee as opposed to Fairtrade coffee. With over 900 stores in 35 countries, Gloria Jean's has become a significant player in the speciality coffee market. In 2004, Gloria Jean's became an Australian-owned company and the majority of the stores are based in Australia. The Coffee Bean and Tea Leaf opened its first store in California in 1963, and now boasts more than 700 stores in around 20 countries. Some of the more unusual types of hot and cold coffee drinks sold at the outlets include: Cafe Mocha, Cafe Vanilla, Cafe Caramel, Cafe White Chocolate Dream, Americano, Iced Cafe Latte and Iced Mocha Latte.

Making Connections with Coffee Events

In order to directly take on the corporate giants of the coffee world, the website 'Delocator' was launched in 2005, allowing users to find an independent café in their local area (as they would through a 'Store Locator' function on a corporate website). Users of Delocator can also modify the website's information and add more independent stores to the database.

The rationale behind the website is that independent coffee shops allow consumers to experience a more 'authentic' café experience and thus promote local culture as opposed to the supposed globalised homogeneity of companies such as Starbucks. The Delocator logo is very similar to that of Starbucks, displaying white writing around the perimeter of a green circle. Both logos also display three stars. The website browser is left with little doubt that Delocator's sights are aimed directly at fighting Starbucks at the grassroots level.

In the USA, 'Car and Coffee' events seem to happen on a regular basis. One such event was advertised as 'Kalamazoo, Cars and Coffee'. Symphony orchestras also promote opportunities for audiences to meet with artists at events such as 'Coffee with the Conductor'. Numerous social coffee groups exist, including 'Freelancers Coffee' – a loose Perth-based group who meet each month. The group is aimed at solo and freelance workers and designed to encourage the networking of freelance workers across a range of industries.

Conclusion

While various coffee-making devices such as the plunger (also known as the French press, press pot or coffee press), espresso pot, percolator

Plate 4.4 A coffee plunger or French press (Source: Leanne White)

Plate 4.5 An espresso pot (Source: Leanne White)

and dripolator devices adorn many kitchens (see Plates 4.4 and 4.5), it would appear that the reality of the home coffee event is largely an 'instant' experience. A recent study found that Australians prefer to drink instant coffee at home, while ground roast coffee was 'linked to an occasion, an atmosphere and an experience' (Australian Associated Press, 2008). Tim Emmerson found that Australia is generally a nation of latte and cappuccino drinkers – a trend that is mirrored across the globe (AAP, 2008).

Coffee events lure the consumer and many millions of small but important coffee events take place across the globe every day, with 500 billion cups of coffee consumed annually (Angelico, 2007).

References

Angelico, I. (2007) *Black Coffee: A Three-Part Documentary Series.* Sydney: Special Broadcasting Service.

Australian Associated Press (2008) Aussies favour instant gratification. On WWW at http://www.smh.com.au/lifestyle/wellbeing/aussies-favour-instant-gratification-20090407-9xhf.html.

Australian Consumer Association (2007) Caffeine. On WWW at http://www.choice.com.au/viewArticle.aspx?id = 105168&catId = 100289&tid = 100008&p = 1&title = Caffeine.

Banks, M., McFadden, C. and Atkinson, C. (1999) *The World Encyclopedia of Coffee.* London: Lorenz Books.

Bar Nine (2009) South Australian AASCA. On WWW at http://barnine.blogspot.com/2009_03_01_archive.html.

Berelson, B. (1952) *Content Analysis in Communication Research.* New York: Free Press.

Berg, C. (2008) Memo Starbucks: Next time try selling ice to Eskimos. *The Sunday Age*, 3 August, 23.

Clarke, T. (2007) *Starbucked: A Grand Tale of Caffeine, Commerce and Culture.* London: Hodder and Stoughton.

Clarke, R.J. and Vitzthum, O.G. (eds) (2001) *Coffee: Recent Developments.* London: Blackwell Science.

Cobley, P. and Jansz, L. (1999) *Introducing Semiotics.* Cambridge: Icon Books.

Cooke, D. (2008) American coffee culture gets roasted. *The Age* (Insight section), 2 August, 3.

Hudson, F. (2009) Purists lay down the law to food philistines: It's our taste, or taste not. *Herald Sun*, 30 May, 21.

Jolliffe, L., Bui, H.T. and Nguyen, H. (2008) The Buon Ma Thuot coffee festival, Vietnam: Opportunity for tourism? In J. Ali-Knight, M. Robertson, A. Fyall and A. Ladkin (eds) *International Perspectives of Festivals and Events: Paradigms of Analysis* (pp. 125–137). Oxford: Elsevier.

Leiss, W., Kline, S. and Jhally, S. (1990) *Social Communication in Advertising: Persons, Products and Images of Well-Being* (2nd edn). Ontario: Nelson.

Moore, G. (2008) OnLatte whips up printer for beer, coffee foam. On WWW at http://www.masshightech.com/stories/2008/11/24/weekly10-OnLatte-whips-up-printer-for-beer-coffee-foam.html.

Munro, P. (2009) That's a red card, Mr Mayor: The coffee clique gives Doyle a roast. *The Sunday Age*, 24 May, 3.

O'Sullivan, T., Hartley, J., Saunders, D., Montgomery, M. and Fiske, J. (1994) *Key Concepts in Communication and Cultural Studies* (2nd edn). London: Routledge.

Pendergrast, M. (1999) *Uncommon Grounds: The History of Coffee and How it Transformed our World*. New York: Basic Books.

Wilkinson, S. (2004) Focus group research. In D. Silverman (ed.) *Qualitative Research: Theory, Method and Practice* (2nd edn) (pp. 177–199). London: Sage.

Chapter 5

Coffee-house Culture and Tourism in Cyprus: A Traditionalized Experience

EVI EFTYCHIOU and NICOS PHILIPPOU

This chapter examines the semiotic value of the *kafeneion* (coffee shop) – as an institution in Cyprus – in various contexts, and the underlying power relations involved in each with emphasis on cultural tourism. In rural Cyprus, a new variation of the kafeneion is emerging; a space perceived to be an 'authentic' and 'traditional coffee shop', which attracts mainly tourists. This new type of enterprise is the product of a process of traditionalization, in which the indigenous kafeneion's contemporary functions as a political, cultural and social space have been deliberately ignored. The traditionalized coffee shop is visually and symbolically purified, in the sense that symbols of cosmopolitanism, modernity and current political affairs are being strategically replaced by signifiers of tradition, rurality and peasantry.

In this chapter, it is suggested that the invented, traditionalized coffee shop is closer to colonial and local romantic photographic depictions of the kafeneion, and not to the indigenous kafeneion, as such. It is argued that the interactive relationship between romantic perceptions about Cyprus and its culture, the product of a local romantic photographic school, along with policies promoted by the European Union (EU) and the state, have as a cultural output the transformation of some indigenous *kafeneia* into 'traditional coffee houses' catering for tourists. The influences of tourism, romanticism and photography can be seen as complementary; constructing dominant representations and simultaneously fulfilling the romantic aspirations of tourists about Cyprus in general and the kafeneion in particular.

The chapter describes the visual traditionalization and purification of Cyprus in general and of the kafeneion in particular. Colonial and local romantic representations from the late 19th century until today are examined in juxtaposition with the significant social, economical and political functions of the indigenous kafeneion.

While we explore the possible internalization by locals of outsiders' fantasies of a Cypriot Arcadia – a Classical Eden – we do not ignore the impact of a local romantic nationalism on how Cyprus is represented by the tourist board and by cultural agencies of the Republic, like the Cultural Services of the Ministry of Education and Culture and the cultural foundations of major banks. Furthermore, the impact of European and national strategies on cultural tourism trends and the semiotic change of the coffee shop are investigated. The social space of the coffee shop and its material culture are examined in relation to issues of politics, cosmopolitanism and modernity.

Visual 'Traditionalization' and 'Purification' of Cyprus and the Kafeneion

Romantic representations of the kafeneion by traveler photographers of the colonial period in Cyprus, the output of a local 'romantic photographic school' and the photographic material widely used within the tourist industry are all aesthetically close to this new traditionalized form of the coffee shop that co-exists with what we call here the 'indigenous' kafeneion – coffee houses frequented by locals.[1] The influences of tourism and photography – combined or independently – can be seen as contributing or simply responding to romantic perceptions about Cyprus in general and the kafeneion in particular.

John Thomson, a prominent 19th-century British travel photographer, produced what seem to be the first photographic representations of Cypriot coffee houses, during his photographic survey of Cyprus in the autumn of 1878. His expedition, immediately after the British acquisition of Cyprus, produced what could be considered as the first attempt toward a comprehensive photographic survey of the island and is in line with Victorian ideologies justifying the colonial project. Though Thomson's photographs of local coffee houses are not worth much in revealing the social and cultural functions of these spaces,[2] his captions provide a valuable insight into British colonial perceptions on the institution of the kafeneion and also the region as a cultural territory.

In the caption of the very first photograph in the 1985 edition of his book, *Through Cyprus with the Camera in the Autumn of 1878*, in which Larnaca Marina is depicted, Thomson makes his first reference to the coffee house:

> Rude jetties invade the sea, while the shore bristles with wooden piles, the wrecks of landing stages, or waterside cafés. Larnaca,

indeed, looks as if it had been groping its way seawards, with a thousand antennae, in search of purer air or social reform. Nevertheless, its old-world aspect, its rich colours, its quaint architecture, and even its decay, all tend to render the place one of the most picturesque of Levantine ports. (Thomson, 1985: plate 5.1)

The coupling of the words *café* and *picturesque* in the same caption, even if not next to each other, is of particular significance. Beyond Thomson's overt political commentary, this paragraph is all about his fascination, as a travel photographer, for the picturesque. The kafeneion was (and still is) often seen as one of those local features that would contribute to the construction of an image of Cyprus as a charming island of the Eastern Mediterranean.

In Thomson's book there is another reference to the kafeneion in a caption next to a photographic depiction of one such establishment. The photograph shows a two-storey structure next to the Gothic Cathedral of Saint Nicholas in Famagusta, which was transformed into a mosque after the Ottoman occupation in 1571. The text is again much more revealing than the photographic representation. In the caption, the kafeneion is presented as a space within which some of the most profound ills of the 'oriental' man would be manifested, and could be observed by the receptive traveler; notably idleness, apathy and fatalism:

On the left, for example, stands one of the most imposing specimens of the present architecture of the place. It is a café, propped upon an old Gothic porch and adorned with a flagstaff. Here worshipers at the shrine of the Prophet meet and sit for hours, smoking their hookahs, and drinking their coffee in silence; for they have long ago exhausted all the subjects of conversation that so lonely a spot can supply. One forlorn individual informed me that he had made arrangements for his funeral many years since, and that his chief wish was to mingle with the surrounding dust as speedily as possible. He was a Turk. (Thomson, 1985: plate 5.2)

Thomson's short and fleeting encounter with Cyprus produced a rather stereotypical and passing account of Cypriot society in the last quarter of the 19th century. His reconstruction of that most important of Cypriot secular cultural institutions was also clichéd and superficial.

The contemporary tourist industry constructs an image of Cyprus that is both romantic and reductive.[3] Tour operator brochures, Cyprus Tourist Organization (CTO) campaigns and postcards sold in tourist areas bring to the fore visual signs of an unspoiled nature and culture. These promotional and souvenir materials thus tend to ignore any signs of modernity that might reduce the intensity of the promise of a pure experience.[4] One of the key brochures of the current CTO campaign is titled 'Authentic Cyprus/Discover it', while the logo at the bottom of the cover reads 'Rural Cyprus/Feel the Experience'. In these materials, authentic Cyprus is portrayed as rural Cyprus. There is no need to make a detailed analysis of the imagery that adorns the pages of this brochure. Such material evidently attempts to satisfy that very common appetite among tourists for the 'authentic', which, in the case of Cyprus, is associated with rustic aesthetics and lifestyle. The paradox here, of course, is in the heart of this process of 'constructing' the 'authentic'.

The kafeneion does not escape the norm of having been construed as traditional and pure, particularly as it is an integral feature in the fantasy of a Cypriot rural heaven in the collective perception of the local urban middle classes who do hold a hegemonic position in the processes of representing local culture. The suggestion here is that this discussion should not focus exclusively on tourism because it is necessary to adopt a more comprehensive perspective, which allows for analysis of the wider ideological context that produces such perceptions and representations. To shed more light on this process of visual 'purification' of Cyprus, it is useful to make reference to the preferred subject matter and the aesthetic of a prominent local romantic school of photography, which is both ideologically and aesthetically closely related to its contemporary respective schools of painting, poetry and literature.

Romantic Cypriot photography emerged and grew along with the new independent state of the 1960s and includes such prominent names as Reno Wideson and Takis Demetriades. The product of this school usually carries the 'seal of approval' of the official cultural agencies of the Republic.

Takis Demetriades, one of the finest examples of this generation of photographers, has recently published a volume entitled *The World of Cyprus 1960–1974 Through the Lens of Takis Demetriades AFIAP* (Demetriades, 2006). The book – as the title reveals – aspires to provide a comprehensive review of Cypriot society and culture during that particular period. The dates that set the chronological limits of inclusion and exclusion of images in the book appear to be marking the period as a specifically distinct one because of the two political events of historical proportions that are associated with these dates: the birth of a new Republic in 1960 and the political and humanitarian disaster of 1974. The years in between are presented as years of innocence. Demetriades'

Cyprus is idealized and appears to be populated by old men and women, peasants, fishermen and artisans that live in a pre-modern paradise.

Modernity and an intensive urbanization process only feature rarely as a de-emphasized and out-of-focus unavoidable annoyance. The political/ideological confrontation that divided the Greek-Cypriot community in the 1960s and 1970s and involved political assassinations and bomb attacks, culminating in a *coup d'état* in 1974, does not feature even in the distant background; nor does the parallel bitter inter-ethnic armed confrontation between the Greek and Turkish Cypriots of the 1960s.

Interestingly, Don McCullin's photographs of the inter-ethnic troubles of the winter of 1963 and 1964 won him the 1964 World Press Photo Award. McCullin's images of Cyprus are as bleak and distressing as any others he has produced in his long career as a war photographer. In his autobiography, the description of his Cyprus project successfully expresses the sense of horror his photographs convey:

> a Turkish villager lying dead on the floor of his house is embraced by his bride; an old man gunned down by snipers in Limassol; a distraught Turkish woman fleeing the village of Gazabaran after her husband has been killed; an eighteen-year-old Turkish girl with shotgun seeking revenge hours after the death of her brother. (McCullin, 1992: 56)

McCullin is evidently sympathetic toward the Turkish Cypriots. It can be discerned that narratives such as his would have no position within the broader scheme of constructing a romantic Cyprus. Sectarian violence, and particularly the kind that may cause embarrassment for the new Republic, would certainly not contribute toward a romantic idealization of the island and its people.

Even the two military interventions by Turkey are reduced to fleeting references in the text that accompanies some of the photographs in Demetriades' book. The air assault of military positions and villages in the region of Tillyria by the Turkish air force using napalm bombs in 1974 is implied in only three captions/titles: *Tillyria: Anguish, Tillyria: Fear* and *Tillyria: Mourning* (Demetriades, 2006: 32–36). The photographs accompanying these captions do not convincingly convey the feelings suggested and the images remain within the aesthetic parameters described above. Had they been detached from the said captions, which add an additional layer of signification and meaning, they could have been interpreted simply as three more aesthetisized, black and white, 'ethnographic' photographs.

Demetriades' review of Cyprus stops at 1974; the year Turkey invaded the island, using as a pretext the Greek Junta-led *coup d'état* against President Makarios, with the well-known disastrous consequences including mass displacement. None of the images in the book tells the story, but in some photograph captions from years prior to the invasion, the forthcoming disaster is referred to in the form of prophesy-like statements. For instance, the caption next to a 1963 photograph of a man sitting at Kerynia harbour, currently still under Turkish occupation, 'foresees' the tragic events of 1974:

> Kerynia Harbour: A Kyrenian takes a rest, gazing at the sea. The shadows which surround him come from the North, from "the beloved sea of Kyrenia" [Turkish invading troops landed ashore at a beach very near Kerynia]. (Demetriades, 2006: 26)

The dominant, widely held and officially sanctioned version of the series of events that led to the 1974 disaster is that Cypriots (Greek or Turkish) and their leaders are largely not accountable for the events, but are merely the victims of external plotting and interventions; an approach that fits in well within the fantasy of Cypriots being a pure and simple people.

Two photographs in Demetriades' book depict kafeneia and are characteristic of the sort of representations discussed. One depicts four elderly men outside a coffee house. Three of them are sitting in the foreground and one is standing by the entrance of the kafeneion in the background; their gaze is directed toward the same point outside the left border of the image. The caption makes a point linking old age, and by synecdoche tradition, with the coffee house:

> An out-of sight friend is relating a story to the old men in the coffee shop. It must be interesting and pleasant, to judge from their expressions. (Demetriades, 2006: 90)

Older men rather than younger ones, and pleasant storytelling rather than politics are interesting narrative-building choices. In addition, the men in the portrait are rather tightly framed and little of the context and its aesthetic is visible. Hence, no political paraphernalia, television sets, radios, refrigerators or any other utilitarian or cultural artefacts that are standard stock in local coffee shops and might evoke modernity are allowed into the frame.

Typical postcards that are displayed in tourist areas are produced by photographers who are equally selective in what enters the frame; it is usually modernity and its manifestations that end up being excluded.

One such example we bought in Laiki Gitonia (the tourist area of the walled city of Nicosia) is credited to Pierre Couteau and is titled 'Traditional Coffee Shop, Pafos, Cyprus'. The postcard depicts an elderly man wearing baggy trousers (a very, very rare sight indeed) and leather boots, sitting on an old rustic chair, his arm resting on a matching table, his face turned toward the lens and with an expression much closer to bemusement than a photographer would wish. The old man is in sharp focus. So is the beautiful, ornamented, tiled floor in the foreground. But the photograph has shallow depth of field. And what falls into the conveniently distant out-of-focus depth of the photograph is a collection of objects that the unaccustomed eye of a non-Cypriot will find very difficult to decipher; a refrigerator and right on top a frame that holds a picture we cannot see, plastic bottles of orange and lemon squash, a plastic water jug, a box of plastic straws, a small pile of aluminium trays. Along with the out-of-focus non-traditional objects, we can clearly see the side of a man standing at the back of the coffee house, whose body and posture tell of a man in the prime of his working years, which the photographer seems to have tried to exclude from his photograph as he is pushed at the top left edge of the frame. We can see how, if all these de-focused and de-emphasized components of the photograph had been highlighted, the constructed image of a *traditional coffee house* embodied by the presence of the old man in the foreground would have been confused.

Contrary to these contemporary traditionalized representations, the kafeneion in its indigenous version is a complex institution, which has long-held multiple social, cultural and political roles and meanings within Cypriot society. During the early colonial period in the last quarter of the 19th century, urban politics only reached the masses through a process of 'translation'. As the press of the period used *katharevousa* (a form of higher and 'pure' Greek language), which would sound foreign and incomprehensible to the ears of Cypriot workers and peasants, it was necessary for the literate – the school teacher or the priest – to interpret and simplify its content. This process normally took place in the kafeneion, which provided the primary forum for political communication and the dissemination of anti-colonial and nationalist ideas sanctioned by urban elites and promoted through a rather vociferous partisan press.[5]

Almost naturally, the space of the kafeneion was later – in the 1920s, 1930s and 1940s – adopted by an emerging leftist labor movement, which began to develop enough confidence to articulate itself and confront dominant nationalist ideology. The establishment of a communist party;

the organization of workers into trade unions in different sectors; and the circulation of leftist press during this period constitute a picture of a rather confident labor movement. The kafeneion lent itself as the obvious arena to contest ideas and subsequently echoed the divisions within Cypriot society, which accumulated into a head-on confrontation in 1948, primarily in the form of long and bitter general strikes.[6] This class conflict caused a complete political and social falling-out between the left and the right and created an ideological split that cut across Greek-Cypriot society – including a fracture along left-right lines of sports clubs and coffee houses; a rupture which gave birth to a local leftist sub-culture that endures to the present day.[7]

Representing Cyprus within the aesthetic and thematic parameters discussed earlier is a highly political process and the persistence of such perceptions of the place, its people and its culture should not be neglected when the aesthetics of tourism are being discussed together, of course, with the economic, demographic and policy dimensions. Further, it is Cyprus as a cultural realm in general that is romanticized and traditionalized and not just the coffee house or any other of those sub-components that make up this perceived-as-uniform culture.

The Politics of Cultural Tourism and the Kafeneion

From the late 1960s onwards, tourism grew rapidly until 1974 when interrupted by the Turkish invasion (Sharpley, 2003: 249; UNEP, 2004: 11). Indicatively, annual arrivals totaled just 25,700 in 1960 and by 1973 the number grew to 264,000. The rapid growth of tourist arrivals discontinued for only two years. However, the Republic could only promote tourism development in the non-occupied coastal zones. The immediate growth was extraordinary. It is indicative that between 1976 and 1989, annual arrivals increased by 700% (Sharpley, 2003: 251). Cyprus is now well established as one of the most popular 'Mediterranean summer sun' destinations (Sharpley, 2003: 251; Peristianis *et al.*, 1996: 483) and evidence of this are the 2,416,081 tourists who arrived in Cyprus in 2007 (CTO, 2007). In the framework of attracting mass tourism, the State did not view culture as a vital 'sellable tourist product', and even though several CTO reports and initiatives in the 1980s promoted and sponsored a more 'balanced [and] sustainable approach to tourism', they were largely unsuccessful at the implementation stage (Sharpley, 2003: 257).

Observing the rapidly increasing international tendency toward cultural tourism (Greg, 2005: 31), and concerned by a potential crisis in the Cyprus tourism industry, the CTO recognized the necessity of promoting culture as part of the Cyprus tourism product. Cultural tourism mainly attracts people who feel nostalgia for the past peasant lifestyle and are in search of the 'picturesque' and 'local colour' that is endangered by modern lifestyle (Smith, 1977: 4). The term cultural tourism refers to the consumption of culture and tradition. In this context, each area is supposed to have 'its own authentic, specific character', which is derived from cultural heritage and preservation of tradition. In other words, each area has to construct, confirm and promote a stable identity, which is verified and authenticated by others, in this case the tourists (McKercher & du Cros, 2002: 1).

The first effort to officially promote cultural tourism was the establishment of the Cyprus Agrotourism Program, launched in 1991 by the CTO with the support of the state. The main objectives of this program were to preserve the natural and cultural environment and 'open up rural Cyprus to nature tourism by capitalising on the island's *people, authenticity, hospitality, culture and unspoiled nature*' [our emphasis] (Saveriades, 2001). Ten years after the launch of the program, 52 traditional houses in 30 villages had been restored and converted into accommodation facilities, catering establishments, craft shops, museums and exhibition halls (Michael, 1998). Similarly, in 50 other villages, a number of other projects were developed, aimed at the preservation of natural and cultural sites (Saveriades, 2001).

Institutionalized efforts to incorporate culture in the Cyprus tourism product could well justify the repositioning statement of Cyprus, which was explicitly acknowledged in the Strategic Plan of Tourism Development 2003–2010, stating that the Cypriot tourism product is facing 'accumulated problems and weaknesses, for example its one-dimensional development and the destruction of natural environment and cultural identity' (CTO, 2003: 1, 3). Taking into consideration the aforementioned problems, the CTO concentrated on repositioning Cyprus on the tourist map as a destination offering an authentic cultural experience to the traveler (CTO, 2003: 1–11).

Within the new trend of cultural tourism, a new type of coffee shop is being developed in rural Cyprus alongside the indigenous kafeneion. This new type, found mostly in rural communities, is designed to evoke tradition in order to appeal to tourists, while not replacing the indigenous kafeneion that still holds its central position within these communities and serves the local population. Traditionalized coffee shops are the outcome of institutional policies as well as local economic concerns and individuals' initiatives.

European and national policies strategically aim at constructing an essentialized, enchanting and authentic Mediterranean identity. The EU and the Cypriot State actively promote and co-finance explicit representations of cultural heritage in rural Cyprus through specific strategies, policies and most importantly through funding schemes. The EU granted a significant amount of money through the Structural Funds to all member states under 'Measure 1.1: Strengthening the Economy of Rural Regions'. Specifically, it was only in 2006 that the EU granted, in the framework of Objective 2, the amount of 10.2 million Euro to Cyprus in order to encourage and support small and medium enterprises to invest in alternative economic activities, targeting the promotion of cultural and environmental resources of rural regions. As stated in the guidelines issued by the Town Planning and Housing Department, the managing authority in Cyprus, their specific objective is to 'rescue, restore, preserve and upgrade the traditional character and authenticity of rural regions and consequently the cultural character of Cyprus' (Town Planning and Housing Department, 2006). It is clearly stated that the traditional communities and the wider cultural and natural environment of Cyprus, along with the *living presence of its inhabitants*, contribute toward an *integrated authentic experience for tourists* (our emphasis) (Town Planning and Housing Department, 2006). Rural residents are eligible to retrieve funds from the Cypriot state for restoration of traditional buildings that will be used as museums, exhibition rooms, agrotourism houses, traditional taverns, traditional coffee shops, wineries and anything that falls under the broad spectrum of cultural tourism.

However, the transformation of some indigenous *kafeneia* into traditionalized coffee shops goes beyond the aforementioned institutionalized policies and funding schemes. It extends to the role of entrepreneurial individuals who observe the demographic changes in rural areas, identify opportunities and needs and promote the new type of traditional coffee shop that fulfils tourists' aspirations. The demographic collapse of rural Cyprus had consequences on the wider socioeconomic situation of the island. From the 1970s until today the population of rural areas is not only shrinking, it is growing older as well. In more detail, the rural population in 1960 was 64% of the total population of Cyprus, while in 2001 it was only 31% (Census of Population, 2001). Several schools have closed down and local family-owned enterprises (e.g. grocery stores, clothing shops, etc.) have been experiencing difficulties in sustaining themselves. Until recently, the state neglected these areas and provided poor public facilities for the inhabitants (Attalides, 1981: 55). In the current climate, cultural tourism is perceived as being 'sold' to locals by the state agencies, the EU and individuals, such as bureaucrats, consultants, politicians, intellectuals and others, as the ideal solution to their economic and demographic problems, through conferences, seminars, lectures, newspaper articles and television shows.

As a consequence, some inhabitants of rural areas, observing the shrinking size of the local population and the increase in the number of tourists in their respective communities, took the initiative to transform their indigenous kafeneion into a 'traditional coffee shop' serving tourists. These initiatives reveal some interesting power relations within this process, which will be examined here.

As noted above, the indigenous coffee shops, for quite some time, have been a politicized social space, in the sense that they are the arenas of political confrontation and that their material culture reflects this dynamic relation to current political affairs (Plate 5.1).

It appears that owners of traditionalized coffee shops, in their quest to attract tourists, are attempting to de-politicize and neutralize them. Neutrality is being unveiled through the aesthetics of the new domain and the constructed social place.

The differences between the material culture of the indigenous coffee shop and the politically neutralized aesthetics of its newborn counterpart, the traditionalized coffee shop, are sharply visible. Political paraphernalia such as national flags, maps, rightwing and leftwing political posters, portraits of Marx, Che, Makarios and Grivas as well as football team emblems[8] (Plate 5.2) are being replaced by politically 'neutral' objects like 'traditional vessels', oil lamps and photographs with rural subject matter, all evocative of a traditional Mediterranean lifestyle (Plate 5.3). This nostalgic and romanticized approach reveals an intention to satisfy tourists' notions of rurality and Mediterranean culture. It seems that locals present themselves in a way that mirrors the desires of the tourists constituting in this way the self as a Western subject (Argyrou, 1996: 183). Consciously ignoring the political and dynamic aspect of the indigenous kafeneion is part of this process.

The de-politicization of material culture and aesthetics is not the only visible change in this new type of coffee shop. Its social space is also being de-politicized. The traditionalized coffee shop, as a social space, has no political affiliation since people visiting it cannot build on a pre-existing notion of community, as is the case with the indigenous kafeneion. As travelers typically, they do not know each other and may not always be interested in getting to know one another. In other words, the function of the tourist coffee shop is focused on leisure and tourism is

Plate 5.1 The interior of a leftist coffee house (Source: Nicos Philippou)

Plate 5.2 Football team posters in a coffee house (Source: Nicos Philippou)

Plate 5.3 The interior of a traditionalized coffee house (Source: Evi Eftychiou)

not directed toward the formulation of a community; a group of people who share a communal and or political identity.

The paradox is that although the locals' intention is to de-politicize the coffee house and transform it into a politically neutral space, this process is political per se. The de-politicization and neutralization of the coffee shop, in effect replicates the romantic images of an 'authentic, traditional coffee house'. This is a process through which locals simulate the romanticized domain in order to provide tourists with opportunities to indulge in their fantasies. It seems that this reinforces the tourists' perceptions of how Cypriots should live: 'pure' from any political expression and confrontation. But it is also a sign of the adoption and internalization of outsiders' expectations or fantasies of how Cypriots and their culture should appear. This is the product of wider cultural and political processes related to Western dominance in the construction of the Other; processes that Said illuminates in his discussion of Orientalism (1978).

Cosmopolitanism, Modernity and Aesthetics

It is not just politics, of course, that get to be de-emphasized in this process of 'traditionalization', it is also any signifiers of modernity and cosmopolitanism within the kafeneion. Until the first half of the 20th century, for Cypriot masses – urban and rural – the coffee house was viewed as a point of contact with the 'outside world'; a world that was perceived as novel, more interesting and wider than the narrow confines of Cypriot traditional community life.

Social and cultural historians note that the kafeneion was a social space within which a working-class counter culture found room to express itself as early as the last quarter of the 19th century. This was a culture that was apparently detested and dismissed as subversive and vulgar by the puritan and paternalistic establishment. The conservative press – an institution itself a child of the local hegemonic culture (Katsiaounis, Bryant, Sophocleous) – condemned the lifestyle of the 'lower' classes, proclaiming that it was decadent and was 'contaminating' Cypriot society and morals. Katsiaounis (1996: 161) reports on reactions to the dawn of this emerging working-class culture, which included the adoption of a new vernacular jargon, and he describes an attack, which lambasted every aspect of working-class belief, behavior and aesthetics, 'all their institutions, folklore, common sense and mentalities'.

Observers, writing about Cypriot culture at the turn of the 20th century, produced descriptions of a rather cosmopolitan atmosphere in the kafeneion. For instance, O-Richter (1913: 174), in her ethnographic work on Cyprus reported that 'magicians, actors, dancers, musicians and singers of both genders' would perform in coffee houses and that theater groups would use the space of the kafeneion for performances.[9] Nevertheless, she complains that locals would waste much time in the kafeneion and spend a lot of money on drinks, smoking narghilehs and gambling (O-Richter, 1913).

When older Cypriots referring to the 1930s and 1940s – decades which are generally considered to be in the heart of the era that have witnessed major structural, social and cultural changes and the advent of Cypriot modernity (Loizos, 2001: 127–138; Argyrou, 1996) – shared their memories of coffee-house experiences, they recounted, with an evident sense of nostalgia, enjoying all sorts of vernacular entertainment within the kafeneion. These included performances by traveling shadow theater artists, storytellers and traveling theater groups.[10] But they also spoke of their enthusiasm for radio, especially during the Second World War; a mass medium they predominantly consumed within the kafeneion's confines.

Furthermore, the kafeneion frequently doubled as a kind of makeshift tavern in the evenings and was frequented by *Apahides*, which were defined by patrons as characters who 'like their drink, do not care much and are worldly-wise' (Philippou, 2007: 30); in other words, a local 'variation' of a Bohemian type. The consumption of *zivania*, a strong local white spirit served chilled and usually accompanied by cold mezze (consisting usually of smoked meat, cheese, nuts and fruits), listening to *laiki mousiki* (Greek urban working-class music) and the smoking of *narghile* (at least up until the 1940s) with sweet-scented tobacco imported from Egypt would all be associated with this lifestyle.

Almost always, older informants placed the kafeneion within a broader narrative of a modernist, urban and cosmopolitan experience, which included the consumption of forms of entertainment in other venues like cinemas, cabarets, theaters and live music and dance taverns. This is in stark contrast to the idealized and constructed nature of the traditionalized kafeneion.

Many of the indigenous kafeneia observed during fieldwork have generally echoed this role of the kafeneion as a social space within which the individual is enabled to transcend boundaries, whether they are the unavoidable boundaries of geography and tradition, or the boundaries that have been erected in the process of imposing hegemonic ideas about appropriate conduct and aesthetics.

The indigenous coffee shops were (and still are) a secular, modern and cosmopolitan realm. Although the modernist vernacular aesthetics reflect the culture still consumed in the confines of the kafeneion by the working class today, the tourism-oriented coffee shops strategically avoid the explicit material expression of modernity. Ironically, these coffee houses have been remodeled so that tourists' yearnings for escaping modernity (Bruner, 2005) by visiting a picturesque, traditional but also 'authentic' coffee house can be satisfied.

The indigenous kafeneion is located in the center of the community, usually not in a illustrious building and frequently with facades on which aluminium-framed glass panels and aluminium-insulated windows and doors are the dominant features. Wooden and plastic furniture are mixed together and placed randomly and spontaneously within the space and with no aspirations to formality. Also, the interior aesthetics are usually a clear signifier of the political affiliation of the owner and the clients. Political paraphernalia, as described above, religious or secular icons, and other objects loaded with political symbolism usually adorn the walls of the kafeneion. Color is an important political signifier too, thus curtains and tablecloths will be strategically blue for right-wing and red for left-wing coffee shops. The walls are decorated with useful information material such as the Euro exchange rate, citizens' service desks and posters announcing governmental and European available funds, but also maps and clocks. Further, newspapers, magazines, a radio and a television set, normally with access to satellite television channels are standard stock; their electricity and antenna wiring, visible on the walls of the kefeneion, can be read as a metaphor for networking, access and 'reaching out' to the rest of the world.

'Traditional coffee shops' are often renovated, housed in well maintained and 'clean' spaces. Earthy colors and wood are predominant in the invented aesthetics. Aluminium windows and doors are replaced either by wooden ones or by aluminium with wood-like finish. The interiors contain wooden furniture, usually well organized within the space. On the walls, political paraphernalia and the like are being replaced by objects – signifiers of tradition and the past. Items that are no longer in use by common Cypriots, such as oil lamps, candlesticks, clay or cucurbit vessels, embroidered curtains, scrimshaw knifes and jib booms, are some of the objects selected to symbolically represent times past. Black and white photographs portray a romanticized perception of Cypriot rural life and activities, while the actual hardship, poverty and difficulties of such lifestyle would not fit in well with this sanitized atmosphere.

Ironically, one of the owners revealed that some of the objects displayed on his walls came from Romania; 'a girl that helps me at the shop brought them back from her country as they are cheaper there' he said. These objects are, however, successful signifiers of local tradition as they are perceived by tourists to be authentic Cypriot traditional objects.

Further, utilitarian objects such as air conditioning, refrigerators or other specialized kitchen equipment are not avoided. A conscious effort has been observed, nonetheless, to 'hide' any of these potentially 'discordant items' behind wooden bars or in spaces out of sight of customers.

The outdoor exterior spaces of these traditionalized coffee shops are again well organized, but usually white or wood-effect plastic chairs and tables adorn the space. Owners felt the need to justify and explain the use of modern plastic rather than traditional wooden outdoor furniture in terms of cost of purchase and maintenance. Interestingly, the CTO (2008: 65), through a funding scheme for beatification and embellishment of the tourism product, strongly encourages the replacement of plastic chairs and tables, in restaurants and coffee shops in rural Cyprus, with wooden ones.

Conclusions

In general, what has been noted during field observation is a conscious and strategic fetishization of a reduced, simplified and de-politicized tradition, which is a synthesis of individuals' efforts and perceptions as well as of institutionalized policies. Local tourism entrepreneurs endeavour to materialize tourists' aspirations of Cypriot tradition in order to successfully attract a new target group in their region. At the same time, the Cypriot state supports and funds the traditionalized aesthetics of rural coffee shops with its own programs and also by promoting specific European funding schemes that support agrotourism entrepreneurships in compliance with set aesthetic criteria. Culture and, consequently, authenticity is continually invented and reinvented (Bruner, 2005: 146), in our case through a dynamic process in which locals, tourists, national and European institutions actively participate.

The material culture adopted within these initiatives is symbolic of a static cultural heritage, perceived as homogenized and fixed. But the 'story' told by the arrangements of objects within the confines of the indigenous kafeneion is a different one. At a surface level, these tableaux can be seen as manifestations of a general Cypriot vernacular culture and aesthetic. Under scrutiny, however, they reveal a multiplicity of cultures and ideologies. Whereas on some occasions these objects and or signs are in agreement with hegemonic values (i.e. religious iconography), they are frequently, if not in sharp contrast, at least indifferent to these. Consequently, the walls of the kafeneion could be seen as a contest ground for antagonistic ideologies, values and aesthetics. But, even when these tableaux of objects do not present such sharp antagonism, observers are still invited to view them as manifestations of idiosyncratic communal identities.

The popularity of cultural tourism reflects the broader ideals of post-modern movements, such as environmentalism (Argyrou, 2005; Theo-dosopoulos, 2003) and cultural preservation (Herzfeld, 1991; Tucker, 1997). Therefore, the development of this new tourism domain is a product of its time. What is important to examine is, first, the meaning of change and, second, the power relations involved in this process.

This chapter attempted to demonstrate that an invented traditiona-lized coffee house is established in rural destinations in Cyprus, mainly to serve tourists. The new version of the kafeneion is visually and symbolically purified, in the sense that symbols of cosmopolitanism, modernity and current political affairs are being strategically replaced by signifiers of tradition, rurality and peasantry.

The meaning of the change in the semiotic value of the coffee shop could be simplistically and naively reduced to a marketing strategy of the state on behalf of the locals. Nevertheless, the detailed examination of this change, in its appropriate context, can reveal significant underlying power relations involved in this process.

This chapter also suggested that the invented traditionalized coffee house is closer to the romanticized photographic depictions of the kafeneion, in the 19th and 20th centuries, which consciously excluded any symbol of modernity and political activity, and not to its indigenous version. Romantic photographers, Westerners and Cypriot elites had the power to represent locals and their culture, from the colonial period until today. It is clearly indicated that the kafeneion's functions have been largely ignored by both romantic photographers and those seeking to enchant tourists.

Tourists' perceptions are constructed by the romantic school of thought, initiated by British colonialists and later by the Cypriot elite. Following Said (1978), it could be suggested that that the longstanding and well-established romanticized representations of Cypriot culture, and by extension of the kafeneion, by Westerners significantly influenced the Cypriot elite, and ironically the Cypriot state, who internalized the dominant representation. The power to symbolically represent the Other as a pure, underdeveloped peasant, not involved or passively uninterested in politics, provides the actor with the authority to refuse the right of the other to live in the present (Fabian, 2002) and be politically active.

Cultural tourists in their search for the *authentic* Other (McCannell, 1976: 3) expect to fulfil their aspirations in order to acquire symbolic capital and culturally differentiate themselves from other tourists (Bourdieu, 1979). It is not surprising that although tourists have the choice between the traditionalized coffee shop and the indigenous kafeneion that locals visit, they consciously select to visit the one that appears to them 'traditional and more authentic'. It seems that in this context, 'the culture of the Other is imagined more than it is actually shared' (Tucker, 1997: 124).

The paradox is that although some tourists are enchanted while visiting the traditionalized coffee shops and perceive them to be an authentic expression of the traditional Cypriot and Mediterranean lifestyle, the respective coffee shops are an invented tradition and a cultural product of modernity. As Hobsbawm (1983) would put it, the concept of tradition itself, is a social product of modernity and as a consequence, 'traditional coffee shops' are paradoxically products of modernity by definition.

Although tourists' imaginations contributed significantly to the invention of the traditional coffee shop, the role of locals should not be neglected. It is acknowledged that locals play an active role in this complex process of traditionalization of rural Cyprus. Locals 'constitute themselves and are constituted as Western subjects' (Argyrou, 1996: 183) by this complex process of traditionalization. Western hegemony is being depicted in the invented coffee shop and on the way locals perceive their identity. It is assumed that traditionalization is considered successful only if the suggested traditional identity is verified and recognized as 'authentic' by Others and not by locals. The emergence of this new type of coffee shop with its traditional aesthetics shows how dominant representations and, consequently, tourists' perceptions have the power to construct cultural domains, landscapes and identities in rural Cyprus.

Acknowledgement

The authors would like to thank Peter Loizos for reading the chapter and giving very useful feedback.

Notes

1. The output of these three 'representational institutions' displays a similar tendency toward a reductive and traditionalized representation of Cyprus as a cultural realm. Nevertheless, it is not implied here that a genealogy of representation of Cyprus has been traced or that a direct link between the three exists. An ongoing PhD thesis (N. Philippou) is exploring this question, but no firm conclusions can be reached as yet.
2. Limitations in his contemporary photographic technology rendered interior photography a challenge.
3. Nicos Philippou, PhD thesis, ongoing.
4. Traditionalization is not the only process or visual category identified. Other categories like 'unspoiled nature', 'monumental heritage', 'hellinisation' as well as depictions of the tourist infrastructure itself were identified, but due to economy of space, they were not expanded on here.
5. This process is a central theme in Rebecca Bryant, 'Signatures and "simple ones": Constituting a public in Cyprus, circa 1900'. See also Katsiaounis (1996: 96) for references to this communication process, plus the book series by Andreas Cl. Sophocleous for a detailed account of the emergence and outlook of early Cypriot press.
6. See Philippou for a more detailed account of the role of the kafeneion as a contest ground for the political/ideological conflict of the period and the attempts of the left to appropriate it and those of the right to re-appropriate it.

7. See Panayiotou's aptly titled article 'Lenin in the coffee-shop' for a thorough and very interesting account of the emergence of a leftist sub-culture in Cyprus as a form of an alternative modernizing movement.
8. Football clubs in Cyprus are strongly affiliated to particular parties or ideological factions since the class conflict of the 1940s.
9. See O-Richter's volume translated to Greek by Marangou (2004: 174).
10. See Philippou (2007) for several oral history accounts of the kafeneion as a space for the consumption of forms of vernacular culture.

References

Argyrou, V. (1996) *Tradition and Modernity in the Mediterranean: The Wedding as a Symbolic Struggle*. Cambridge: Cambridge University Press.
Argyrou, V. (2005) *The Logic of Environmentalism: Anthropology, Ecology and Postcoloniality*. New York and Oxford: Berghahn Books.
Attalides, M. (1981) *Social Change and Urbanization in Cyprus: A Study of Nicosia*. Nicosia: Zavallis Press.
Bourdieu, P. (1979) *Distinction: A Social Critique of the Judgement of Taste*. New York and London: Routledge.
Bourdieu, P. (1980) *The Logic of Practice*. Stanford, CA: Stanford University Press.
Bryant, R. (2006) Signatures and 'simple ones': Constituting a public in Cyprus, circa 1900. In H. Faustmann and N. Peristianis (eds) *Britain in Cyprus/ Colonialism and Post-Colonialism, 1878–2006* (pp. 79–97). Mannheim and Mohnesee: Bibliopolis.
Census of Population (2001) Statistical Service. Republic of Cyprus.
Cyprus Tourism Organization (2003) Strategic Plan for Tourism Development 2003–2010.
Cyprus Tourism Organization (2008) Scheme for promotion of investments in sustainable enriching and improvement of the tourism product. First Call for Proposals, December 2008.
Demetriades, T. (2006) *The World of Cyprus 1960–1974 Through the Lens of Takis Demetriades AFIAP*. Nicosia: Armida.
Fabian, J. (1983) *Time and the Other: How Anthropology Makes its Object*. New York: Columbia University Press.
Greg, R. (ed.) (2005) *Cultural Tourism in Europe*. Wallingford: CABI.
Herzfeld, M. (1991) *A Place in History: Social and Monumental Time in a Cretan Town*. Princeton, NJ: Princeton University Press.
Hobsbawm, E. and Ranger, T. (eds) (1983) *The Invention of Tradition*. Cambridge: Cambridge University Press.
Katsiaounis, R. (1996) *Labour, Society and Politics in Cyprus during the Second Half of the Nineteenth Century*. Nicosia: Cyprus Research Centre.
Loizos, P. (2001) *Unofficial Views/Cyprus: Society and Politics*. Nicosia: Intercollege Press.
McCannell, D. (1976) *The Tourist: A New Theory of the Leisure Class*. London: University of California Press.
McCullin, D. (1992) *Unreasonable Behaviour/An Autobiography*. London: Vintage.
McKercher, B. and du Cros, H. (2002) *Cultural Tourism: The Partnership Between Tourism and Cultural Heritage Management*. New York: Haworth Press.

O-Richter, M. (1913) *Griechische sittten und Gebrauche auf Cypren* [*Greek Customs in Cyprus*]. Greek translation by A. Marangou (2004) Ελληνικά 'Ηθη και 'Εθιμα στην Κύπρο [*Greek Customs in Cyprus*]. Λευκωσία: Πολιτιστικό Κέντρο Λαϊκής Τράπεζας [*Nicosia: Cyprus Popular Bank Cultural Centre*].

Panayiotou, A. (2006) Lenin in the coffee-shop. *Postcolonial Studies* 9 (3), 267–280.

Peristianis, N., Akis, S. and Warner, J. (1996) Resident's attitudes to tourism development: The case of Cyprus. *Tourism Management* 17 (7), 481–494.

Philippou, N. (2007) *Coffee House Embellishments.* Nicosia: University of Nicosia Press.

Said, D.E. (1978) *Orientalism* (F. Terzakis, trans.). Athens: Nefeli Publications.

Saveriades, A. (2001) Developing the agrotourism (rural tourism) product: The Cyprus experience. International Conference on the Development of Ecotourism, Greece, 2–4 November 2001.

Sharpley, R. (2003) Tourism, modernisation and development on the Island of Cyprus: Challenges and policy responses. *Journal of Sustainable Tourism* 11 (2 & 3), 246–265.

Smith, V. (ed.) (1977) *Hosts and Guests: The Anthropology of Tourism* (1989 edn). Philadelphia, PA: University of Pennsylvania Press.

Sophocleous, A.Cl. (1995–2006) Συμβολή στην Ιστορία του Κυπριακού Τύπου [*A Contribution to the History of Cypriot Press*] (4 vols). Nicosia: Intercollege Press and IMME Publications.

Theodosopoulos, D. (2003) *Troubles with Turtles: Cultural Understandings of Environment on a Greek Island.* Oxford: Berghahn Books.

Thomson, J. (1985) *Through Cyprus with the Camera in the Autumn of 1878.* London: Trigraph Limited.

Town Planning and Housing Department (2006) Scheme for funding small and medium size enterprises for alternative economic activities related to agrotourism. Ministry of Interior.

Tucker, H. (1997) The ideal village: Interactions through tourism in Central Anatolia. In S. Abram, J. Waldren and V.L.D. Macleod (eds) *Tourists and Tourism: Identifying with People and Places* (pp. 107–128). Oxford: Berg.

UNEP (United Nations Environment Programme) (2004) *Guide to Good Practice in Tourism Carrying Capacity Assessment.*

Part 3

Coffee Destination Experiences

Chapter 6

Coffee in Vietnam: International Tourist Experiences

LEE JOLLIFFE, KAREN KWAN and GIANG KHONG YEN

Coffee is a globally recognized commodity, but because a suitable climate is required for production it is locally produced in the tropics. Vietnam has such a climate and coffee was introduced by French missionaries in the 19th century (between 1865 and 1866) and a plantation was established in 1887 (Thorn, 2006). Thereafter, French colonists and entrepreneurs exported coffee grown here (Murray, 1997). After the Vietnam War of the 1970s, the government established coffee plantations in the Central Highlands (Tay Nguyen).

Later, small-scale coffee-holder production was stimulated by institutional reforms at a central level and by *doi moi* – the 1986 policy directed toward the move to a market economy, as well as by socio-economic tools (such as demographic resettlement) and legislation toward land tenure (Tan, 2000; D'haese *et al.*, 2005). Production here is now reportedly from small farms with the government having some involvement in a number of plantations and in processing (Thorn, 2006). In addition, rising prices on international markets for coffee have stimulated increases in production of coffee in Vietnam (McCargo, 2004).

The Vietnam National Coffee Corporation (Vincafé) oversees 50 coffee plantations (http://www.vinacafebienhoa.com) and also operates a coffee institute. According to the company website, the Vincafé brand of processed coffee has 45% of the domestic Vietnamese coffee market share. Another major player in the Vietnamese coffee business is Trung Nguyen Corporation, a coffee manufacturer headquartered at Buon Ma Thuot in the coffee-producing Central Highlands, and the developer of cafés in Vietnam and the surrounding countries. The company is developing the image of Vietnamese coffee, for example (http://www.trungnguyen. com.vn) establishing the Trung Nguyen Creativity Club House in Hanoi where people can visit and experience coffee culture.

As a consequence of increases in coffee production in Vietnam, according to Euromonitor (2007) the country is now the second largest coffee exporter in the world. Coffee produced here is mostly Robusta, serving major world markets for blending (Thorn, 2006), although at times there has been some investment in the cultivation of Arabica (Murray, 1997). The government is now reported to be encouraging the production of Arabica as a way of adding to the value of the coffee produced.

Domestic consumption of coffee within Vietnam is small compared to its export and most coffee-producing companies concentrate on production for export. However, beyond production there is potential for developing the domestic coffee market as evidenced by the rise of the local Trung Nguyen coffee chain in Vietnam and the surrounding countries (Jolliffe & Bui, 2006).

Coffee, first introduced by the French, is now part of the beverage tradition of the country. In a previous paper, the overall potential for branding the coffee tourism experience in Vietnam was examined (Jolliffe & Bui, 2006; Jolliffe, 2007). Subsequent work focused in on the role of a coffee festival in branding Buon Ma Thuot – the central city of the coffee-producing Central Highlands – as an emerging coffee destination (Jolliffe *et al.*, 2009). This chapter considers another dimension of tourism related to coffee, as international visitor encounters with coffee in Vietnam are documented and discussed.

Experiencing Coffee in Vietnam

In Vietnam, coffee is locally produced and uniquely prepared, thus forming part of the culinary experience of international tourists visiting local cafes, restaurants and hotels. While tea is the traditional drink in the north of the country, coffee is positioned as a habitual drink of the Vietnamese (Euromonitor, 2008) and since coffee is produced in the country, tourists consuming coffee here are experiencing a local product and tradition. This reflects global trends in culinary tourism with growing emphasis on 'local authentic food and drink of the place' (Boniface, 2003: 28).

In commercial hospitality, outlets (such as cafés and restaurants) prepare coffee using a small, metal, one-cup drip filter (known as *ca phe phin*) perched on top of the cup or glass, and the coffee may or may not be dripped over ice and/or sweet condensed milk. The process is longer than what most tourists would expect, producing a small amount of very rich coffee (Berger, 2005) with a uniquely Vietnamese flavor (Stirling,

2000). Zolf (2001) observes of the experience 'There's an aspect of ritual to it: sitting, waiting, watching the coffee brew right over your own glass'.

According to Berger (2004), Vietnam is recognized as having one of the great cuisines of the world. Food and drink form part of the tourism product (Stewart, 2000), although coffee is not directly promoted as a tourism attraction (Jolliffe & Bui, 2006). However, since the Vietnamese appreciate coffee, as reflected by the distinct coffee preparation and vibrant café culture (Berger, 2005; Stirling, 2000), this coffee theme as part of local culinary experiences may appeal to tourists as authentic. As Long (2004) notes, foodways provide an entry into participating in and understanding other cultures.

As Richards (2001) indicated, food structures the tourists' day, and for those who consume coffee at home, experiencing local coffee at new tourism destinations is a logical extension of the daily routine. Coffee as an internationally recognized beverage with a local culture, therefore it has the potential to be an attraction for the growing numbers of international visitors in Vietnam, reaching 4 million in 2007 (Vietnam Administration of Tourism, 2008).

Visitors to Vietnam could consider the consumption of coffee, with its unique preparation and local origins, to be a local product, just as Smith and Xiao (2008) indicate that visitors from the USA to Canada may consider a Canadian wine to be local. However, in some cases, international visitors and tourists may not be aware that coffee is produced in Vietnam because the country is a newcomer as a global coffee producer.

The coffee heritage and culture of the country is well represented by Hanoi's vibrant café culture, especially in The Old Quarter of Hanoi (Berger, 2005) as well as by other cafés throughout the country. The coffee-growing regions of the country offer visitors the opportunity to experience coffee at its origins and to gain insights into the growing, harvesting and production processes. In the case of the Central Highlands, where much of the coffee in Vietnam is grown, coffee festival establishment during the coffee harvest period (2005) and associated coffee destination development is emerging, as documented by Jolliffe *et al.* (2009). In the latter work, the authors identified the potential for a parallel festival and related tourism during the coffee blossom period.

Furthermore, in 2007, Dak Lak Province held coffee weeks in both Ho Chi Min City and Hanoi. These coffee-week celebrations included a model coffee farm, a coffee road with cafés, coffee games, meetings about the coffee industry, exhibitions and films on coffee production and cultural performances from the coffee-producing region (Vietnam.net, 2007). A byproduct of this branding promotion for Buon Ma Thuot coffee is the encouragement of coffee-related tourism. At the 2007 coffee week, 2008 was declared the year of coffee, to continue to promote the Buon Ma Thuot coffee trademark and profile. In addition, Dak Lak Province organized and held the Buon Ma Thuot Coffee Festival again in 2008.

At Buon Ma Thuot City, in part as a result of the initial Buon Ma Thuot Coffee Festival in 2005, opportunities are emerging for international tourists to join coffee tours (organized on demand for example by Damsun Travel) or to independently visit (with a tour guide) coffee farms and potential production facilities. The first festival in 2005 stimulated the establishment of a variety of local café outlets in the city of Buon Ma Thuot, which is becoming known as a coffee town. Many are located in garden settings. Here, the entrepreneur who owns Trung Nguyen Coffee reportedly also has plans to leverage local coffee resources to turn the region into a 'coffee paradise', with a company-operated coffee institute and coffee-themed resort (http://www.trungnguyen.com.vn).

In addition, the material culture associated with coffee in Vietnam (such as the coffee beans and metal coffee filter) can play a role in this culinary tourism experience. It is known that shopping is a popular tourist activity (Timothy, 2005) and this coffee-related equipment has potential for the production of souvenirs for tourists. For example, Berger (2005), writing about his own tourism encounters in Vietnam, portrays the purchasing of coffee beans and a coffee filter from Vietnam, as souvenirs obtained so that he could enjoy Vietnamese coffee and its associated memories once he had returned home.

Methodology

Information was collected by a survey conducted in English by the researchers of a sample of 271 international tourists visiting Vietnam during October 2007 to May 2008. Convenience sampling was used because it has been recognized as being of use for exploratory research, as it is, to a large extent, dependent on respondents who are available at the location at the time of research (Hemmington, 1999). A brief, structured questionnaire was administered in the context of culinary tourism, in interview settings at major historic sites frequented by international tourists in Hanoi, e.g. the Temple of Literature and the park outside the Ngoc Son Temple at Hoan Kiem Lake. In terms of the survey sites chosen, there is a potential bias toward cultural tourists visiting these cultural sites. However, since culinary tourism is recognized as a subset of cultural tourism and coffee tourism as a subset of culinary tourism, the researchers considered the site selection to be appropriate.

The survey questionnaire focused on questions about the type of trip, the culinary tourism and coffee experiences and demographics of the tourist. It included both fixed and open-ended questions. It was administered by the researchers acting as face-to-face interviewers, a method traditionally acknowledged as being the most reliable for collecting attitudinal, opinion and other forms of factual data (Rossi *et al.*, 1983).

The survey was supplemented by participant observation of coffee environments (café settings and retail outlets) in Hoi An, Hue, Hanoi and Buon Ma Thuot, during a four-month stay in Vietnam (fall of 2007). Participant observation is acknowledged as being a valuable secondary source of information, especially in exploratory research. In addition, secondary information from guidebooks (such as the Lonely Planet etc.), media reports and sectoral food studies (Euromonitor, 2007, 2008) were also used to interpret the state of coffee-related experiences in Vietnam. In the latter case, Wood (2007) notes the limitations of such sectoral surveys of the food industry, in this case of hot beverages, as tending, for the most part, to description rather than analysis.

The research is limited by the small sample size (271) as well as the single survey location of Hanoi. Another limitation is the fact that the survey interviews were only completed with international tourists who spoke English. However, even with this language limitation, the sample size is a beginning and should be enough to provide some indication of the interests of international tourists in coffee in Vietnam. Hanoi, as a survey site, is a city that is on the itinerary of many international visitors to the country and it has an established café tradition in the historic Old Quarter and other parts of the city.

Findings

The results provide a very preliminary profile of the interests of international tourists in coffee as part of culinary tourism in Vietnam. A visitor profile was derived by analysis of 240 useable surveys. The respondents were fairly split between female (53%) and male (47%). In terms of age (Table 6.1), only a few were under 20 (3%), the largest groups were in the age range of 20–29 and 30–39 years and only a few were from the 50–59 and 60 years or above age ranges.

The visitors reported a high level of education, as is typical with culinary tourists (Boniface, 2003) with 44% having a Bachelor's degree, 44% holding a Master's degree and 4% having Doctoral degrees. Notably, 34% were first-time visitors, while 66% were repeat visitors, indicating the potential for creating repeat visitation to the country.

Table 6.1 Age of survey respondents

Age range	%
Under 20	3
20–29	36
30–39	28
40–49	19
50–59	7
60 or above	8

In terms of the origin of visitors, the largest destination origin groups were from the USA (13%), France (9%), Australia (8%), Sweden (7%), Japan (6%) and China and Thailand (5% each). There were a few visitors from a number of other countries: Canada, Spain, South Korea, Germany (4% each); Russia, Singapore, Netherlands (3% each); UK and Malaysia (2% each), with other countries reporting at 19%. The average length of stay was reported as 32 days, however there was an educational tourist bias, as some international students surveyed were staying in the country for up to 365 days.

Participants were asked about the purpose of their trip and the largest group identified with being on a cultural holiday (28%) followed by the touring holiday (25%), the sun/beach holiday (17%) and the ecotourism/ nature holiday (16%). All these former visitor segments would be interested in coffee tourism experiences. Smaller numbers reported being on a health/sport holiday (6%), a city holiday (4%) or a rural holiday (1%). Other types of holiday trips were reported at 3%.

While coffee is an internationally known beverage, Vietnam is a newcomer as a coffee-producing country (Jolliffe, 2007). Nonetheless, 65% of those international tourists surveyed were aware that coffee is produced here. This could be, in part, due to the mentioning of coffee production in guidebooks such as the Lonely Planet and to international press about the role of Vietnam in the global coffee crisis (see Chapters 11–13 for detail about the crisis).

An overwhelming percentage of those surveyed (84%) reported drinking coffee at home, while fewer (16%) were not coffee drinkers. Predictably, as the sample was dominated by coffee drinkers, the majority (77%) reported trying coffee in Vietnam with fewer (23%) not trying it. There are four standard coffee (*ca phe*) drinks in Vietnam, hot black coffee, iced black coffee, hot black coffee with sweet milk (condensed milk) and iced black coffee with sweet milk (Zoepf, 2001). In addition, egg coffee (*ca phe trung*, literally egg coffee) is a traditional concoction of coffee, whipped egg white, sugar and milk, and is only found at Cafe Giang and other cafés in the Old Quarter of Hanoi. Of those trying coffee, the largest group (53%) reported trying coffee (*ca phe*) served in the traditional Vietnamese manner, served black, hot and/or with ice (Table 6.2). A slightly smaller group (44%) consumed coffee dripped over sweet (condensed) milk and/or ice.

In an open-ended question, participants were asked about their favorite café in Hanoi. Common responses were coded and the results were Cafe Mai (9%), Mocha Cafe (14%), Highlands Cafe (16%), Trung Nguyen Cafés (9%) and other cafés (52%). Both Cafe Mai and Mocha Cafe are old traditional cafés located in the Old Quarter of Hanoi. Highlands Cafe is a modern café chain serving both Vietnamese (*ca phe* variations outlined in Table 6.2) and Western coffee preparations (such as cappachino and café au lait). Trung Nguyen is a fast-growing coffee company based in Vietnam and franchises its name and products to other café outlets in the country and in Cambodia, Thailand and Singapore.

In Vietnam, coffee, like tea, may be offered to guests as a sign of hospitality. However, of the international tourists surveyed, only 39% had been offered coffee, while 61% had not been offered coffee in situations where a beverage might be offered as a sign of hospitality. In Vietnam, it is common for tea to be offered as a sign of hospitality, for example when checking into a hotel or when making a business transaction in a shop. It could be significant that this hospitality tradition to some extent has transferred over to the offering of coffee.

Table 6.2 Type of coffee preparation experienced

Type	%
Hot black coffee (*ca phe den nong*)	34
Iced black coffee (*ca phe den da*)	19
Hot black coffee with sweet milk (*ca phe sua nong*)	31
Iced black coffee with sweet milk (*ca phe sua da*)	13
Coffee with egg (*ca phe trung*)	2
Other	1

Source: Zoepf (2001)

Coffee experiences can be situated within the broader context of culinary tourism. As to their generalized experience with cuisine while visiting Vietnam, an overwhelming majority (93%) of those surveyed stated they seek out local food and drink experiences when traveling, reflecting the willingness of tourists to discover the culture of others through food, as discussed by Long (1994). However, while the vast majority of those surveyed were willing to experience new food and drink, over half of the respondents (60%) look for a combination of strange and familiar in their culinary choice, while 27% seek out strange food experiences and 13% seek out familiar ones. This parallels Long's (1994) comments and the observations of Kivela and Crotts (2006) that many tourists will seek out familiarity in food experiences as they travel away from home. Most of the international tourists surveyed (88%) will recommend Vietnam to others as a destination for food and drink experiences, indicating they had a positive culinary experience in the country. In terms of souvenirs, over half of those surveyed (54%) would purchase coffee beans or coffee-related accessories as a souvenir and just over half (51%) reported being interested in coffee-related tours.

Vietnam is therefore a culinary destination with potential in the area of food and drink experiences, including those related to coffee, as the survey results indicate that local culinary traditions are being transformed for tourism.

Discussion

Among the international tourists surveyed, many were aware that Vietnam produces coffee. A large majority of respondents reported drinking coffee at home, but only a slightly smaller group of these coffee drinkers tried coffee in Vietnam. Capitalizing on this awareness of Vietnamese coffee and the profiles of coffee drinkers there, may be the opportunity for proposing and developing forms of coffee tourism targeted at international visitors to the country. In addition to these results, potential for developing the market for coffee-related souvenirs is shown by the fact that over half of the respondents, reportedly, would purchase coffee beans or accessories as a souvenir. Similarly, the case for further investigating the development of the coffee-related tour product is supported by the result that over half of those surveyed would be interested in such tours. At present, few dedicated coffee tours exist, so the results identify possible opportunity for tour companies to develop coffee tour packages.

Results from this exploratory study indicate that the Vietnamese coffee experience forms part of the international tourist's culinary tourism experience in Vietnam. For the most part, international tourists surveyed were reportedly attracted to the local cuisine and to coffee experiences. Those surveyed recommend Vietnam as a culinary destination. The survey results indicate the potential for coffee to play a role within the culinary heritage available for tourism.

In summary, international tourists surveyed indicate that they are somewhat aware of Vietnam as a coffee destination, both for the coffee consumed and for potential new tour products (such as tours of Hanoi café district) that could address this interest. While survey findings reflect some demand for coffee-related souvenirs (such as coffee beans, coffee filters, coffee cups and pots), for this market the researcher found only one shop in Hanoi now has this exclusive focus, mainly for Japanese clients. However, long-established café outlets such as Cafe Mai with their separate retail store and department stores that sell the Vincafé and Trung Nuygen coffee beans and accessories are also positioned to cater to this interest.

In conclusion, the chapter relates coffee consumption and production heritage to culinary tourism in the experience of international tourists visiting the coffee-producing country of Vietnam. It confirms that international tourists have an interest in coffee in Vietnam and points to the potential for the development of product offerings for them, such as souvenir production and tours, related to Vietnamese coffee heritage and production. It positions coffee heritage experiences currently available within the context of Vietnam and its developing international tourism, providing a starting point for further research and development in this area.

Acknowledgement

Research funding was provided by the University of New Brunswick, Canada. Assistance with survey work in Vietnam was provided by Giang Khong Yen, Hang Nguyen and Huong Do, all of Hanoi University. An earlier version of this chapter was presented by Lee Jolliffe and Karen Kwan at the TTRA Canada Conference in Victoria, BC, Canada in October 2008.

References

Berger, A.A. (2005) *Vietnam Tourism*. New York: Haworth Press.

Boniface, P. (2003) *Tasting Tourism: Travelling for Food and Drink*. Aldershot: Ashgate.

D'haeze, D., Deckers, J., Raes, D., Phong, T.A. and Loi, H.V. (2005) Environmental and socio-economic impacts of institutional reforms on the agricultural sector of Vietnam: Land suitability assessment for Robusta coffee in the Dak Gan region. *Agriculture, Ecosystems & Environment* 105 (1–2), 59–76.

Euromonitor (2007) *Hot Drinks in Vietnam*. London: Euromonitor International.

Euromonitor (2008) *Hot Drinks in Vietnam*. London: Euromonitor International.

Hemmington, N. (1999) Sampling. In B. Brotherton (ed.) *The Handbook of Contemporary Hospitality Management Research* (pp. 244–262). Chichester: John Wiley and Sons Ltd.

Jolliffe, L. (2007) Coffee and tourism: A research framework. Presented at the Second International Conference on Tourism and Hospitality, Universiti Utara Malaysia and The Department of National Heritage, Ministry of Culture, Arts and Heritage Malaysia, Putrajaya, Malaysia.

Jolliffe, L. and Bui, T.H. (2006) Coffee and tourism in Vietnam: A niche tourism product? Presented at the Travel and Tourism Research Association – Canada Chapter Conference at Montebello, Quebec.

Jolliffe, L., Bui, H.T. and Nuygen, H. (2009) The Buon Ma Thuot coffee festival, Vietnam: Opportunity for tourism? In J. Ali-Knight, M. Robertson, A. Fyall and A. Ladkin (eds) *International Perspectives of Festivals and Events* (pp. 125–136). London: Elsevier.

Jolliffe, L. and Kwan, K. (2008) Blending coffee and tourism: International tourist experiences in Vietnam. TTRA Canada Conference, Victoria B.C. On WWW at http://www.linkbc.ca/torc/downs1/JolliffeKwan.pdf.

Kivella, J. and Crotts, C. (2006) Tourism and gastronomy: Gastronomy's influence on how tourists experience a destination. *Journal of Hospitality and Tourism Research* 30, 254–377.

McCargo, D. (2004) *Rethinking Vietnam*. London: Routledge.

Murray, G. (1997) *Vietnam Dawn of a New Market*. Basingstoke: Palgrave MacMillan.

Richards, G. (2001) Gastronomy: An essential ingredient in local culture. In A.M. Hjalger and G. Richards (eds) *Tourism and Gastronomy* (pp. 1–20). London: Routledge.

Rossi, P.H., Wright, J.D. and Anderson, A.B. (1983) *Handbook of Survey Research*. London: Academic Press.

Smith, S.L.J. and Xiao, H. (2008) Culinary tourism supply chains: A preliminary examination. *Journal of Travel Research* 46, 289–299.

Sterling, R. (2000) *World Food Vietnam*. Australia: Lonely Planet.

Tan, S.B.H. (2000) Coffee Frontiers in the Central Highlands of Vietnam: Networks of Connectivity. *Asia Pacific Viewpoint* 41 (1), 51–67.

Thorn, J. (2006) *The Coffee Companion: A Connoisseur's Guide*. London: Quintet.

Timothy, D. (2005) *Shopping Tourism, Retailing and Leisure*. Clevedon: Channel View Publications.

Vietnam Administration of Tourism (2008) 2007 Annual Report. Hanoi.

Vietnam.net (2007) Cofffee Culture Week to be held in HCM City, October 14, 2007. On WWW at http://english.vietnamnet.vn/biz/2007/10/749294/. Accessed 31.7.09.

Wood, R. (2007) The future of food and beverage management research. *Journal of Hospitality and Tourism Management* 14 (1), 6–16.

Zoepf, K. (2001) *Hanoi's Café Society. The New York Times*, September. On WWW at www.nytimes.com.

Chapter 7

Coffee Culture, Heritage and Destination Image: Melbourne and the Italian Model

WARWICK FROST, JENNIFER LAING, FIONA WHEELER and KEIR REEVES

In 2008, the media reported on growing concern that international inbound tourism to Australia was stagnating. The malaise was highlighted by a succession of mediocre marketing campaigns that spectacularly failed to reverse the trend. Christopher Brown (of the industry body Tourism and Transport Forum or TTF Australia) complained that there was a '"cargo cult mentality", where the industry relied on advertising rather than developing new products and experiences to attract tourists… the country has sat around for 20 years waiting for another great ad to come along and save us'. According to Brown, the only exception to this stagnation was continuing growth for Melbourne, where for the first time ever, international tourists spent more money than in Sydney. For Brown, the secret of Melbourne's success was its linking of marketing campaigns to experiences: 'Melbourne has things to do, not just things to look at – that's its strategic advantage'. Chief among these attractive experiences were events and a 'unique café culture' (quoted in Topsfield, 2008: 3, see also Walker, 2008).

Some cities have 'place luck'; historical buildings or spectacular natural settings that attract strong flows of tourists. By contrast, 'cities that lie outside this orbit must take steps to transform themselves into tourism sites' (Fainstein & Judd, 1999: 11). Melbourne belongs to this latter group. It lacks Sydney's attractive harbour, and it does not have built icons such as Sydney's Harbour Bridge or Opera House. In the 1970s and 1980s, Melbourne toyed with the idea of a competition to design a suitable landmark, although apart from a certain notoriety, nothing was achieved (Holcomb, 1999). Instead, since the 1990s, Melbourne's destination marketing has increasingly focused on culture, cuisine, popular culture, fashion and lifestyle – a sophisticated modern city rather than one with one or two tangible icons (Adams, 2005; Frost, 2008).

A *high-quality* coffee culture is seen as a keystone of this sophisticated image and one of the main destination attributes of Melbourne and its surrounding region. As the *Lonely Planet* guidebook on Australia observes: 'Expect the best coffee in Melbourne... Melbourne's café scene rivals the most vibrant in the world' (Lonely Planet, 2004: 73). Quality is, of course, a subjective term. In this context, it refers to small-scale, independently owned coffee shops, with distinctively quirky (even eccentric) décor, ambience, staff and patrons. The style of coffee and visitor experience in these coffee shops draws heavily on an 'Italian Model', where the drinks, food and even the staff are named after their Italian equivalents – 'latte', 'macchiato', 'foccacia', 'barista' (Frost *et al.*, forthcoming). The dominance of the Italian model in central Melbourne is in sharp contrast to an 'American model', characterised by chain stores, brewed coffee, free refills, takeaway containers and flavoured coffees. This chapter will focus on the role of coffee in marketing Melbourne to visitors, including the background to its adoption of the Italian model of coffee and the way that this coffee culture is increasingly used to project an attractive image to tourists of a cosmopolitan and stylish city.

The Italian Model

For much of the 19th and 20th centuries, Australians were a nation of tea-drinkers; part of a 'cultural baggage' that accompanied immigrants from the UK (Symons, 2007). It was not until after the Second World War that coffee consumption in Australia began to rise. As late as 1958–1959, Australians consumed per capita 2.7 kg of tea per annum, but only 0.6 kg of coffee. By 1968–1969, coffee consumption had doubled and by 1978–1979, the two beverages were approximately equally favoured. In 1998–1999 (the latest figures available), coffee consumption was 2.4 kg, a fourfold increase in 40 years. By contrast, tea had declined to 0.9 kg, a third of its level in 1958–1959 (Australian Bureau of Statistics, 2000). As with many countries, intriguingly, this increase in coffee consumption contrasted with the decline in the USA (Pendergrast, 1999).

This increased coffee consumption is often linked with the post-War surge in migration from continental Europe, particularly Italy. Melbourne, with its strong manufacturing base, was a major destination for Italian migrants. Even today, Italians are the largest non-British ethnic group in the city. In the 2006 census, some 260,000 people identified themselves as of Italian ancestry, nearly 8% of the city's population (Australian Bureau of Statistics, 2007). In the popular imagination,

Melbourne acquired its café culture as part of the cultural baggage of Italian migrants (Brown-May, 2001).

However, Melbourne's coffee heritage was not simply imported from Italy. While Italy is seen as the source of espresso-style coffee, the café culture that evolved in Melbourne was influenced by a range of cultures and was adapted for local conditions. Packaging this café culture as Italian heritage recognises one of its major sources, but there is also a recognition that, as with many so-called 'traditional' ethnic cultural practices, it has been heavily modified (Frost *et al.*, 2009). This hybrid amalgam of cultures was noted by food historian Michael Symons (2007: 324), who argued that 'Australians have followed the Italians in making espresso, and the French in sitting around in cafés'.

The multicultural origins of Melbourne's coffee culture are well illustrated by the 1950s introduction of Gaggia espresso machines (Brown-May, 2001). The espresso machine, whereby coffee is made by steam forced through the coffee grounds, was first patented in Italy in 1901. Giovanni Gaggia perfected the process with a machine patented in 1947. The first of these machines arrived in Melbourne in 1954. It was introduced by Peter Bancroft, a Melbourne teenager who had holidayed in London after finishing school. Hanging around the West End theatre district, he had become entranced by the latest fad for espresso cafés. Seeing their potential, he persuaded his father to back him in taking on the Gaggia distribution rights for Australia.

Back in Melbourne, the Bancrofts opened a café – Il Capuccino – to showcase their machines. As well as Italian coffee, they sold snacks, such as open sandwiches, based on their experience in London. A great success, the café was quickly imitated. By 1957, the Bancrofts had imported 400 Gaggia machines and many were purchased by recent migrants, who were attracted by the prospect of running their own small businesses, rather than remaining as factory workers.

It is important to note the multicultural origins of these cafés. The original template was a London café. The distributors were Anglo-Australians. Their prototype café had an Italian name and coffee machine, but the chefs and their cuisine were Dutch. Having established the demand for Gaggia machines, the Bancrofts sold Il Capuccino within a year. The new owners were Czech.

The Café Revolution

While the rise of cafés was popularly imagined to be due to Italian immigrants, other forces were at work. The rise in coffee drinking was part of a global trend of increased consumption of convenience foods and eating out, features of post-War prosperity (Symons, 2007). The build-up to the 1956 Olympic Games in Melbourne promoted a sense of the city needing to interact with the rest of the world and a broader range of cultures. The economic boom was characterised by a wider range of economic, strategic and cultural linkages, again forcing Australians to look beyond traditional links with the UK. Continuing prosperity allowed young Australians to reflect upon and reinterpret their culture. Critics of a seemingly sterile culture (such as Barry Humphries, a writer/ satirist and creator of the Bazza McKenzie and Dame Edna characters) encouraged a search for new models.

The Italian-inspired cafés of the 1950s provided a basic foundation for future developments. They form a striking contrast to the US situation. There, the 1950s and 1960s saw a steady decline in coffee consumption. Coffee was brewed, cheap, consumed in bottomless cups at diners and was often of very poor quality (Pendergrast, 1999). When specialised coffee shops developed in San Francisco and Seattle, they did so as a reaction to the lack of good coffee. In Melbourne, the base of small specialised cafés endured and provided the model for later developments.

In the 1980s, the café revolution began to change the face of Melbourne (Adams, 2005). Much of this was due to deliberate government policy. Enthusiasm for an iconic structure – a 'Monument for Melbourne' – dwindled as the concept was increasingly ridiculed (Holcomb, 1999). A change in direction came with the appointment of Don Dunstan as head of the Victorian Tourism Commission (1982–1986). Previously the Premier of the neighbouring state of South Australia, the high-profile Dunstan championed a greater emphasis on food and wine. Indeed, as Premier, he had campaigned strongly for footpath cafés, using his position to write and publish a government booklet, *Open Air Restaurants and Cafés in Adelaide* (1973) (Symons, 2007). Such ideas were quickly transplanted to Melbourne.

The revolutionary change came with the 1988 reforms to liquor licensing, which allowed cafés to also serve wine and other alcoholic beverages. The changes arose from a government enquiry headed by economist John Nieuwenhuysen:

> Before his reforms, Victorian-era wowserism ruled. Hotels had a monopoly on serving alcohol and restaurants wanting a liquor licence had to submit to a lengthy, expensive, cumbersome and paternalistic application process. Nieuwenhuysen... had a vision of

European-style liberalisation, of civilised drinking and freedom of choice. (Wilden, 2006: 10)

The changes were aimed at encouraging the spread of small cafés and restaurants. Nieuwenhuysen promoted his concept of European-style lifestyles, built on the existing foundations of small cafés. He advocated a city of cafés that:

> can serve you a drink without necessarily serving you a full meal; you can have a glass of wine with a piece of cake if you want. These little premises that serve 30–40 people, that's exactly what we were looking for in the liquor review. (Quoted in Wilden, 2006: 11)

These reforms encouraged cafés to serve food and wine, increasing their yield per customer and their overall viability. Furthermore, government costs were deliberately set low. For example, a small café in Melbourne can acquire a liquor licence, allowing customers to have a glass of wine with or without a meal, for a cost of only $567. In Sydney, the same licence costs $10,500, approximately twenty times more (Evans, 2007). In Melbourne, the low regulatory costs and greater potential yield encouraged small proprietors to open cafés. The result was a large increase in the number of small premises. In 1986 there were only 571 licensed restaurants in the state, by 2004 there were 5136, many with longer European-style trading hours (Wilden, 2006: 10).

The Café Experience

Cafés in Melbourne are typically small and independently owned. There is a strong tendency for clustering of cafés and complementary retailers, now marketed by the city as boutique 'precincts' such as the Block Arcade (see Figure 7.1). In the city centre, many cafés are located in laneways and alleys – originally built for goods delivery, but increasingly pedestrian-only. Centre Place, for example, is only 50 m long, but contains 14 cafés. Individual cafés are characterised by quirky décor and design, many striving for an ambience variously perceived as 'alternative', 'funky', 'grungy' or 'bohemian'. Competition pushes design to the limits. Perhaps the most extreme is a café in a converted shipping container, placed in a parking space in a small lane (Smith, 2006).

Coffees are generally made by professionally trained baristas (the various hospitality colleges run a range of courses). Cups and glasses are used in preference to paper cups. Servings are small; the ubiquitous café latte is a single 30-ml shot of espresso topped with foamed milk in a 200-ml glass (see Figure 7.2). The provision of table service is common.

Figure 7.1 Photo of the Block Arcade. The Block Arcade in Melbourne - cafe culture

Figure 7.2 Photo of café latte. Notice the heart on the top of the milk - Melbourne loves its coffee!

Serving staff sport an eclectic fashion range. Unlike the chain coffee stores, there is no conformity or consistency of style, which is part of the charm.

There is now a spillover of this café culture into nearby rural areas of Victoria. The tourist visiting heritage sites is increasingly attracted by the juxtaposition of associated shopping opportunities, cafés and restaurants. The availability of good coffee is thus a factor in creating a sophisticated ambience and some heritage towns such as Maldon and Castlemaine have been advertising their 'Melbourne-trained baristas' (Frost, 2006; Frost *et al.*, 2009). Young entrepreneurs have turned small town general stores into facsimiles of city cafés, making what were struggling businesses viable by catering for day-trippers (Thomas, 2008). Accordingly, the rural tourism experience is changing:

> Where inland towns are growing and prospering now, it often seems, it is by assimilating themselves to a metropolitan ideal. Walk down the main street of Daylesford, Beechworth or Castlemaine and it's the sweet aroma of coffee and incense rather than the pungent tang of sheep and horse manure that you are most likely to notice. Country life now comes attractively packaged with many of the cultural attractions of the big city – cafes, bookshops and health resorts. (Davison, 2005: 01.13)

The Tourist Experience

To understand the appeal for tourists of Melbourne's cafés, it is useful to analyse them by utilising two quite different theoretical approaches. The first is Oldenburg's theory of the *third place*. The second is Pine and Gilmore's *experience economy*.

Cafés, shops and other communal spaces are examples of the *third place* in modern society, existing apart from and distinctively different to the home and the workplace (Oldenburg & Brissett, 1982; Oldenburg, 1999, 2001). Their importance has increased with modern tendencies for greater isolation, particularly with smaller families, single-person households and telecommuting, resulting in:

> the attrition of situations in which people can become involved in freewheeling associations with others. The range of available arenas for social participation has narrowed to the point that for many people life has come to offer a very restrictive two-stop model of daily existence. The office or shop and the home, joined by the ordeal of commuting, tend to absorb people's time and interest... Neither

place, nor even the two together, seems to provide satisfying experiences and relationships. (Oldenburg & Brissett, 1982: 266)

Cafés and other third places fill an important role of providing sociability and a feeling of communitas. There is a sense in which this is nothing new. The Parisian cafés frequented by Sartre and de Beauvoir or the Viennese *kaffeehaus* were an oasis for discussing the affairs of the day or socialising. Oldenburg and Brissett (1982: 269) refer to the coffee house in literature as providing a setting for 'escape' from domestic dramas and demanding employers, but more importantly facilitating 'important experiences and relationships'. There is the feeling that the unexpected might occur; 'a vital part of experiences in the third place' (Oldenburg & Brissett, 1982: 274).

While this theory has been developed in terms of a resident population, it can also be extended to a city's tourists. For a tourist, their accommodation may be analogous to 'home' and visiting attractions their 'work'. In both spaces, they may be trapped in a 'tourist bubble' with very limited human interactions, mainly with service workers and other tourists. However, cafés offer the third place experience. Here they can relax and interact with other people and feel a sense of connection with the destination they are visiting. Instead of being outsiders, they can imagine themselves as insiders. Their social mixing might be with other tourists, as in cafés next to backpackers, or it might only be observing others ('peoplewatching'), and the promise of interacting with the host community might be illusory, but it is a welcome and comforting alternative.

The eclectic style and ambience of Melbourne's cafés suggest that they are examples of the new 'experience economy', where businesses attract customers with the promise of 'enjoying a series of memorable events that a company stages – as in a theatrical play – to engage him [sic] in a personal way' (Pine & Gilmore, 1999: 2). There is much that is theatrical in these cafés and the experience is as much a part of their appeal as the quality of the coffee. The quirkiness of café design, the emphasis on Italian culture and the flamboyant costumes of staff and some customers all suggest the theatrical experience. Furthermore, the customer/tourist enjoys the experience by being part of the production, of being personally engaged, rather than merely being in the audience.

However, rather than following Pine and Gilmore's strategy of tightly planned and scripted interactions with customers, the independent cafés of Melbourne instead offer more satisfying unscripted experiences. Conformity and formulaic experiences may be dull and unappealing, and seemingly customers in Melbourne value spontaneity, authenticity, variety, perhaps even chaos. As Oldenburg and Brissett (1982: 277) observe: 'People are so given to rationality that they tend to think all worthy experiences can be prefabricated. We seem to forget that the most enjoyable and memorable moments of our lives were not really planned'. This freewheeling ingredient contributes to 'quality of place' according to Florida (2002), where the street becomes the locale for a cornucopia of dynamic and diverse experiences. Finding the 'right' café is a quest tantamount to seeking the Holy Grail for dedicated coffee drinkers, and involves an anarchic blend of the hip aesthetic and the quality of their coffee.

Paradoxically, Tourism Victoria and Walt Disney have attempted to recreate Melbourne's laneways and café culture in the Epcot International Food and Wine Festival at Disney World (Ridge, 2008), one of the most staged tourist 'bubbles' on the planet, complete with 'cast members' as helpers. This 'mock' Melbourne urbanscape pays tribute to Melbourne coffee culture, within the commodified and safe environs of the Disney industry.

Coffee and Reimaging/Reimagining the City

Coffee, in both creating a cosmopolitan atmosphere (Oldenburg & Brissett, 1982 refer to this as 'color') and enhancing the tourist experience, has become a key and successful destination attribute for Melbourne. A city without any clear 'place luck', Melbourne has used a combination of events, popular culture, ethnic heritage and shopping to reimagine itself and provide a new and attractive image to tourists. In doing so, risks have been taken, with policy makers introducing major changes (as in the Nieuwenhuysen reforms) and highlighting unusual and quirky features (Frost, 2008).

Melbourne's use of coffee as a point of brand differentiation is an example of the growing use of lifestyle within place promotion (Gold, 1994; Wheeler & Laing, 2008). The logic is that cities that are 'liveable', through being vibrant and cosmopolitan, attract not only residents, but also tourists. A successful café scene underpins a whole range of liveable attributes. In recent years, both Vancouver and Melbourne have topped lists of being 'the world's most liveable cities' and have transferred this essentially domestic label to their destination marketing (Adams, 2005).

The attractiveness of liveability to tourists may also be tied to Florida's (2002, 2005) concept of 'creative cities'. Florida's thesis (which has been enthusiastically embraced by policy makers in Melbourne) is that cities are economically successful if they are able to attract creative people. This appeal may be measured by instruments such as a 'coolness index', which includes the number and quality of cafés and a 'Bohemian index', which counts writers, artists and actors (Florida, 2005: 41, 74–76).

Such concepts warn against the dangers of sameness. Fainstein and Judd (1999: 12–13) see a potential paradox in the reimagining of cities, 'whereas the appeal of tourism is the opportunity to see something different, cities that are remade to attract tourists seem more and more alike'. Florida (2005: 35–36) also sees major 'iconic' developments as a trap; 'attractions that most cities focus on building – sports stadiums, freeways, urban malls, and tourism-and-entertainment districts that resemble theme parks – are irrelevant, insufficient, or actually unattractive to many Creative Class people'.

In emphasising a sophisticated café culture (see Figure 7.3), Melbourne has successfully reimagined and reimaged itself for international tourists. In particular, key market segments such as young affluent tourists from Europe and North America are attracted by a city that appeals to their sophisticated self-identities rather than emphasising mass tourism experiences.

Figure 7.3 Photo of the Block Arcade. Melbourne GPO - coffee

Postscript: The Failure of Starbucks

The case of Starbucks is a valuable lens through which to view the café culture of Melbourne. Certainly, Starbucks draws on an Italian heritage. Its chief, Howard Schultz, talks of a trip to Milan in 1983 as providing an epiphany as to how cafés should be modelled (Pendergrast, 1999: 368; see also Williams, 2006). It also fits well with theories of the third place and the experience economy. However, Starbucks has not been very successful in Melbourne.

Starbucks opened its first store in Australia in 2000. In 2008, it closed 61 of its 84 stores. In explaining the decision, Howard Schultz cited 'challenges unique to the Australian market' (quoted in Miletic *et al.*, 2008: 3). Retail analyst, Barry Urquhart, argued that Starbucks was unable to compete in an entrenched market of established, high-quality, independent cafés, stating that: 'In America, Starbucks is a state of mind. In Australia it was simply another player' (quoted in Miletic *et al.*, 2008: 3). Elsewhere in the world, Starbucks expansion seemed indicative of the standardising force of globalisation (Lyons, 2005; Mordue, 2007; Williams, 2006). In Melbourne, its failure indicates the strength of an independent and diverse café culture.

References

Adams, R. (2005) Melbourne: Back from the edge. In E. Charlesworth (ed.) *Cityedge: Case Studies in Contemporary Urbanism* (pp. 50–64). Oxford: Architectural Press.

Australian Bureau of Statistics (2000) *Apparent Consumption of Foodstuffs*. Canberra: Australian Bureau of Statistics, catalogue no. 4306.0.

Australian Bureau of Statistics (2007) *2006 Census Tables*. Canberra: Australian Bureau of Statistics, catalogue no. 2068.0.

Brown-May, A. (2001) *Espresso! Melbourne Coffee Stories*. Melbourne: Arcadia.

Davison, G. (2005) Country life: The rise and decline of an Australian ideal. In G. Davison and M. Brodie (eds) *Struggle Country: The Rural Ideal in Twentieth Century Australia* (pp. 01.1–01.15). Clayton: Monash University ePress.

Evans, M. (2007) How Sydney Harbours Deep Pub Envy. *The Age*, News section, 18 August, p. 3.

Fainstein, S.S. and Judd, D.R. (1999) Global forces, local strategies, and urban tourism. In D.R. Judd and S.S. Fainstein (eds) *The Tourist City* (pp. 1–17). New Haven, CT: Yale University Press.

Florida, R. (2002) *The Rise of the Creative Class: And How It's Transforming Work, Leisure, Community and Everyday Life*. Cambridge, MA: Basic Books.

Florida, R. (2005) *Cities and the Creative Classes*. London and New York: Routledge.

Frost, W. (2006) From diggers to baristas: Tourist shopping villages in the Victorian goldfields. *Journal of Hospitality and Tourism Management* 13 (2), 136–143.

Frost, W. (2008) Popular culture as a different type of heritage: The making of AC/DC lane. *Journal of Heritage Tourism* 3 (3), 176–184.

Frost, W., Reeves, K., Laing, J. and Wheeler, F. (2009) Villages, vineyards and Chinese dragons: Constructing the heritage of ethnic diasporas. *Tourism, Culture & Communication* 9, 107–114.

Gold, J.R. (1994) Locating the message: Place promotion as image communication. In J.R. Gold and S.V. Ward (eds) *Place Promotion: The Use of Publicity and Marketing to Sell Towns and Regions* (pp. 19–37). Chichester, New York: John Wiley and Sons Ltd.

Holcomb, B. (1999) Marketing cities for tourism. In D.R. Judd and S.S. Fainstein (eds) *The Tourist City* (pp. 54–70). New Haven, CT: Yale University Press.

Lonely Planet (2004) *Australia* (12th edn). Melbourne: Lonely Planet Publications.

Lyons, J. (2005) Think Seattle, Act Globally': Specialty coffee, commodity biographies and the promotion of place. *Cultural Studies* 19 (1), 14–34.

Miletic, D., Arup, T. and Emerson, D. (2008) Hundreds of Jobs Lost as Starbucks Shuts 61 Shops. *The Age*: News section, 30 July, p. 3.

Mordue, T. (2007) Tourism, urban governance and public space. *Leisure Studies* 26 (4), 447–462.

Oldenburg, R. (1999) *The Great Good Place: Cafés, Coffee Shops, Bookstores, Bars, Hair Salons, and Other Hangouts at the Heart of a Community.* New York: Marlowe.

Oldenburg, R. (2001) *Celebrating the Third Place: Inspiring Stories about the Great Good Places at the Heart of our Communities.* New York: Marlowe and Co.

Oldenburg, R. and Brissett, D. (1982) The third place. *Qualitative Sociology* 5 (4), 265–284.

Pendergrast, M. (1999) *Uncommon Grounds: The History of Coffee and How it Transformed Our World.* New York: Basic Books.

Pine, B.J. and Gilmore, J.H. (1999) *The Experience Economy: Work is Theatre & Every Business a Stage.* Boston, MA: Harvard Business School Press.

Ridge, V. (2008) Backstreet Bacchanal. *The Age*: Epicure section, 23 September, p. 8.

Smith, B. (2006) Don't Blink or You'll Miss the Latest Trend – Pop-Up Stores. *The Age*: News section, 20 March, p. 2.

Symons, M. (2007) *One Continuous Picnic: A Gastronomic History of Australia* (2nd edn). Melbourne: Melbourne University Press (first published 1982).

Thomas, G. (2008) Supplies in Demand. *The Age*: Epicure section, 29 January, pp. 4–5.

Topsfield, J. (2008) A Country in Pursuit of the Vanishing Tourist. *The Age*: News section, 4 June, p. 3.

Walker, F. (2008) Sydney Suffers and the Winner is... Melbourne. *Sun Herald*, 14 September, p. 8.

Wheeler, F. and Laing, J. (2008) Tourism as a vehicle for liveable communities: Case studies from Regional Victoria, Australia. *Annals of Leisure Research* 11 (1&2): 242–263.

Wilden, N. (2006) Here's Cheers to 20 Years. *The Age*, Epicure section, 21 March, pp. 10–12.

Williams, A. (2006) Tourism and hospitality marketing: Fantasy, feeling and fun. *International Journal of Contemporary Hospitality Management* 18 (6), 482–495.

Chapter 8
Coffee and Coffee Tourism in Kona, Hawai'i – Surviving in the Niche

CHARLES JOHNSTON

Newcomers to Hawai'i quickly learn that this place is farther from anywhere than anywhere. Surrounded on all sides by thousands of kilometres of ocean, the Hawaiian Island chain has existed for hundreds of millions of years because of the volcanic activity of the hotspot below. Although Hawai'i is considered tropical, in fact many environmental niches exist, based on topography and climate. Over the eons, life has arrived only sporadically. Whether by wind, ocean current, bird flight or human transport, once a life form reaches Hawai'i, it must then be lucky enough to find its niche. Many species have not survived. Those that do often have to adapt – this has given Hawai'i one of the highest rates of endemism on earth.

The organic analogy – surviving in the niche – has been chosen as the theme around which this chapter will be constructed. As a plant species, coffee was brought to Hawai'i by people. As a commercial crop, those who grow it have had to find a niche both locally and globally, to survive economically. This has been an on-going struggle for about 190 years; ecologically quite a short period. As recently as the mid-1980s there was considerable concern that Kona's coffee landscapes would become extinct because economic and cultural conditions had become so unfavourable. This trend was reversed in the 1990s, partially by allowing coffee tourism to become a part of the product. The situation today looks more favourable and stable. Having a niche in the tourism industry has permitted survival once again. Yet booms and busts are the norm for coffee, thus survival into the indefinite future remains speculative. As in the past, growers must continue to successfully adapt to both the changing nature of coffee consumption and the Hawaiian socio-economic situation in order for coffee to survive.

In a recent book on niche tourism, Robinson and Novelli (2005: 2) have noted that a niche relates to an 'optimum location' from which an organism can exploit resources successfully while still being in the presence of competitors. The ecological concept of niche has itself found a niche in business studies. A niche is something a company or a product finds. Niche products are conceived as rather small. There is a relationship between the product and the customers. In general, the concept suggests companies produce products that are bought directly. This does not mean unsophisticated; Robinson and Novelli (2005: 9) note there is a 'knowledge process' that links the producing company to customers having specific needs and this creates relationships between the producers and the consumers. Successful niche products are created by businesses that know their customers intimately and can adapt quickly when the environment changes. The authors further note there are three approaches to niches: geographical, product-related and customer-related (Robinson & Novelli, 2005: 9). These three approaches have been chosen as a structure for this chapter. Kona will first be described as a geographic niche. Kona coffee will then be discussed as a niche product. Developing Kona coffee experiences for tourists-as-consumers will then be examined as a new-found survival strategy. The chapter will conclude with some thoughts on survival into the future.

Kona as a Geographic Niche

Figure 8.1 shows the Hawaiian Island chain. The state is in fact named for Hawai'i Island, which is larger in size than all the other islands combined. Within the state, local residents universally refer to the island as the 'Big Island', but confusion has led the Hawai'i Visitors and Convention Bureau (2009) to market it as 'Hawaii's Big Island'. The Big Island Visitors Bureau (2009) currently calls it the 'island of adventure' on its website.

As a word, 'kona' is often translated as 'leeward', but the full meaning invites explication. The word is of ancient origin and exists across the Austronesian language family in other forms (Fornander, 1980; Pukui *et al.*, 1974). For example, further south it is spoken as 'tonga', and thus the name of a South Pacific island chain and nation. What kona land areas are leeward of is the direction of the trade winds. Within the Hawaiian island chain, four of the six major islands contain a district named Kona by the original Hawaiian settlers. The indigenous geographic concept of kona is more than simply a directional relationship. Kona districts have particular environments created by the specific microclimates that exist from being leeward. These districts tend to be less rainy, hence more desirable as places to live. Hawaiian kings often

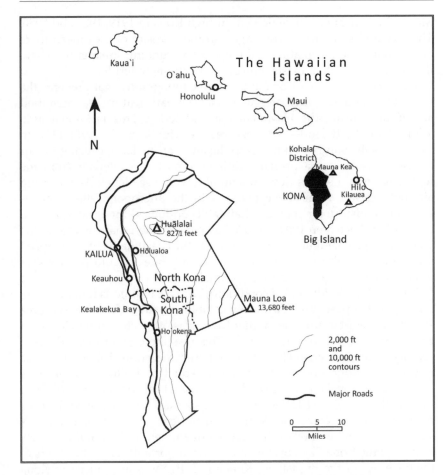

Figure 8.1 Kona within the Big Island and the State of Hawai'i

chose to reside in Kona districts (see Kamakau, 1961). Tourists also prefer these conditions. It is no accident that Honolulu and Waikiki are in the Kona district of O'ahu Island.

Figure 8.1 shows the Kona districts of the Big Island to be on the central western side. The trade winds blow in from the northeast; they are entirely blocked by the volcanic massifs of Mauna Kea and Mauna Loa. The topography of Kona is relatively steep and rises unceasingly from the sea floor up to the summits of Mauna Loa and Hualālai. Peterson and Moore (1987) have noted both these volcanoes are still considered active. Hualālai is the older of the two; it last erupted in 1801.

Mauna Loa eruptions have flowed through Kona in 1919, 1926 and 1950. The recentness of surface coverage and the porosity of lava mean there has been little soil formation and there are no running streams anywhere in Kona. The soil that exists, however, is extremely fertile.

In the central part of Kona, the volcanic topography that prevents the flow of the trade winds creates an unusual climatic feature that permitted agriculture during the Hawaiian era and today. This is known as a 'diurnal localised land-sea breeze regime' (Juvik *et al.*, 1978: 131). In essence, as the sun rises it heats up the air over the land, causing the air to rise. This creates a pressure difference so that cooler air from the higher mountain slopes flows downhill towards sea level. As the rising air cools, clouds form above the land in the afternoon. Often there is sufficient moisture for showers. Rainfall is optimised for agriculture in a narrow band between 1000 and 3000 feet in elevation that runs along the volcanic slopes parallel to the ocean. Thus, the coastline (Hawaiian *makai*) is dry and amenable to sun-oriented tourism, while agriculture flourishes upland (*mauka*) where rainfall is optimal.

The dry but cloudy makai conditions, with a continuous hint of breeze during the hot part of the day, when combined with a nearby mauka area suitable for agriculture, meant that Kona was often chosen by Hawaiian chiefs for their seat of government. This was the case in the early 19th century; after Kamehameha had conquered the entire island chain, he returned to Kona and established his capital at Kailua. The gardens above fed his royal entourage and the thousands of commoners who also lived makai. Kirch (1984: 194), noting the size and intensity of cultivation, referred to this area as the 'Kona Field System'. When Kamehameha's successor, Liholiho, moved the seat of government to Honolulu in 1820, Kona and the Kona Field System remained important due to the efforts of the governor of the Big Island, Kuakini. Coffee was introduced to Kona during this period. After Kuakini's death in 1844, Kona quickly became a backwater, a by-passed district with a vastly reduced population. In 1848, throughout Hawai'i, land reform was instituted through what was called the Great *Mahele*. The Kona Field System was abandoned at this time, replaced by ranches and gardens owned and leased by individuals. This is when coffee's story begins.

After the abandonment of traditional agriculture, the 'coffee belt' gradually replaced what had been the 'taro belt' for Hawaiians (see Kelly, 1983; Schilt, 1984). This 'belt' today is a stretch of terrain about 20 miles long and 2 miles wide, running parallel to the coastline, at an elevation between 700 and 3000 feet. This amount of land is miniscule by world standards, yet the rugged volcanic terrain and specific microclimatic conditions do not permit agricultural expansion. Masuda (2007) has noted coffee requires five conditions, related to temperature, rainfall, soil, slope and shade. Within this narrow belt of land, Kona's situation is near-ideal for all of them – afternoon cloud cover providing the needed shade. As a geographic niche, then, a small part of the Kona landscape is almost perfect for growing coffee. Yet, not even this 40-square mile niche is completely usable. The volcanic terrain is very uneven and thus not suited for monoculture. Small holdings represent the best human adaptation. Further, conditions are also ideal for growing a variety of crops (papaya, avocados, cut flowers). Coffee must also compete with other potential land uses. Though parts of the Kona landscape are an ideal niche for coffee as a plant, its survival is contingent on many factors – economic, environmental and socio-cultural.

Kona Coffee as a Niche Product

Coffee growing in Kona has gone through a set of stages. Table 8.1 shows the core features of each stage and the major reasons for transition. Overall, it is a story of booms, when coffee growing expanded and the growers did well economically, followed by busts during which agricultural production systems went extinct, individuals left coffee and Kona, and those remaining suffered great financial hardship. This section of the chapter will elaborate on the details shown in Table 8.1. Special attention will be paid to the second stage – leasehold farms – because a coffee 'way of life' emerged that has become an important component of Kona's heritage and therefore is important to tourism.

Goto's (1982) research indicated that coffee was brought to Hawai'i at least four times between 1810 and 1830. The seedlings were from Brazil, Batavia (Java) and the Philippines. Goto (1982: 113) considered the latter to have been the source that grew most successfully; it formed the 'parent stock' that spread throughout the islands. It is well established (Bingham, 1981) that the missionary, Ruggles, first took coffee to Kona in 1828. It was not initially cultivated as a commercial crop, however Hawaiian people grew it in the Kona Field System lands because the Hawaiian government allowed taxes to be paid in coffee (as well as pigs – Goto, 1982: 113). Brazil became established as the world leader in coffee production during this period (see Luttinger & Dicum, 2006).

The transition into the Plantation Stage occurred because of the Great Mahele, which affected the entire island chain. The Great Mahele permitted land to be sold to *haoles* (Caucasians) and a number bought land in the Kona Field System area. They established coffee plantations

Table 8.1 Stages in Kona coffee's niche development

	Global	Regional – Island chain	Regional – Big Island	Kona
1. Hawaiian beginnings (1820s–1850)	Brazil becomes world leader	Coffee brought to Hawai'i	Coffee brought to Big Island	Hawaiian traditional land system. Coffee brought to Kona
Reasons for transition		Great Mahele enables plantation agriculture		Great Mahele allows Kona Field System land to be bought and converted to coffee plantations
2. Commercial establishment (1850–1899)	Price booms and busts in Brazil	Plantation agriculture system for sugar and coffee	Plantation agriculture system for sugar and coffee	Plantation agriculture system for sugar and coffee
Reasons for transition	1898–1899 world glut causes price bust	1850s white scale insect damage everywhere but Kona		1850s initial plantations extinct 1890s second generation plantations go bust
3. Survival at the bottom (1899 to Second World War)	Coffee becomes a modern commodity	Big 5 companies control economy		Two companies control coffee. Japanese lease 5-acre plots; coffee way of life established

Table 8.1 (*Continued*)

	Global	Regional – Island chain	Regional – Big Island	Kona
Reasons for transition		Decline in Big 5 control of economy		Second generation Japanese improve economic situation
4. Improving niche position (post-Second World War to 1980s)	Coffee still a modern commodity; extreme price fluctuations			Tourism exacerbates labour shortages. Leasehold system under threat from suburbanisation
Reasons for transition	Coffee decommodifies into a gourmet product			'Kona' identity becomes possible for coffee
5. Sustainability at the top? (1980s to present)	Specialty coffee niches partially replace generic coffee	Coffee plantations open, especially on Kaua'i island	Coffee growing begins again in Hamakua district	Kona identity emerges; counterfeit scandal; internet and tourism permit stability

that were initially successful. However, an introduced environmental predator, the white scale insect (*Pulvinaria psidii*) wreaked havoc on the coffee plants throughout the Kingdom during the late 1850s (Kinro, 2003). Coffee plantations, as an agricultural production system, were wiped out. On most islands, coffee did not survive. The insect did less damage in Kona because the rugged terrain limited its spread, yet its presence was sufficiently pervasive to put the coffee plantations out of business. For the next 30 years, coffee growing wild or in gardens was picked as a cash crop by Hawaiians (Jean Greenwell, Kona Historical Society, personal papers, n.d.). This became known as 'Kanaka Koppe' (Hawaiian coffee) (Drent, 1994).

Prices for coffee rose gradually during the late 1880s and this created a world-wide boom during the 1890s (Kinro, 2003). In Hawai'i, the independent nation run by Queen Lili'uokalani was overthrown in 1892. Government-owned lands were sold and some were turned to coffee, on several islands. Coffee plantations, this time run by both haoles and Chinese, again emerged in Kona. Japanese, often workers who had run away from sugar plantations elsewhere, formed the bulk of the labour force. Another severe drop in world prices in 1898 again forced plantation agriculture into extinction. During this time, coffee production went extinct everywhere in Hawai'i except Kona. For nearly a century, when plantations re-emerged on Kauai'i island, Kona has been Hawai'i's only niche for coffee.

In a discussion of coffee as a niche product, the first point for the next stage must be that the source plant used to grow coffee changed at this time. Plants from Guatemala had been brought into Kona during the 1890s and these were perceived to produce more beans and a higher quality beverage. Farmers converted completely and by 1920, 'Melikan' (American) had entirely replaced 'Kanaka' coffee. This strain, known as *Kona typica* has been used since (Drent, 1994). The original coffee brought during the 1820s is thus extinct, except as wild plants growing in gullies and other inaccessible niches.

Coffee had been subject to boom and bust periods during the previous half-century and this cycle would continue, as it still does. Expansion in Brazil and Colombia created a highly developed plantation agriculture system that permitted coffee to be sold as a cheap commodity item to consumers, mainly in the USA. Cartels and corporations arose and consolidated (Luttinger & Dicum, 2006). Yet price fluctuations continued. A period of relatively high prices occurred after the First World War and into the 1920s; the number of farms in Kona increased and coffee growing brought a modicum of prosperity. The bust occurred after the

1929 stock market crash and brought terrible conditions during the 1930s (Lind, 1967).

Within Hawai'i, sugar and pineapple plantation agriculture became established as major export crops. A production system based on plantation agriculture emerged; this would dominate for most of the 20th century. In Kona, a variation of this system developed. One of the former plantation owners, W.W. Brunner, subdivided his land and began leasing it to tenant farmers (Waiaha River Coffee Company, 2009). These were mainly Japanese who had previously been plantation labourers. The leases were around 5 acres as this was considered the optimal size for one family. Brunner also provided housing and other necessities in exchange for one third of the crop (Royal Kona Coffee, 2009). This arrangement caught on and by 1910 virtually all coffee was grown using this system. Two companies, Captain Cook Coffee Company and H. Hackfield (later Amfac) came to control 70–80% of the coffee leases. The sharecropping system evolved somewhat. Families paid the lease in cash, but were required to sell their entire crop to Captain Cook and Amfac. Further, 'company stores' predominated, meaning the families had to buy all their supplies from the companies to whom they sold their crop. Individual families lived in debt for decades.

The situation invites comparison with the worst excesses of American rural industry, for example, Appalachian coal-mining towns. Kinro (2003) has provided a detailed story. Families lived in small metal shacks with dirt floors. All slept in one room on futons. Wood fireplaces were used for cooking and for reading at night as there was no electricity. Water came from a catchment tank, filtered through a tobacco bag. There was little money.

The agricultural system that developed was equally impoverished. All family members helped tend the lands and pick the crop. Child labour became necessary for economic survival so the school calendar was altered in 1932 in order that children could be at home between September and November to help with the harvest (Lind, 1967). This became known as the 'coffee vacation'. After picking, the coffee was dried on the ground. It was covered by a movable roof – *hoshidana* – at night. Braying donkeys – 'Kona nightingales' – carried the crop to the mill. It was then shipped to San Francisco to be used as a nameless flavouring additive to American coffee.

Lind (1967) has noted that immigrants initially occupy the bottom rungs of the economic ladder and then work their way up. The version of this period told by growers themselves (see *Communities*, 2009) is considerably more optimistic. Much less desirable working conditions existed in rural Japan and on the sugar plantations. Coffee as a crop required the patience and diligence of rice growing in Japan, something growers' families had been doing for generations. Growing coffee was an opportunity for a kind of independence and dignity, if not the road to riches. A rich spirit developed, as exemplified by the *kumi*, community level organizations that helped individuals in times of need.

Coffee production expanded during the First World War and especially after 1918, when a severe frost destroyed the crop in Brazil (Luttinger & Dicum, 2006). The number of families increased to around 1000 as prices rose and stayed high. The Great Depression brought debt and despair. Many hung on because of the independence compared to life on the sugar plantations. They adapted by growing additional crops, weaving *lauhala* baskets; public works projects provided a source of cash. It was not enough. By the late 1930s, the leasehold system was on the verge of extinction. What saved it was an act of corporate generosity – in 1938 Amfac forgave growers 98% of their debt (see *Communities*, 2009). They were not forced off the land and coffee as a niche crop survived.

The situation changed for the better and after the Second World War, prices were again on the rise. They held throughout the 1950s, peaking in 1957 (Royal Kona Coffee, 2009). The second generation (*Nisei*) replaced the aging parents (*Issei*) and had bigger ideas. Infrastructure progress came in the form of electricity and municipal water supplies (Kinro, 2003). At the economic level, the control of Captain Cook and Amfac waned. Some farmers were able to buy their land (Drent, 1997). Stores worked on a cash-and-carry basis, rather than credit. By the 1960s, growers had formed co-operatives that owned independent mills, which paid higher prices. Hawai'i, now a state, instituted quality control through creating standards for grading coffee (Kinro, 2003).

The latter half of the 1960s saw another downturn in prices. Families turned to other crops – particularly macadamia nuts and bananas – which paid better (see *Communities*, 2009). So did marijuana (Drent, 1997). During this period, tourism had become established along the coastal zone and jobs also paid better than coffee (see next section). The entire crop was still sold as a commodity for flavouring and remained at the mercy of world price fluctuations (Masuda, 2007). Kinro (2003: 95) argues that coffee was on its 'deathbed' by 1972. The situation was touch-and-go into the 1980s, as the set of factors against coffee's survival continued to worsen. Many felt it was just too hard to make a go of hand picking coffee.

Then the world of coffee began to change in the 1980s: the uniform commodity beverage drunk democratically began to go upscale. This trend has not likely finished yet. More change occurred in Kona coffee in the last 20 years of the 20th century than had occurred in the previous 80 years.

Worldwide, coffee labelled by place of origin began to be sold in specialty food shops, as discussed in Chapter 1. It was possible to choose between Costa Rican, Kenyan or Indonesian rather than be limited to generic mixes of Brazilian and Colombian. This made the unthinkable possible – Kona coffee could be marketed as a place-brand product, not sold off in bulk as a flavouring agent. This possibility began to be practiced by mainland haole newcomers who had gravitated to Kona for the tropical rural lifestyle – the first 'new blood' since the Japanese 80 years earlier (Drent, 1994). These farmers had more marketing savvy and took their cue from the Napa Valley wine region (Kinro, 2003). By the 1990s they had started opening shops on the roadside. Individual farms became 'estates' and sold coffee grown only on that piece of property. Tourism became an ally; tourists were now seen as people having enough money to pay premium prices. With the internet came direct on-line sales. Education campaigns extolling the virtues of pure Kona were launched. Farmers began to grow organic coffee to raise quality even further. There have been many positive changes.

There have also been many negatives. At the world scale, as discussed further in Chapter 13, production in Vietnam expanded hugely, resulting in the lowest prices, adjusted for inflation, in the history of coffee (Luttinger & Dicum, 2006). Yet, because of direct selling, this did not impact Kona to the same extent as earlier price crashes. Most of the problems have been of local origin. In the late 1980s, coffee began being grown outside Kona for the first time in 90 years. Modern plantations were opened on Kaua'i Island; newly arrived farmers also began growing coffee in Hamakua District of the Big Island (Drent, 1995/1996). Kona no longer has the local market to itself. Blends from Kona and other locations are now called 'Hawaiian' coffee. An unusual problem occurred in the 1990s – a large grower was found to be counterfeiting coffee by mixing locally grown Kona with cheaper varieties grown internationally. This damaged Kona coffee's image as a high-quality varietal. A third major issue has been that truth-in-labelling laws in Hawai'i have not changed with the times. The larger local producers import coffee but are legally able to call it 'Kona' on packages. A law was passed requiring 'Kona blend' to have only 10% Kona coffee. The small farmers do not have the economic wherewithal to challenge the larger producers in court (see *Independent Voice*, 2007). This situation remains unresolved in 2009.

Kona Coffee tourism as a consumer niche

Tourists began arriving in Kona around the same time that coffee arrived. Previous research (Johnston, 1995) has shown that since then tourism in Kona has gone through a complete set of Butlerian (1980) life cycle stages. Table 8.2 provides an overview of the main stages and features. This section begins with a brief elaboration of the Table 8.2. Following that, the symbiotic relationship that has developed since the 1990s will be discussed.

Table 8.2 Kona's tourism area life cycle

Stage and substage	Dates	Core and reason for change
Exploration A. Royal Hawaiian Capital B. Agricultural Hinterland	1779–1927	Cook is killed at Kealakekua Bay. King Kamehameha establishes government at Kailua. Liholiho moves government to Honolulu; Kona declines. 1844; Kona becomes agricultural hinterland after death of Governor Kuakini.
Response A. Early B. Late	1928–1963	Kona Inn opened in Kailua; lures domestic tourists. Old Kona airport opens (1949); initiates involvement of locals in tourism businesses in Kailua.
Development A. Domestic B. Linked	1964–1985	Development boom in accommodation begins along coast. Multi-story hotels constructed. Hotel construction ends (1975); condominium numbers increase until 1985.
Maturity A. Consolidation B. Resource diversification	1986 to present	Kona residents reject big resorts; these are built in Kohala District. Big Island promotes itself as 'Hawaii's Island of Adventure'; sun-sand-sea tourism replaced with emphasis on diversity of experiences (including coffee).

Both coffee and tourism can be shown to have gone through stages of development, however, a comparison of Tables 8.1 and 8.2 indicates there was very little relationship after the end of the Hawaiian period. The stages have not changed at the same time during this period, nor for any common reason. Coffee and tourism have mostly had parallel, not overlapping, existences on the Kona landscape. The experience of coffee has been one of boom and bust, of repeated need to adapt to survive. This has not been the case for tourism. There have been periods when growth came to a standstill, or declined slightly, but tourism in Kona has never been threatened with extinction in the same way as coffee. With each change in stage, the numbers of both visitors and accommodation units have risen. Tourism began in a small number of locations on the Big Island, but this has gradually increased. At present, tourism is larger and more diversified than ever, in terms of resources used to create experiences.

During the 19th century, Kona went from being the centre of Hawai'i – with Kailua as the capital and the Kona Field System producing food for tens of thousands – to one of the most isolated areas of the island-chain. After Liholiho (Kamehameha II) moved the government to Honolulu, coastal Kona became synonymous with 'Old Hawai'i' (Stewart, 1831), an image it retains to this day. As Governor of the Big Island, Kuakini built Hulihe'e Palace for his residence and also Mokuaikaua Church, structures that added to Kailua's historic landscape. During a visit in the 1860s, Twain would remark that Kailua was 'the sleepiest, quietest, Sundayest looking place you can imagine' (Clemens, 1966: 202). By the 1850s, tourists were coming to the Big Island to visit Kīlauea Volcano, whose constantly boiling lava lake was one of the major attractions on the planet for Romantic era tourists interested in the sublime. On the return voyage, ships stopped briefly at Kealakekua Bay for tourists to experience the site where Captain Cook had been slain (see Johnston, 1995).

During the 1920s, Kailua's and Kona's image and importance changed dramatically. In 1924, Kīlauea's lava lake hardened over. Tourists could still see the volcano, but they now needed more to do. Offshore from Kailua, it was discovered that game fish such as marlin, tuna and barracuda could be caught in abundance. The sleepy coastal zone was also the one spot left where Hawaiians still lived fairly traditionally and the authentic landscape of the Hawaiian kingdom was made tangible by the historic buildings constructed by Kuakini. Finally, the Kona Inn was constructed on Kailua Bay, providing a relaxing getaway for Honolulu residents.

After the Second World War, tourism expanded throughout Hawai'i. Because of its 'Old Hawai'i' image, Kailua was considered the number two resort spot in the islands, hence destined for development. Enough occurred to spoil much of the ambience; Caen (1956) wrote that the town had been 'made miserable by progress'. Yet the big story of the 1950s through the 1980s is not about what was built, but what was not. Residents bitterly, and mainly successfully, contested developers' plans to build tall hotels in Kailua and large resort enclaves on isolated beaches to the north. By the 1970s, government plans stipulated Kailua maintain its village atmosphere and high rises were prohibited. Few hotels were built, though resort condominiums were constructed in large numbers up until the mid-1980s and 'linked' Kailua with Keauhou Resort four miles south. Kailua maintains its peaceful 'old village' ambience very carefully.

One or two big projects have occurred along the coastline north of Kailua since the 1990s, but as a whole, resort tourism had reached its maturity stage and had stabilised. Without ever going into stagnation, Kona since then has gradually become enveloped into the Big Island, a much larger, more diversified destination. As one destination among several, Kona now exists in a situation of co-opetition with other localities. The Big Island is marketed as 'Hawaii's Island of Adventure' (Big Island Visitors Bureau, 2009). This includes the again-active Kīlauea, visiting world-class astronomical facilities atop Mauna Kea and riding with *paniolo* – Hawaiian cowboys – in Kohala District. Kona is now a place for whale watching and diving with manta rays, as well as the best spot in the state for cultural and heritage tourism. Coffee is a part of the adventure, but it is somewhat buried as a component of 'ag-tourism' on the promotional websites. It must compete against locations providing experiences with traditional Hawaiian agriculture, cattle ranches, macadamia nuts and farmers' markets.

Throughout Kona's tourism life cycle, tourists have gazed at coffee and frequently commented upon it. A circle-island road was constructed during the 1850s and this enabled tourists to visit the coffee belt. Being elevated, the cooler temperatures of mauka Kona were in fact preferred by 19th-century tourists, who were lodged at early hotels such as Miss Paris' and the Mahealani (Jean Greenwell, Kona Historical Society, personal communication, November 1991). Early guidebooks (e.g. Whitney, 1875: 97) included the coffee zone as a component of the 'luxurious vegetation' of the uplands. Individual tourists wrote travel narratives that often included some aspect of a coffee experience. Cheever (1851) described his visit to one of the first coffee plantations, run by an ex-sailor from Maine. Chaney (1879: 201) wrote of his daily rides on the mules that hauled the coffee to the mills. Musick, aboard a steamer, described the dock at Ho'okena village as full of 'white coffee planters', whose 'plantations' were 'four-acre plots, plus visions of more to come'. He travelled inland during the picking season and found there were 'vast forests of wild coffee' and 'hundreds of Japanese were picking the berries' (Musick, 1898: 219). Kona coffee gained its reputation for quality during this stage in tourism. Twain provided an early celebrity endorsement, noting 'Kona Coffee has a richer flavour than any other' (Clemens, 1966: 202). By the end of the 19th century, magazines about Hawai'i, such as *Paradise of the Pacific* (see January 1899 issue), had spread the word that Kona was the only location in the USA where coffee was grown. By the 1920s, writers such as Morrill (1919) and Harlow (1928) could comment they had seen the 'famous' Kona coffee growing on the mountainside during their visit. Coffee was a well-understood component of the experience of a trip to Hawai'i and, while falling short of being an attraction with a great deal of pulling power, Kona was a region that was known for growing high-quality coffee and tourists who visited Kona expected to see it and taste it. These features continued to be of interest during the 20th century. In addition, seeing the Japanese growing the crop and the children picking it during the 'coffee vacation' were notable ethnic features (Gessler, 1937; Deubner, 1938) that added to the overall experience.

As the coastal regions of Kona developed, tourism and coffee became competitors for labour. By the mid-1950s, speeches were being made that tourism was the industry of the future, not coffee or ranching (Gaspar, 1955). The 'coffee vacation' was considered obsolete in the face of such a future: children would be better served being educated to work in tourism. Jobs in tourism paid better than coffee, and so did jobs in construction that became available because of tourism (Smyser, 1972). The worst threat, however, came from exploding land prices caused by tourism development. Increasing urbanisation from subdivision construction, housing the new tourism workers and retirees who had originally visited as tourists, created a situation where Kona agricultural land was more valuable by itself than it was with coffee grown on it (Yim, 1981; Harada-Stone, 1989a, 1989b). The many farmers who still leased their land did so with the knowledge that new lease prices might see them replaced by new lessees who did not work the land.

In the latter part of the 1980s, the situation was improved by the world-wide trend that made coffee a gourmet product. With a reputation for high quality firmly established, growers could change markets without great difficulty. However, realising that tourists were an ideal market came slowly to farmers who had been used to the idea of their coffee being a nameless commodity. The 1990s saw this transition occur. Since then, the gaze between tourists and growers has become much more mutual (see Maoz, 2006). Coffee tourism is now established as one niche among many tourism niches on the Big Island.

Luttinger and Dicum (2006: 156) assert that the new era for coffee is one of 'decommodification'. The relevant qualities are origin, bean quality, methods of cultivation and processing. There is greater choice in types of roasts and grinds. Overall, they suggest there exists a 'much richer, personal coffee landscape'. For the world at-large, they suggest, this has resulted in greater profits for the countries of consumption, not production, because more of the value-added occurs to businesses in the consuming nations. However, what might be a deteriorating situation for growers in producing countries such as Brazil or Colombia has in fact led the latest boom for Kona growers, who find themselves situated much closer to the consumers (tourists). Masuda (2007) modelled the sales points in the production process. Coffee can be sold as 'cherries', these can be 'pulped' then sold as 'parchment'; this can be milled and the beans sold as 'green'; or, finally, the beans can be roasted and sold as a finished product. The recent change in the production system has in fact been for farmers to hold on to the coffee past the parchment stage. However, farmers have the choice to sell their lower grade coffee locally to companies who will roast it and blend it with others into a generic 'Hawaiian' coffee, a 'Kona blend' or a '100% Pure Kona' blend. They also have the choice to keep their 'estate' grade completely separate and sell this according to type of roast. Of course, value-added occurs with each step and so farms make the most money from selling roasted coffee beans directly to tourists and tourism industry operators.

The current status of coffee tourism is that Kona coffee is available to residents and tourists throughout Hawai'i. Within Kona there are currently five aspects to having a coffee experience: buying coffee retail (either as a package in a shop or as a drink in a café); visiting a coffee farm; seeing coffee roasted at a mill; staying overnight at a coffee farm; visiting a coffee museum. Plate 8.1 is a 'driving tour' map of Kona's coffee belt, which has been created for tourists wishing to explore Kona in a manner equivalent to wine tourism (Kona Coffee Cultural Festival, 2009). The map lists 56 venues for Kona coffee, where the five kinds of experiences can be had. Examination of the list of venues indicates there are 45 retail outlets, 36 coffee farms open to the public; 25 places where coffee roasting can be watched; three coffee museums; two coffee accommodation facilities. Five of these also have other attractions, such as pottery studios and a doll museum.

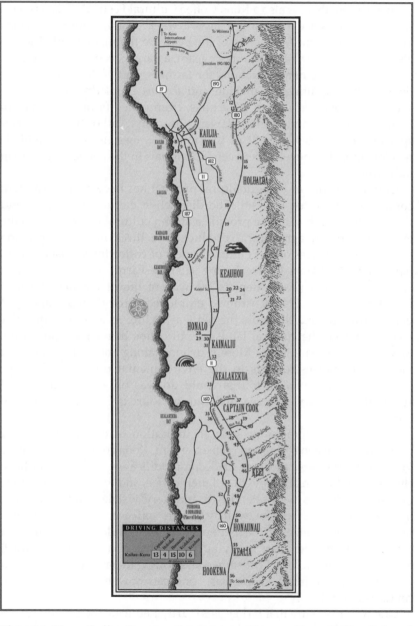

Plate 8.1 Kona Coffee Country driving tour (Source: Kona Coffee Cultural Festival, 2009)

In addition, there is also a Kona Coffee Cultural Festival. This has been held annually since 1970 and it lasts a week. Coffee cuppings, which award prizes for the best coffee of the year, are the main event. There is also the Miss Kona Coffee Beauty Pageant, a parade, cooking contests, art exhibits, scientific demonstrations for farmers, and cultural demonstrations such as quilting, lei-making and *ikebana* floral displays. Specific events take place at dozens of venues, from coffee farms to lobbies of luxury resorts. Though the Hawai'i Tourism Authority is a major sponsor, the greatest benefit of this impact comes from the symbiotic relationships that develop between individuals in the coffee and tourism industries.

Coffee's history as an agricultural product has become an important component of coffee tourism. The distinctive cultural landscape and way of life described above provide a strong cultural component to the experience of an agricultural product. The three museums provide learning experiences of this cultural aspect of coffee for tourists. One in particular, the 'Kona Coffee Living History Farm', run by the Kona Historical Society (2009), depicts the way of life of Japanese farmers between 1920 and 1945. Costumed employees provide tours and give demonstrations that illustrate the old way of life. At a more vernacular level, however, the cultural landscape of coffee in mauka Kona is the essence of the experience. Merely driving along the route shown in Plate 8.1 immerses tourists in the environmental presence of coffee. For over a century, all a tourist could do was observe. In this latest stage, the industry has reached out to tourists, enabling them to interact, as well.

The above paragraphs provide an indication of the currently solid connection between coffee and coffee tourism. Kona coffee would appear to be surviving well in times of decommodification. All farmers have choices about when and how to sell their coffee, and to whom. The coffee tourism product is well established and very visible. Tourists driving through the coffee belt know they are in coffee country and have a multitude of chances to experience coffee. World-wide trends in consumption would seem to favour the selling of a gourmet product, for which decommodified consumers are willing to pay top dollar. Given the hardships endured in the past, one can only hope this situation continues indefinitely.

One way to ensure that it does is to further educate the consumers. In business, niche theory asserts that the most successful niche products will be those whose consumers are educated to the nuances of the product. Current tourism theory shows that more can be done for coffee.

In a recent chapter on gastronomic tourism, Hall and Mitchell (2005) have developed a model showing the relationship between number of tourists and motivation for 'gourmet' and 'cuisine' tourism. The model indicates that these niches require tourists' primary motivation to be to want these specific experiences. However, for 'culinary' tourism, only secondary motivation is required. In a similar vein, McKercher (2002) developed a model for identifying cultural tourists in Hong Kong. This model is a matrix based on (1) depth of experience by (2) importance of culture in the destination decision. Through surveys, he was able to identify five types of cultural tourists. The purest type was named 'purposeful' on the basis that culture was an important factor in their decision and they had had deep cultural experiences during their visit. At the other end, 'incidental' cultural tourists had not come to Hong Kong for culture and had only shallow experiences while there. Together, these models suggest that motivation, decision making and depth of experience are all important variables for the coffee tourism industry to consider. It is probably the case that the percentage of 'purposeful' coffee tourists is low, as McKercher found for cultural tourists. The job for the coffee tourism industry is therefore to educate as completely as possible, to increase this number.

One unlikely factor might have the potential to reduce Kona coffee's survival capability: milk. The Kona Coffee Cultural Festival website (2009) refers to the 'espresso revolution' and provides recipes for the 'specialty coffees' – cappuccino, latte, etc. These drinks require milk and the art of making them – barista – involves getting the milk right. By contrast, the coffee component is relatively straightforward. This situation would not seem ideal for a varietal coffee such as Kona, for which growers can charge double or more the price for generic coffee. Will consumers want to pay very premium prices for a product that loses its distinctiveness when blended with milk? Kona coffee as a gourmet product is reliant upon the rather American custom of drinking coffee black. Were milk coffee drinks to pervade America, Kona growers might have to go back to the days of selling their coffee as a commodity rather than as a gourmet product. This makes education through tourism experience even more essential. Tourism's main product might be memories, but sipping a delicious cup of Kona coffee that has been bought on-line from the farm the tourists visited a decade earlier is something very tangible.

Conclusion

Coffee and tourism arrived around the same time in Kona. Each adapted to the niches available. The life cycle pathways of each have been, until recently, quite separate. Of the two, the survival of coffee has been the most precarious and most in doubt. Extinction was forecast as recently as the 1980s, with tourism and tourism-induced land-use changes functioning as both competitor and predator. The world-wide change in coffee consumption preferences has lessened the threat, for the moment. Tourists have always taken an interest in coffee and the way of life of the farmers, but the tourism industry focused on a completely different set of resources. Tourism in Kona has grown to the point where it probably won't expand a great deal more. Resorts on prime locations have been built; locals will likely fight vigorously to prevent other coastal areas from being taken. As part of tourism at-large in Hawai'i and the Big Island, Kona has seen its tourism industry become incorporated into broader marketing designs. Tourism in Kona is now part of a set of niche activities, doing business in a state of co-opetition with other districts against Maui, O'ahu and Kaua'i. This is only likely to intensify.

Coffee tourism only began when coffee itself became a decommodified, gourmet item around 30 years ago. Coffee growers realised, quite suddenly, that there was a desirable market segment right in their midst that they had ignored for over a century. Coffee thus opened itself to tourists, not the other way around. Tourism did not suddenly discover coffee and Kona will never be solely a coffee destination. Yet, as the situation stands today, coffee tourism is in a good position. Huge expansion will not be possible as Kona's geographical conditions prevent it. However, stability for coffee farmers now seems a reality rather than a dream. As long as Kona farmers can maintain their status as gourmet producers, tourists finding special coffee experiences are likely to help the coffee industry stay on solid economic ground. This may require more education, so that the percentage of purposeful coffee tourists continues to increase. Let us hope this eventuates because Kona coffee, as a delightful beverage, deserves to survive in its very small niche.

References

Bingham, H.A.M. (1981) *A Residence of Twenty-One Years in the Sandwich Islands: Or the Civil, Religious, and Political History of Those Islands.* Rutland, VT: Charles E. Tuttle Company.

Big Island Visitors Bureau. On WWW at www.bigisland.org/. Accessed 15.5.09.

Bryan, J. (1970) Kona residents, council ponder problems of growth. Honolulu *Star-Bulletin*, 16 April, C3.

Butler, R. (1980) The concept of a tourist area cycle of evolution: Implications for management of resources. *Canadian Geographer* 24, 5–12.

Caen, H. (1956) Baghdad—by the bay. Hawai'i *Tribune Herald*, 18 August, A9.

Chaney, G.L. (1879) *Alo-ha! A Hawaiian Salutation*. Boston, MA: Roberts Brothers.

Cheever, Rev. H.T. (1851) *Life in the Sandwich Islands: Or, the Heart of the Pacific.* New York: A.S. Barnes & Co.

Clemens, S.L. (1966) *Mark Twain's Letters from Hawai'i.* Edited with an Introduction by A. Grove Day. London: Chatto & Windus.

Communities. A Social History of Kona. University of Hawai'i at Mānoa, College of Social Sciences, Center for Oral History. On WWW at http://www.oralhistory.hawaii.edu/pages/community/kona.html. Accessed 13.5.09.

Deubner, W.H. (1938) *Deubner's Daily Doings*. Privately published.

Drent, L. (1994) State of the Bean Address. *Coffee Times*. On WWW at http://www.coffeetimes.com/state.htm. Accessed 15.5.09.

Drent, L. (1995/1996) What you don't know about coffee. *Coffee Times*. On WWW at http://www.coffeetimes.com/konacoffee.htm. Accessed15.5.09.

Drent, L. (1997) Kona Coffee Booms but...Can there be peace, stability, and prosperity in our industry. *Coffee Times*. On WWW at http://www.coffeetimes.com/oct97.htm. Accessed 15.5.09.

Fornander, A. (1980) *An Account of the Polynesian Race: Its Origins and Migrations.* Rutland, VT: Chas. E. Tuttle Company.

Hawai'i Visitors and Convention Bureau website. On WWW at www.gohawaii.com/big_island. Accessed 10.5.09.

Gaspar, E.A. (1955) Tourism's place in Kona education is stressed. Honolulu *Advertiser*, 10 November, D5.

Gessler, C. (1937) *Hawai'i: Isles of Enchantment.* New York: D. Appleton-Century Company.

Goto, B. (1982) Ethnic groups and the coffee industry in Hawai'i. *Hawaiian Journal of History* 16, 111–124.

Greenwell, J. n.d. Kona Historical Society. Personal papers.

Hall, C.M. and Mitchell, R. (2005) Gastronomic tourism – comparing food and wine tourism experiences. In M. Novelli (ed.) *Niche Tourism: Contemporary Issues, Trends and Cases* (pp. 1–14). New York: Elsevier.

Harada-Stone, D. (1989a) Kealakekua ranch's plans worry neighbors. Hawai'i *Tribune Herald*, 10 January, 1.

Harada-Stone, D. (1989b) Land board to consider swap of Kona lands. Hawai'i *Tribune Herald*, 2 August, 1.

Harlow, G.S. (1928) *Hawai'i: By a Tourist.* Los Angeles, CA: West Coast Publishing.

Hawai'i Visitors and Convention Bureau. On WWW at www.gohawaii.com. Accessed 8.5.09.

Independent Voice (2007) Newsletter of the Kona Coffee Farmers Association. February. On WWW at http://konacoffeefarmers.org/docs/newsletter-0207.pdf. Accessed 25.5.09.

Johnston, C.S. (1995) Enduring idylls? A geographical analysis of Kona, Hawai'i. PhD dissertation, University of Hawai'i at Mānoa.

Juvik, J.O., Singleton, D.C. and Clarke, G.G. (1978) Climate and water balance on the island of Hawai'i. *Mauna Loa Observatory, a 20th Anniversary Report* (pp. 129–139). National Oceanic and Atmospheric Administration.

Kamakau, S.M. (1961) *Ruling Chiefs of Hawai'i.* Honolulu, HI: The Kamehameha Schools Press.

Kelly, M. (1983) *Nā Māla o Kona: Gardens of Kona – A History of Land Use in Kona, Hawai'i.* Honolulu, HI: Bernice Pauahi Bishop Museum, Department of Anthropology. Report 83-2.

Kinro, G.Y. (2003) *A Cup of Aloha: The Kona Coffee Epic.* Honolulu, HI: University of Hawai'i Press. A Latitude 20 Book.

Kirch, P.V. (1984) *The Evolution of Polynesian Chiefdoms.* Cambridge: Cambridge University Press.

Kona Coffee Cultural Festival. On WWW at www.konacoffeefest.com. Accessed 10.6.09.

Kona Historical Society. On WWW at www.konahistorical.org. Accessed 12.6.09.

Lind, A.W. (1928) Occupational trends among immigrant groups in Hawai'i. *Social Forces* 7 (2), 290–299.

Lind, A.W. (1967) *Kona: A Community of Hawai'i. A Report for the Board of Education.* Honolulu, HI: State of Hawai'i.

Luttinger, N. and Dicum, G. (2006) *The Coffee Book: Anatomy of an Industry from Crop to the Last Drop.* New York: The New Press.

McKercher, B. (2002) Towards a classification of cultural tourists. *International Journal of Tourism Research* 4, 29–38.

Maoz, D. (2006) The mutual gaze. *Annals of Tourism Research* 33 (1), 221–239.

Masuda, T. (2007) Economic analyses of organic farming – the case of kona coffee industry in Hawaii. PhD dissertation, University of Hawai'i at Mānoa.

Morrill, G.L. (1919) *Hawaiian Heathen and Others.* Chicago, IL: M.A. Donahue & Co.

Musick, J.R. (1898) *Hawai'i. Our New Possessions.* New York: Funk & Wagnalls Company.

Paradise of the Pacific (1899) Coffee in the Kona District. Vol. 1 2 (1) (January), 6.

Peterson, D.W. and Moore, R.B. (1987) Geologic history and the evolution of geologic concepts, island of Hawai'i. In R.W. Decker, T.L. Wright and P.H. Stauffer (eds) *Volcanism in Hawai'i* (pp. 149–189). Washington, DC: US GPO (USGS Professional Paper 1350).

Pukui, M.K., Elbert, S.H. and Mo'okini, E.T. (1974) *Place Names of Hawai'i.* Honolulu, HI: University of Hawai'i Press.

Robinson, M. and Novelli, M. (2005) Niche tourism: An introduction. In M. Novelli (ed.) *Niche Tourism: Contemporary Issues, Trends and Cases* (pp. 1–14). New York: Elsevier.

Royalkonacoffee. On WWW at http://www.royalkonacoffee.com/LearnMore/AboutKonaCoffee/tabid/76/Default.aspx. Accessed 23.5.09.

Schilt, R. (1984) *Subsistence and Conflict in Kona, Hawai'i: An Archaeological Study of the Kuakini Highway Realignment Corridor.* Honolulu, HI: Bernice Pauahi Bishop Museum, Department of Anthropology. Prepared for the State Department of Transportation. June.

Smyser, A.A. (1972) Changing Kona's Uncertain Future. Honolulu *Star-Bulletin*, 19 February, A11.

Stewart, C.S. (1831) *A Visit to the South Seas in 1829 and 1830.* New York: John P. Haven.

Waiaha River Coffee Company. On WWW at www.konaroast.com/local_hist.html. Accessed 8.5.09.

Whitney, H.M. (1875/1890) *The Tourist's Guide Through the Hawaiian Islands, Descriptive of their Scenes and Scenery.* Honolulu, HI: The Hawaiian Gazette Company.

Yim, S. (1981) The Good Old Days Down in Kona. Honolulu *Star-Bulletin,* 25 June, C1.

Chapter 9
Serendipitous Coffee Experiences in Papua New Guinea

WENDY S. SHAW

> If this were anywhere else, Club Med, the Hilton chain, McDonald's and Starbucks would have taken over... but this is Papua New Guinea, one of the **last frontiers** and, remarkably, **one of the least visited countries**. The perceived dangers of... Port Moresby, keep travellers at bay, as does the difficulty getting around... [The attractions are] the world's most untouched islands... [and] the experiences we share with the people of this land.
> I notice the passenger beside me is crying and the one beside her too... she says "These kids just make me blubber, look at them, are they really real?"... One day soon, villagers may abandon their traditional ways for the new... surely it can't be long before mass-tourism operators discover this wonderland... It is nice to know paradise does still exist on this war-ravaged planet, at least for now. (Excerpt from Tansley, 2009, **emphasis added**)

Wake up and smell the coffee in the highlands of Papua New Guinea (PNG), where tourism in the usual forms barely exists. There are remote coastal and island locations, which are visited for their pristine environments, and for unique experiences. Activities such as snorkelling, scuba diving and big game fishing attract the adventurous traveller (Abe & Vincent, 2006). Or, as described in the account above, those with the funds to travel on an expensive cruise ship can find somewhere that appears to be so untouched by the outside world that the place and the local people provide transformative, even emotional, moments.

The coffee-growing regions in the far-flung highlands of PNG do not offer quite the same ideal of paradise. Visitors usually come in search of other things, such as employment, research data and, often, salvation as part of the multitude of missionary work currently underway following the establishment of a German Catholic missionary, The Society of the Divine Word, in 1896, and the Anglican 'Project Canterbury', in 1883

(Chignell, 1913). In the remote mountains, in the East and West Provinces, and Simbu, a tourism experience is often *incidental* to other activities, much of it involving missionary work with the more than 85% of Papua New Guineans who now identify as Christian (Smith, 2002). Some exceptions include participation in what could be described as *hard-core* 'adventure' tourism. One such adventure is an arduous pilgrimage to the remote Kokoda Track. According to one trekking tour company 'the difficulty of the track should never be underestimated' (PNG Trekking Adventures, 2006). Some undertake this experience in remembrance of its importance to Australian soldiers during the Second World War. For others, the experience of the trek itself – this contested,[1] ecologically sensitive track – that is the attraction. Other motivations for visiting this highland attraction include the 'focus on the military history of the Kokoda campaign and follow[ing] the footsteps of the brave [soldiers] over the entire 150 km *"wartime trail"* as opposed to today's easier and more popular 96 km *"eco-tourist track"'*, according to one trekking company (Kokoda Treks, 2009).

This niche market type of tourism rarely includes an encounter with the largest industry in the highlands, which is the production of some of the world's best coffee, apart from the morning cup. Good locally grown coffee is always on the tourist menu. Tourism with a coffee focus does exist, but only in the form of a one day annual event titled the 'PNG Coffee Festival and Trade Fair', which has been held in Goroka since 2001. The festival aims to bring together all aspects of the coffee industry, and as the website promotes: 'provide an opportunity to showcase... products and services'. It brings local people together with industry, is a day out for all concerned and includes a 'miss coffee festival pageant' as well as traditional dancing (PNG Coffee Festival, 2008). The national airline, Air Niugini, advertises this festival on its calendar of events. There is also the annual Goroka Show (2008), which is sponsored by Kokoda Coffee and Goroka Coffee Roasters; both companies advertise at the Goroka Show and have web links on the Goroka Show website for the sale of their coffees. Coffee tourism in PNG is otherwise informal or incidental. There are, of course, many incidental tourism 'experiences' that occur in the highlands and I discuss some of these later.

Context

This chapter considers visitor activities in the coffee-growing highlands of PNG with a view to expanding the notion of (coffee) tourism to include more incidental moments. In so doing, it reflects on how the prospect of travel for 'work', or other non-tourist activities in these parts, includes an almost mandatory form of adventure travel for those who visit from other places, particularly from other countries.[2] Far from the usual forms of tropical tourism, replete with images of swaying palm trees, lazy beach activities and resort holidays, PNG is not a common holidaying destination for foreigners as the travel journalist, Craig Tansley, emotively observed (above). Once a destination for foreign visitors to the luxurious plantation homes of British, German and Australian ex-patriots during colonial times (see Bulbeck, 2002, on lives of ex-patriot women), PNG now holds a dangerous reputation. PNG is simply no longer *on* the beaten track as a tourist-oriented destination regardless of its many attractions; its environmental and cultural uniqueness, replete with wide-eyed innocent children (as depicted above). Moreover, the images of PNG have not been fed by the same heady enthusiasm for other Pacific places. The accounts of European explorers during imperialist expansion and invasion of Pacific lands provided a basis for current understandings of 'paradise' (think of de Bougainville's 1771 drooling accounts of Tahiti, particularly Tahitian women). Populist accounts of PNG, in the late 19th and early to mid 20th centuries reflected warrior cultures, and a familiar ideal of the 'noble savage' (e.g. Chapter 8, Angas, 1866). This morphed into a gentler image of the 'fuzzy wuzzy angels' who supported Australian soldiers during invasion attempts by Japanese soldiers in the Second World War, and who were revered for their bravery. More recent accounts have departed somewhat from this celebration of the relationship between Papuans and Australian soldiers during that war.

From outside PNG, images of the wild and dangerous dominate popular understandings. The marauding hoards of unemployed and criminal 'raskols' – which is Tok Pisin for the word 'rascal' in English – seem to be holding the country to ransom. Raskols are often associated with gang membership and/or criminal activities (Flickling, 2004). Stories of corruption and loss of control have escalated since PNG gained independence from Australia in 1975. In 1993, a non-government organisation, Transparency International, formed to assist in the prevention of corruption in PNG. Stories of violence are almost a daily event, with the international media reporting on, for instance, 'Witches put to death in Papua New Guinea as mob rule takes hold' (Parry, 2009) and 'Doctors evacuated from remote PNG post' (Anonymous, 2009).

Underpinning the perceptions of danger and violence in PNG are references to a seemingly unshakable primitivism. The use of biological determinism easily explains this kind of primitivism, which is similar to the use of narratives of racialised genetic inferiority, deployed to explain Indigenous intolerance to alcohol. Compounding these kinds of representations is the idea that 'civilisation' was tried during colonisation but was lost with independence.[3] This appears to be a culture that cannot 'look after itself', with reports of 'lost tribes' and acts of cannibalism (Marriot, 1887)[4] occasionally emerging to verify this failure (Palmer & Lester, 2007). And then, very occasionally, we read stories of the purity of unblemished remoteness, of *true* unsullied paradise in 'one of the [world's] least visited countries', a 'final frontier' soon to be lost (Tansley, 2009, above). Although the basic premise of primitiveness prevails – as a paradise locked away in time according to this rendering – this is a more positive spin for tourism than spiralling under-development and tribal anarchy.

A methodology

To write this chapter, I draw on observations that I have made as a collaborator on two internationally based research projects on coffee production in the PNG highlands. Both projects are working towards improving the overall conditions of the production of mostly high-grade, organic Arabica coffee, which is PNG's largest agricultural cash-crop, grown in small household gardens in the remote highlands. One project is concerned with identifying best practice methods to control a particularly insidious coffee pest (insect) know as Coffee Green Scale (CGS) – *Coccus celatus* in this case – which has been estimated to account for 10–50% of current crop losses in PNG (CAB International, 2005). Integrated approaches to pest management, including the use of biological controls, are being developed and tested to compliment or enhance existing farmer practices and knowledge about pest control. The other research project aims to work with farmers to improve the quality of the coffee harvest. This project is assessing current systems used to get the coffee crop from the coffee trees to market. The aim is to assist in improving what have been dubbed 'postharvest systems', from the harvest stage to storage, through to appropriate local processing systems and crop transport. A premise to both research projects (herein dubbed collectively as ACIAR coffee research projects, after the funding body, the Australian Centre for International Agricultural Research), is that the socio-cultural and economic contexts of coffee production are integral to progressing the aims of these otherwise highly scientific and technical efforts to improve life in these highlands (ACIAR, 2009a, 2009b). As a geographer, I have ensured that this part of the research has been operationalised. I have drawn on correspondences and discussions with colleagues, who also travel from elsewhere to engage in other-than-tourism activities, but like me, end up drinking excellent coffee in sometimes unexpected circumstances, and sometimes encounter other serendipitous travel experiences while engaged in the activities associated with action-based research on PNG's coffee industry. I have focussed on 'outsiders' (foreigners) who are informed by external portrayals of PNG before they arrive. I do acknowledge that my PNG colleagues also engage in tourism, but it is differently informed, and for future investigation.

As a contribution to a book on coffee and tourism, this chapter is a little unusual because of the minimal presence of formal coffee tourism in PNG. Part of the aim of writing this chapter therefore is to showcase the existence of a thriving coffee industry in PNG, as well as to consider the kinds of tourist experiences associated with the crop and its production. As a contributor to the global coffee supply (over 1%), and in particular to the bourgeoning organic and boutique coffee market, with Starbucks as a main purchaser (Batt & Murray-Prior, 2007), it can be argued that the experience of coffee tourism extends to its consumption destinations. However, in this chapter I focus on PNG. I provide a short history of the coffee industry in PNG, followed by a discussion of the study of tourism, particularly from within the discipline of geography. I consider formal and informal meanings of tourism and the sometimes unexpected nexus of coffee (research) and tourism in PNG. This chapter concludes by arguing that because tourism in the highlands of PNG tends to sit outside conventional definitions, coffee tourism will remain somewhat accidental. At present, this form of tourism is mostly informal and very often serendipitous. McKercher (2002: 33) has identified the 'Serendipitous Cultural Tourist' for whom 'cultural tourism plays little or no role in the decision to visit a destination, but while there this type of cultural tourist... ends up having a deep [cultural] experience'. This certainly rings true for a group of coffee researchers who work in the PNG highlands.

Coffee in Papua New Guinea

PNG consists of numerous islands and approximately half of the island of 'New Guinea' (Figure 9.1) – the other half, West Papua, is currently part of Indonesia. The highland provinces on the PNG side of New Guinea are now the home of PNG's most important export industry.

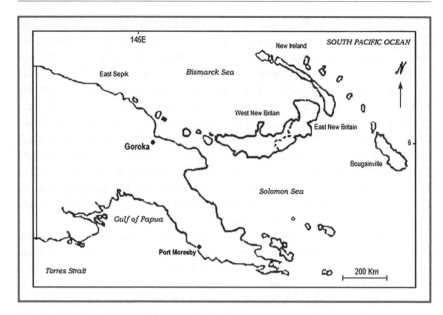

Figure 9.1 Map of Papua New Guinea

Coffee exports constitute the highest foreign exchange earnings within PNG's agricultural sector and the bulk of this is grown in the Eastern Highland Province, the Western Highland Province and Simbu (Batt & Murray-Prior, 2007).

Contrary to many other coffee-growing circumstances, where a legacy of colonialism has left a culture of plantation-based production, PNG coffee is overwhelmingly produced by smallholders in isolated highland locations. Most growers in PNG have 'coffee gardens'. These gardens are small plots of land with as few as 20 coffee trees growing alongside subsistence crops. Because of locational remoteness and low-tech production, most PNG coffee is 'organic' by international standards. Along with a continued demand for coffee, and subsequent growth in production levels, interest in organic produce is also increasing, which certainly bodes well for PNG's coffee industry (Bacon, 2005; CAB International, 2005) with The International Coffee Organization (2009) reporting that coffee production nearly doubled between 1977 and 1999 globally, and continues to rise with increasing demand. There is, however, a fine balance between maintaining the 'pristine' nature of PNG coffee and the suitability of its current means of production for local growers. The local ecologies of food and coffee agriculture mean that growers continue to live close to subsistence with little surplus income for inputs to improving or maintaining coffee production. Smallholder coffee growers simply cannot afford commercial pest management controls or more efficient processing facilities (Maika, 2007). Fluctuations in coffee quality and quantity are commonplace and impact upon the reliability of supply and cash payments to growers (Batt & Murray-Prior, 2007). Another major problem with coffee growing is the issue of coffee theft, which has impacted significantly on grower household incomes. A recent survey conducted for the ACIAR coffee research projects (described above) identified that theft was a main cause for concern for growers. The crop is often carried to a local roadside buyer, which means that the carrier and the crop are vulnerable. At other times, coffee cherries are simply stolen from the trees (cf. Shaw *et al.*, 2008).

The remoteness of much of PNG's highland population has created difficulties for gathering information about them. The *CIA World Factbook* (2008) estimated that unemployment in PNG in 2004 ranged from 2 to 80% – the last figure applied to urban areas. Although smallholder coffee growers in the remote highlands are far from unemployed, there is widespread under-employment and poverty. A 2002 estimate put 37% of the population of PNG below the poverty line (CIA, 2008). Compounding the issues of unemployment, under-employment and poverty, is the sporadic nature of income from coffee production. Coffee theft usually occurs at harvest time, when the coffee cherries are ripe, or just harvested. It has become a somewhat reliable source of instant cash for thieves and a consequent loss for growers who have worked for the income (Maika, 2007; Simbiken, 2006). Concerns about safety, shared by tourist advisories – including the Australian Government's 'smartraveller' website, which provides a stern warning for travel in PNG – are compounded for highland coffee growers by theft-related income insecurity; coffee is a valuable commodity. In short, coffee is grown in rugged, remote PNG highland locations where the usual provisions for tourism, such as accommodation, transport and leisure activities, are outside the orbit of concern for coffee farmers, or the industry more generally. This commodity represents an essential cash supplement for these farming communities. The lack of tourism infrastructure means that few tourism operators include the highlands on their routes. For travellers to these highlands, transport and accommodation usually need to be organised well in advance, and independent of tourism agencies. At the same time, travellers need to be adaptable to the vagaries of this kind of travel.

Geographies of Travel and Tourism

By dint of the discipline's name and pre-occupation, geography – the writing/study of the earth (and its people) – has a long-standing interest in mobility as well as origins and destinations. 'Tourism Geography' as a field of study began to appear after the Second World War (see Gibson, 2008, for an empirical overview). According to a *Progress in Human Geography* review of Tourism Geographies, Del Casino and Hanna (2000) identified that with an emphasis on positivism, the interests at that time were rather simplistic with a focus on tourism planning. A major development in Tourism Geographies was the adoption of McCannell's (1976) 'theory of the leisure class', which posited that:

> The tourist is engaged in a modern form of religious ritual. The tourist seeks out an **"authentic" other** in an attempt to order and structure the world. Authenticity can never be fully realized, however, because it is constantly staged through the process of creating representations for tourists... these material and social practices banish the real or authentic to the backstage, outside the sight and reach of the tourist. Therefore, **spaces of tourism hide the reality of everyday life under a myriad of representations**. (Del Casino & Hanna, 2000: 26; **emphasis added**)

The search for *an authentic other* can be found in the accounts of 'travellers', particularly during the imperial expeditions from Europe. The flamboyant Louis Antoine de Bougainville, as mentioned earlier, waxed lyrically about Pacific peoples. Clearly enthralled with the 'noble savage', de Bougainville (and many others) found a sense of authenticity that could be compared to the European self. Indeed, this search for authenticity was a fundamental question of the Enlightenment, where the meanings of purity and civilisation were challenged (see Gascoigne, 2002, for the Australian context). Perhaps 'they' (the Pacific *others*) represented the true authentic human, unadulterated by the ravages of 'civilisation'. The highlands of PNG certainly offer an image of authenticity. The few tourism agencies that do operate in the highlands include the experiences of intact 'tribal' cultures and pristine environments on their menus (e.g. see McKinnon *et al.*, 2008).

Del Casino and Hanna (2000) observed that more recent studies of tourism (which now include more recent conceptualisations of the 'traveller', which I return to shortly) have considered representations of the gazed upon, and the commodification of peoples and cultures that accompany tourism. Challenges to essentialist identity politics in cultural studies, postcolonial and poststructuralist literary theory, and in geography, have questioned the universalist notion of 'the tourist', particularly as an opposite to the non-tourist worker in a location (Franklin & Crang, 2001, provide an overview). Of course, many who work in tourism, which can be seasonal and involve travel, also engage in tourism activities during their breaks from work, such as in the ski-fields of Europe and elsewhere. Many have had the experience of travelling, then stopping for work when funds needed to be 'topped up'. There are also business tourists who engage in tourism during business activities (and 'down' times), and there are people like me now, who are researchers.

And for those of us (researchers) who engage with cultural and/or social theory of various disciplinary persuasions, we now acknowledge that identities are not fixed for the tourist, or for the researcher. After all, tourism experiences are not always leisure based. Moreover, what constitutes leisure for one person is not necessarily on the list of another (think again of de Bougainville in Tahiti). The notion of 'adventure tourism' has also shifted. Once the domain of the wealthy eccentric – the Freya Starks of the past – travel to remote locations (Geniesse, 2001), which are far from home and the familiar, now attracts a range of 'independent travellers', including holiday-makers, the *working* holiday-makers and the working *travellers* who engage in a little downtime here and there. The following, which distinguishes the traveller from the tourist, also pinpoints an interesting dilemma for researchers (in this case, ethnographers).

> The traveler was associated with the broadening of the mind, cultivation of taste, and respect for other cultures. In contrast, the tourist lacked imagination, initiative, and knowledge of the travel destination... [anthropologists and others] thus viewed travelers as superior to the tourists... Ethnographers now argue that many concepts in tourism discourse – such as longing for primitive, exotic, and authentic travel experience – reflect [this kind of] Western hierarchical and binary thinking. ... [Conversely] some ethnographers have found their personal, private touristic selves increasingly mixed with their professional, ethnographic selves to the point where they are unsure if any such distinction actually exists. (Markula, 1997: 208–209)

The search for authenticity reminds me of my own heady days as a young 'traveller' who sought out journeys that were decidedly *off* 'the beaten track'. Along with McCannell (quoted above), I believed that away from the trappings of tourism, where cultures seemed to be artificially (mis)represented, I could find less corrupted, more *authentic* cultures/environments. Along with many others, I too have engaged in adventurous kinds of 'independent travel'. A combination of personal politics, and wanting to travel without huge reserves of cash, meant that I had joined the armies of travellers from 'first world countries' who sought out 'third world' experiences, from the late 1970s. Now a geographer who engages in a range of professional travel, for conferences, guest presentations and ethnographic research, I draw on my experiences of travelling 'rough'; I tend also to find my personal, private touristic self immersed within my professional self. According to Timothy and Teye (2005), there is a distinction between formal and informal tourist sectors, which are of particular relevance to the 'first world' traveller (and/or researcher) wandering around in 'developing' nations.[5] I can now identify that much of the travel I engaged in – before becoming an ethnographic researcher – would be classified as 'informal' tourism because I generally avoided the trappings of *mainstream* tourism. Being largely unaware of this categorisation, I was, of course, oblivious to my tourist gaze (Urry, 1990), and the commodifications of cultures and locations that I participated in, just by being there and following the few that had gone before, or carving out new 'tracks', to be followed by others.

Tourist offerings are also not always easy to distinguish from non-tourism. For instance, the point at which eating in a local eatery or drinking in a bar frequented by locals becomes tourism is open to conjecture. Also, formal and informal tourism activities often overlap. Drawing on a range of debates, Timothy and Teye (2005) surmised the 'formal sector' in tourism as officially recognised, licensed, taxed, enumerated and often regulated, whereas the informal sector usually involves people and incomes that are none of the above and sometimes, not legal. Mostly, tourism spaces include both the formal and informal and, of course, where there is tourism of any sort, there will be trade – formal and/or informal. As Davidson (1994) suggested, *business* travel might indeed be one of the earliest forms of tourism because people have always travelled for the purpose of trade. And the researcher, engaged in travel-based research, must engage in the business of trade.

In a different treatment of the business of travel and trade, Sikes (2006) considered her own position as a traveller/tourist researcher during a visit to Bangkok. To deal with what appeared to be a mix of discomfort and fascination, and justify her decision to stay when she inadvertently found herself in a 'girlie [sex act] bar', Sikes decided to write about the experience, and the way she defaulted to a professional explanation for her presence, regardless of it not being part of any research. Sikes identified that she had stayed at the bar, and 'taken it all in':

> Partly because that's what I always do [as a researcher] but I [was] also using it... [as an exercise in] detaching me, my "self" from [such a] situation. Being [there] in a professional sense seem[ed] to give legitimacy to my presence. I [was] a "scientific," "objective" observer, there for a proper purpose with the task of documenting and analyzing what I [was] seeing... To my mind, there was an immediate and intimate connection between my experience of being a visiting scholar overseas in an unfamiliar setting and... being an academic and doing research in a more general sense. (Sikes, 2006: 528, 290)

In the next section, I consider the reverse situation. Unlike Sikes, who is a tourist who reverts to a researcher position, I discuss some of serendipitous tourism experiences of researchers working in the highlands of PNG. Specifically, I draw on the experiences of a group of scholars of varying disciplinary persuasions who all work in coffee research – there are entomologists, food technologists/engineers, economists, agronomists and a human geographer, to name a few. I do recognise that travel and tourism are also practices of local people, but in this chapter I consider 'my own kind' (foreign researchers). As Galani-Moutafi observed,

> Overall, as the postmodern world – because of travel and mobility – is undergoing a continuous readjustment of cultural geographies, the formerly stable distinctions between the familiar and the foreign, the self and Other, as well as the conventional views about the "field" where... research takes place, have been undermined. A reaction to these conditions is an increasing reorientation of the ethnographer's gaze towards the self, as the appropriate place for interpreting cultural experience. (Galani-Moutafi, 2000: 216–217)

Building on Markula's (1997) observation that tourism research can provide unique insights into the researcher as tourist position, I push the notion of 'tourism' to include a largely non-acknowledged form of adventure travel that accompanies 'out of country' research (but see Halvaksz, 2006, on 'in country' tourism in PNG). By doing this, I hope to expand the orbit of the definition of 'tourist' to include the traveller/tourist researcher.

Serendipitous Tourism Experiences in Papua New Guinea

> Tourism [is] any visit to the [PNG] highlands...[it is] an amazing landscape. (Australian food scientist, 2008)

> Most of the foreign tourists are researchers... from European countries like the Netherlands, France, Germany, Belgium and the UK... the obstacles in developing [ordinary] tourism [in North Sulawesi]... [are] the lack of infrastructure including transportation means, telecommunications, and roads. (Excerpt from Anonymous, 2008)

The last quote supports the idea that in certain contexts the tourists *are* researchers. This is particularly the case in remote locations where conventional tourism is yet to occur, as has been observed in Sangihe, in North Sulawesi, Indonesia. I begin a process of exploring the researcher position to include identifications of traveller and tourist in this chapter by following Sikes' lead. I include my own experiences[6] of research-related travel/tourism, which began in PNG in 2006. Like most, I visited PNG for reasons other than tourism, but arrived wide-eyed with curiosity. My first response to seeing the highlands echoed that of my colleague (quoted first, above). The purpose of my first visit was to participate in the commencement of the two ACIAR coffee research projects (see Introduction), which are based in Aiyura, near Kainantu, in the East Highlands Province. On this occasion, I arrived after a long day of travel from Sydney, Australia, and had spent the night at a hotel near Jackson's Airport in Port Moresby.

My immediate impression upon arrival at the hotel in Port Moresby was that the surrounding impoverished neighbourhood was a stark juxtaposition to its relative luxury, high fences and armed guards. Forewarned of the dangers of travelling to and within PNG, my reaction to Port Moresby was not one of fear but acknowledgement of the high level of segregation between local residents and visitors. Armed officials (were they police, security guards or military?) patrolled the airport and the roads. Hotels seemed highly organised; drivers fetched visitors from the airport and would not leave for the hotel until every booked passenger was located. Upon my arrival, I too was securely escorted to the hotel, which sat within a fortified compound. In compliance with various instructions I received before leaving Sydney, I had familiarised myself with the relevant Australian Federal Government websites, including the official travel site, 'Smart Traveller', which suggested that travellers exercise a 'high degree of caution' while in PNG, as does the adventure guidebook, *The Lonely Planet*, which warns travellers against visiting the highlands. I am familiar with travelling to 'risky' destinations. My usual response is that this kind of travel includes a tension between being a female foreigner who, in this context, would probably be highly visible and likely viewed as 'affluent', and engagement with people who live their lives in risky contexts (albeit slightly different to the risks I face as a 'white' woman travelling alone). I am always cautious in such circumstances and ensure that I have made careful calculations about the risks involved, but I try to not let this interfere with my encounters with local people or the work I have to do.

Before boarding the local aircraft the morning after my first night in PNG – for a notoriously late and harrowing but thankfully short one-hour flight to Goroka, in the highlands – I noticed the gift shops at Jackson's Airport were spilling over with handicrafts. What really stuck me, however, was a wondrous variety of mostly organic coffees, which were one of the most prominent items on sale. As an amateur coffee connoisseur and home barista, I eagerly purchased the strongest espresso blend. I was in PNG on 'coffee business' and my research association with the Coffee Industry Corporation (CIC) was to be my key into the world of one of PNG's, and perhaps the world's most celebrated industries. For instance, PNG Tourism offers advice on 'what to buy in PNG', and coffee is included. It was a moment of Gruen Transfer,[7] and I felt that I was in the right place, for a range of reasons. Upon arrival in the domestic departure lounge, I was greeted by what seemed a most incongruous sight for the location. Two women wearing barista uniforms were promoting PNG coffee, which was freshly ground and served straight from a large commercial espresso machine, for free (there was to be a charge in future). And, the coffee was divine. As a coffee researcher, who likes a little of the unexpected, this was a most serendipitous moment, though, sadly the coffee machine has remained unattended on subsequent visits.

Regardless of how 'experienced' outsiders may be, there are always stories about travelling in PNG. As a colleague remarked, 'it [PNG] is well known as the land of the unexpected' (Australian Agronomist, 2008). There is an accepted logic that the more one travels to PNG, the higher the odds of 'an event'. The more experienced outsider will offer a gamut of PNG travel tales, experienced personally, or 'heard' from someone else. Such stories usually involve experiences of thrilling moments, of intimidation by 'raskols', of being held-up (at gun or knife or machete-point), robbed, mugged or worse. Tales of magnificent landscapes and friendly local people are also told. But visitors to PNG do tend to arrive braced for the prospect of danger, as discussed at the beginning of this chapter. Before my first visit, I was warned about the mishap of a colleague who carries a scar that runs from ear to ear – the result of a machete attack in the highlands. Because of the Australian Government's Smart Traveller warning (above), I need considered permission by my employer – an Australian university – for travel to PNG.

Thus far, my tourism experience in PNG has been somewhat varied and definitely adventurous. The journey from Sydney includes the mundane stresses of travel involving connecting flights (which happens everywhere). Once in PNG, the reminders of danger are ever-present, from the moment of arrival at Port Moresby, and particularly when in the highlands, where I travel in an armoured vehicle (Plate 9.1), in a convoy. I have walked from a private house to my hotel in Goroka with armed bodyguards and been heckled by groups of men (possibly because of the bodyguards). On one visit, staying in a hotel in downtown Port Moresby, in 2007, I arrived a day before my colleagues in the hope of getting to know Port Moresby a little better, and on foot. However, as I checked into the hotel, the two women at the reception desk warned me not to walk around the Central Business District alone, at any time. Compounding the danger narrative that keeps tourists at bay, a UK

Plate 9.1 Well-secured research vehicle with Coffee Industry Corporation logo, Kainantu Lodge, Papua New Guinea

broadsheet, *The Guardian*, reports regularly on 'the world's most dangerous cities'. In 2004, Port Moresby held that most dubious of reputations. At breakfast the next morning, as I sipped on my very drinkable PNG-grown coffee, I happened to find the *same* news sprawled across the front page of that same newspaper. Port Moresby had won the title of *The World's Most Dangerous City* again! After a momentary stomach somersault, and a side glance at the women at the reception desk who had given me such a stern warning, I quickly dismissed the headline; I was there 'on business', for work purposes, and not some form of extreme or 'danger' tourism that involved unnecessary risk taking. I would simply spend the day working in my pleasantly air-conditioned hotel room with its nice view of the city. I did go for that walk the next day. I mentioned the warning to a colleague – a young Papuan woman who had studied at the University of Papua New Guinea in Port Moresby – and she laughed and assured me that I could have gone and just taken a few precautions (such as staying in the main areas with other people, especially women).

During research for this chapter, I invited a group of colleagues to think about and try recalling any serendipitous experiences of tourism that they might have experienced in PNG, and specifically while doing coffee research. Although we all cited 'coffee research' as our purpose for visiting PNG (none of us cited experiences of engaging in formal tourism), it did not take much probing or prompting for 'adventure travel' tourism stories to emerge.

We all cited similar pastimes such as shopping, wandering streets and taking photos while in the highlands or elsewhere in PNG. This is understandable as the sights of women selling colourful billums (woven bags), handicrafts and other goods, such as betel nuts, and the setting generally is often breathtaking. One of my informants provided a lengthy account of a first encounter with living and working in PNG. As well as the story of getting set up for work, and the amusing accounts of the tribulations of adapting to daily life in PNG, the text included descriptions of scenery and side trips, which were reminiscent of travel diary entries. Scenery descriptions included:

> The drive was magnificent, seventy-five km along the coast of a slightly uplifted coral reef. This coastal drive is quite reminiscent of Samoa – except that... is limestone rather than basalt... The... estate looked like well tended gardens... Visited a limestone cave that the Japanese used in the war time to get inland from the coast. (Australian agronomist, 2008)

Another informant (Australian food scientist, 2008) cited 'watching the Rabaul volcano [erupting] and driving through the devastated Rabaul below [the volcano]' as an example of engagement in informal tourism. Another (Australian coffee expert and former plantation owner, 2008) reported that visiting PNG:

Is always exciting as it is a unique and interesting place. The law and order situation also adds a degree to excitement to any trip... I also enjoy the scenery, the people, the culture.

For another colleague, informal tourism experiences included some familiar kinds of downtime (from work) activities. These included:

Golfing at Goroka; [I was really angry that] I didn't get time to play Mt Hagen... having a quiet drink or two at the Goroka Golf Club [which] has to be one of the most spectacular settings for a club house. Drinks at the Aero club and other notorious spots such as Bird [Hotel], the Highlander and Hagen Club. [I also] buy presents at markets etc... [and] take walks around Goroka and Aiyura. (Australian coffee marketing expert, 2008)

The same respondent included the following informal tourist experiences:

Meeting some of the security guards with their bows and arrows... [and] trying to shoot with a bow and arrow.

Upon reading this, I remembered that on my first visit to Goroka, I was sitting in an open-air bar with a colleague when just over his shoulder I noticed a man armed with a bow and arrow, standing a few metres away. I whispered to my colleague 'don't look now but there's a dude with a bow and arrows behind you'. Of course my colleague laughed. He knew the situation. The armed man was a security guard who patrolled the boundaries of the hotel compound. After a very friendly exchange (in Tok Pisin, which I could not) and several photos, he went back to his patrol. When I woke the next morning, I discovered that he had stationed himself outside my door.

The aforementioned respondent also noted coffee-related informal tourism activities:

Visiting coffee plantations, processing plants and mills, [and] cupping coffee... – in a couple of locations – with exporters and CIC [PNG's Coffee Industry Corporation].

And assured me that all of the activities s/he engaged in were:

Directly or indirectly related to coffee research – either where we were staying or taking the opportunity to meet the locals – even shopping because [we usually] observ[e] other aspects such as coffee buying at the markets.

When asked about serendipitous or accidental (including 'adventure') tourist moments, one colleague responded with the kind of story one expects, but hopes not to hear:

Accidental? I had heard stories of the dangers in travelling around PNG from a colleague, but didn't expect to be involved in [an incident] myself. I asked to visit a local coffee orchard in order to talk to local farmers, and on the trip in we travelled as a safe "convoy" (two cars). After completing discussions, we headed off, but the lead car (with the local extension trainers) disappeared before we could complete turning around. About one km down the road, we were ambushed by two local "rascals". The first walked onto the road in front of us, a large rifle aimed at the driver. [The driver] opted to try and run down the gunman, who jumped for his life. There was a loud bang, and then we were driving away. About this time I started to realise sticking my head up and watching was not a good idea, but by the time I hit the floor it was all over anyway. And the loud bang? I thought it was the gun going off, but in fact it was an angry rascal bashing the side of the car with his gun, which was empty [not loaded]. (Australian food scientist, 2008)

When reading this passage, I remembered that I was there when this incident occurred. I was about to jump into the vehicle (Plate 9.1) to visit the coffee orchard when the team from the other ACIAR coffee project appeared, unexpectedly, from the UK. I decided to catch up with them about that project – I could go to the orchard another time. Of course, after the convoy returned with the news of the 'hold up' (retold above), with the team clearly shaken by the incident, that particular destination was struck off the list for me. I have also noticed tighter security, around the foreign visitors at least, since that incident. I was very glad not to have shared that particular encounter/adventure, but do recount it to those who like a good story (and I am sure my colleague enjoys retelling it). There was quite a lot of excitement in the coffee research camp after this event. We all congratulated the brave driver and were very relieved that no-one had been hurt (including the raskols).

In another account of serendipitous or accidental tourism, a respondent reported:

> Getting the [largish vehicle] bogged twice in one day and having difficulty getting out of a couple of other tight spots [on the road]. Paying highway extortion [which could include being held up for money to cross a bridge] – and [then deciding to] drive straight through highway extortion attempts [in defiance of the extortionists]. (Australian coffee marketing expert, 2008)

And another cited:

> Driving from Goroka to Mt Hagen through Chimbu – exciting mountain scenery and the prospect of robbery around every corner... Going out to the villages to see farmers, how they live and to be involved in the processes of coffee – growing, harvesting processing. (Australian coffee expert and former plantation owner, 2008)

As I read through the accounts and thought about my own autobiography of experiences, it became clearer to me that this group of coffee researchers do engage in, and sometimes enjoy, their adventure tourism experiences while working in PNG. I began to think more of my own 'moments' in the PNG highlands, some of which were adventure tourism, while other moments were less adventurous, but just as exciting. In the end, some of travel experiences I tell include:

> Upon arriving at Goroka Airport, in the highlands, the first time, a coffin arrived with the luggage, which all went onto a rickety timber luggage rack. Just as I was taking that sight in, my luggage – a battered travel case that obviously did not belong to a local – disappeared into the crowd. Much to horror of my PNG-savvy colleagues, I made chase and retrieved it, to the amusement and approval of the local onlookers. My next interesting moment occurred as we left the airport. After a very warm welcome by the Papuan colleagues, I was escorted to the security-grille clad vehicle, while some of the colleagues I had just met sat on the backs of other vehicles, in convoy. Then, we sped further into the mountains, on a rough and dangerous highway; the plane was late in and we simply had to get to Kainantu before dark. It was a bone-shaking drive.

Ultimately, for foreign researchers who work in the coffee-growing highlands of PNG, our visits are always full of a myriad of mostly incidental, but not necessarily completely unexpected, tourism experiences. However, for all the serendipitous 'adventures' we encounter, it is the warm and caring hospitality of our Papuan colleagues, who are our hosts, that must not be understated. Apart from carrying out the day-to-day research activities, our hosts ensure that each visit is highly organised; they become like tour operators, ensuring that all aspects of the travel experience are arranged for, including the transport, accommodation, meals and so on, and above all, our personal security (not to mention organising the research meetings, field and laboratory work for the coffee projects). My Papuan colleagues have also arranged many enjoyable extra-curricular coffee experiences, from visiting coffee growers to learning cupping techniques in the highly controlled laboratories of coffee exporters. During the cupping sessions, we learned about the difference between the taste, aroma and colour of both Arabica and Robusta coffee. Some of us became quite adept at discerning quality. We also learnt how easy it is to taste too much coffee – it is very important to spit the coffee into specially provided spittoons after tasting. But, as one of my Australian colleagues reminded me, the boundary between coffee researcher and traveller/tourist is blurred because, ultimately, a highlight of being in the highlands of PNG is:

> Going out to the villages to see farmers, how they live and to be involved in the processes of coffee – growing, harvesting [and] processing. (Australian coffee expert and former plantation owner, 2008)

For an outsider, travel in the coffee-growing highlands of PNG is an experience that is hard to compare with any other.

Conclusions

Formal tourism in PNG is a small, specialist industry. Coffee tourism in PNG exists only in the form of a festival, and a presence at the Goroka Show. Presently, tourism marketing tends to focus on PNG's natural beauty and associated wilderness adventures. Overall, PNG is perceived to be a 'wild' landscape inhabited by tribal peoples; an environmental final frontier that is still largely intact. Although this bodes well for the production of organic coffee, grown in the picturesque highlands, the contours of coffee production are yet to be included within the formalised or usual tourist trails. In this chapter, I have 'publicised' a form of coffee tourism that remains largely informal, and unacknowledged. I have endeavoured to bring the idea of tourism in touch with the traveller-researcher identity. In so doing, I hope to have contributed to the project of prizing open the definition of 'tourism' and in particular, 'coffee tourism'.

For the comparatively wealthy 'Western' researcher, the prospect of carrying out research in 'other', less traversed places carries an element of excitement that is not dissimilar to the trepidations and anticipations associated with other forms of independent travel. Carrying out research in a destination like PNG, as an employee of an Australian university or research centre, brings its own set of hurdles to be crossed before the journey can begin. Apart from gaining visas and permissions, the institutional fears of litigation associated with 'risk management' ensure that such work is not taken on lightly. In short, we are primed before we arrive.

In the meantime, the priority in the highlands of PNG is simply not tourism, though a colleague in the highlands, in Aiyura, has told me that coffee tourism is certainly 'on the agenda' for the CIC.[8] Overall, efforts are generally focused on improving the lives and livelihoods of the coffee growers and those dispossessed of lands to grow coffee, who resort to desperate measures, including coffee theft. Less formal forms of coffee tourism are likely to prevail in the short term, however, if the production of PNG coffee expands, as it needs to do to meet demand, and if 'business' tourism, including visits by coffee researchers and others in the coffee business, continues or expands, then there are many opportunities for coffee and other areas of PNG tourism.

In the meantime, I hope to be able to offer more 'return' hospitality for Papuan colleagues who occasionally visit Sydney from the coffee-growing highlands of PNG. On a previous visit, Sydney's coffee (a la café) was graded as 'too bitter, thumbs down', or at best 'ok' by my Papuan colleagues. It seems work needs to be done. My next venture might just be to find out about the serendipitous tourism experienced by my Papuan colleagues when travelling to Sydney, Australia, on coffee-related business.

Notes

1. The traditional landowners of The Kokoda Track closed the track in protest over the Australian Government's plan to have the track listed as a World Heritage site; the owners had agreed to allow copper mining in the area. The issue was resolved by a PNG Government decision to halt the mining venture (Kokoda Track Protest Stage-Managed, by Greg Roberts, 8 February 2008 – On WWW at http://www.theaustralian.news.com.au/story/0,,23178324-31477,00.html?from = public_rss).

2. Although beyond the scope of this chapter to consider in depth, the foreign gaze over 'the other' is present for researcher and tourist alike. Those who visit 'poorer' nation states, gaze and consume (be it leisure or data), then jet out, and return to the contrasting comfort of their everyday (working) lives (cf. Said, 1978; Urry, 1990).
3. Elsewhere, I have discussed the ascription of biological inferiority and failed independence attempts with reference to Indigenous Australians living in the inner-city neighbourhood of Redfern, Sydney (Shaw, 2007).
4. On 17 September 2006, a media frenzy erupted in Australia over a '60 Minutes' story titled 'Last Cannibals', which was about a Korowai boy named Wawa, who was allegedly at risk of being cannibalised in his village in West Papua (Indonesia), and then the attempted 'rescue' by the anchor of another television programme, Today Tonight (for analysis see http://www.abc. net.au/mediawatch/transcripts/s1743768).
5. I use terms such as 'first world' and 'third world', 'developed' and 'developing' reservedly. In Australia (as with all other 'first world' nations), first world and third world conditions exist within the same country. The erosion of welfare states has resulted in what are sometimes referred to as 'fourth world' conditions, i.e. for Indigenous peoples in contemporary settler societies (such as Australia and the USA).
6. I have used autobiography in other work (Shaw, 2009). I do acknowledge, and am mindful of the trap of narcissistic navel gazing. Here, I have used my own experiences to help me interrogate the traveller-researcher position, and then find out about the experiences of others.
7. Gruen Transfer' is the moment of consumer 'capture' associated with 'cues in the environment', which lead to purchase (see http://en.wikipedia.org/ wiki/Gruen_transfer). An Australian television infotainment programme also carries the same name with panel discussions on the power of advertising (http://www.abc.net.au/gruentransfer).
8. The Coffee Marketing Board, which became the Coffee Industry Board (CIB), was formed in 1964 to centralise PNG's coffee industry. In 1991, the Coffee Industry Corporation, CIC (Statutory Powers and Functions) Act was passed by the PNG Parliament. CIC Ltd. is largely self-financing (http://www.cof feecorp.org.pg/abotus.html).

References

Abe, T. and Vincent, P. (2006) *Papua New Guinea Tourism Sector Review and Master Plan (2007–2017): 'Growing PNG Tourism as A Sustainable Industry'*, Final Report. Independent Consumer and Competition Commission PNG and the Tourism Promotion Authority, Government of Papua New Guinea. On WWW at http://www.iccc.gov.pg/publications/DraftPNGTourismSectorReview& MasterPlan.pdf.

ACIAR (2009a) Sustainable management of Coffee Green Scales in Papua New Guinea project. On WWW at http://www.aciar.gov.au/project/ASEM/2004/ 047.

ACIAR (2009b) Assessment and improvement of quality management during postharvest processing and storage of coffee in Papua New Guinea. On WWW at http://www.aciar.gov.au/project/ASEM/2004/017.

Angas, G.F. (1866) *Polynesia: A Popular Description of the Physical Features, Inhabitants, Natural History and Productions of the Islands of the Pacific*. London: Society for Promoting Christian Knowledge.

Anonymous (2008) Researchers dominate tourists to Sangihe, North Sulewesi, Indonesia. Antara News Agency, September 21. On WWW at http://www.indonesia-ottawa.org/information/details.php?type = news_copy&id = 5358.

Anonymous (2009) Doctors evacuated from remote PNG post. *The Age*, 17 February.

Bacon, C. (2005) Confronting the coffee crisis: Can fair trade organic and specialty coffees reduce small-scale farmer vulnerability in northern Nicaragua? *World Development* 33 (3), 497–511.

Batt, P. and Murray-Prior, R. (2007) Emerging possibilities and constraints to PNG smallholder coffee producers entering the speciality coffee market. *Australian Centre for International Agricultural Research*. Canberra: Australian Government.

Bulbeck, C. (2002) *Australian Women in Papua New Guinea: Colonial Passages 1920–1960*. Cambridge: Cambridge University Press.

CAB International (2005) Project document, Sustainable management of Coffee Green Scales in Papua New Guinea. *Australian Centre for International Agricultural Research*. Canberra: Australian Government.

Central Intelligence Agency (2008) *The World Factbook: Papua New Guinea*. On WWW at https://www.cia.gov/library/publications/the-world-factbook/print/pp.html.

Chignell, A.K. (1913) *Twenty-One Years in Papua: A History of the English Church Mission in New Guinea (1891–1912)*. Milwaukee, WI: The Young Churchman.

Davidson, R. (1994) *Business Travel*. Harlow: Longman.

de Bougainville, L.A. (1771) *Voyage Autour du Monde par la Frégate Du Roi La Boudeuse et la Flûte L'étoile; En 1766, 1767, 1768 & 1769*. Paris: Saillant & Nyon.

Del Casino, Jr. V.J. and Hanna, S.P. (2000) Representations and identities in tourism map spaces. *Progress in Human Geography* 24 (1), 23–46.

Flickling, D. (2004) Raskol gangs rule world's worst city. *The Guardian*, 22 September. On WWW at http://www.guardian.co.uk/world/2004/sep/22/population.davidfickling.

Franklin, A. and Crang, M. (2001) The trouble with tourism and travel theory? *Tourist Studies* 1 (1), 5–22.

Galani-Moutafi, V. (2000) The Self and the Other: Traveler, ethnographer and tourist. *Annals of Tourism Research* 27 (1), 203–224.

Gascoigne, J. (2002) *The Enlightenment and the Origins of European Australia*. Cambridge: Cambridge University Press.

Geniesse, J.F. (2001) *Passionate Nomad: The Life of Freya Stark*. London: Modern Library.

Gibson, C. (2008) Locating geographies of tourism. *Progress in Human Geography* 32 (3), 407–422.

Goroka Show (2008) Goroka, EHP, Papua New Guinea. On WWW at http://www.gorokashow.com/.

Halvaksz, J.A. (2006) Becoming 'local tourists': Travel, landscapes and identity in Papua New Guinea. *Tourist Studies* 6 (2), 99–117.

International Coffee Organisation (2009) Statistics: Coffee prices. On WWW at http://www.ico.org/coffee_prices.asp.

Kokoda Treks (2009) The real experience. On WWW at http://www.kokoda treks.com/.

Maika, N. (2007) ACIAR ASEM/2004/017 Project Progressive 2nd Quarter Report. Aiyura, Papua New Guinea: Coffee Research Institute.

Markula, P. (1997) As a tourist in Tahiti: An analysis of personal experience. *Journal of Contemporary Ethnography* 25 (2), 202–224.

Marriott, E. (1997) *The Lost Tribe: A Harrowing Passage into New Guinea's Heart of Darkness*. New York: Henry Holt and Co.

McKercher, B. (2002) Towards a classification of cultural tourists. *International Journal of Tourism Research* 4, 29–38.

McKinnon, R., Barillet, J-B. and Starnes, B. (2008) *Papua New Guinea and Solomon Islands Travel Guide*. Victoria: Lonely Planet.

Palmer, C. and Lester, J.O. (2007) Stalking the cannibals: Photographic behaviour on the Sepik River. *Tourist Studies* 7, 83–106.

Parry, R.L. (2009) Witches put to death in Papua New Guinea as mob rule takes hold. *The Times*, 13 February. On WWW at http://www.timesonline.co.uk/tol/news/world/asia/article5720698.ece.

PNG Tourism (2009) Frequently Asked Questions. On WWW at http://www.png-tourism.com/default.asp?action = article&ID = 61.

PNG Trekking Adventures (2006) The Kokoda Track. On WWW at http://www.pngtrekkingadventures.com/pngta_kokoda_track.html.

Said, E. (1978) *Orientalism: Western Conceptions of the Orient*. London: Penguin.

Shaw, W.S. (2007) *Cities of Whiteness*. Oxford: Blackwell-Wiley.

Shaw, W.S. (2009) Riotous Sydney: Redfern, Macquarie Fields and (my) Cronulla. *Environment and Planning D: Society and Space* 27, 3.

Shaw, W.S., Inu, S. and Smart, G. (2008) Ethnographic geographies of coffee production in Papua New Guinea. *INSULA: International Journal of Island Affairs* (Dossier: Island Sustainable Development) 17 (1), 13–22.

Simbiken, N.A. (2006) *Preliminary Survey of Coffee Green Scale Report*, 6–10 November. Aiyura, Papua New Guinea: Coffee Research Institute.

smartraveller.gov.au. Australian Government Department of Foreign Affairs and Trade: Papua New Guinea. On WWW at http://www.smartraveller.gov.au/zw-cgi/view/Advice/?topic = Papua_New_Guinea.

Sikes, P. (2006) Travel broadens the mind or making the strange familiar: The story of a visiting academic. *Qualitative Inquiry* 12 (3), 523–540.

Smith, M.F. (2002) *Village on the Edge: Changing Times in Papua New Guinea*. Honolulu: Hawai'i University Press.

Tansley, C. (2009) Treasure islands. *Sydney Morning Herald*, Traveller, Weekend Edition, 24–25 January, 10–11.

Timothy, D.J and Teye, V.B. (2005) Informal sector business travellers in the developing world: A borderlands perspective. *The Journal of Tourism Studies* 16 (1), 82–92.

Transparency International PNG Inc. (2007) Annual Report 2007. On WWW at http://www.transparencypng.org.pg/downloads/Annual%20Report%202007.pdf.

Urry, J. (1990) *The Tourist Gaze*. London: Sage.

Part 4

Responsible Coffee Tourism and Cultural Change

Chapter 10
Blending Coffee and Fair Trade Hospitality

C. MICHAEL HALL

Fair trade is a social and economic movement with respect to the trading of commodities between the developed and developing nations. Originally, fair trade was primarily a European social justice movement that sought to ensure a fair and equitable price for products imported by the West (often from former colonies), but the notion of fair trade has since expanded to include concern over the environment as well as general principles of sustainable development (McDonagh, 2002; Jones *et al.*, 2003; Wright, 2004; Giovannucci & Ponte, 2005; Muradian & Pelupessy, 2005; Alexander, 2006; Grankvist *et al.*, 2006; Fridell, 2007; Hall & Sharples, 2008). Fair trade was defined by FINE, the four major international groups associated with fair trade (International Fair Trade Association/International Federation for Alternative Trade (IFAT) [now renamed the World Fair Trade Organization (WFTO)], Fair Trade Labeling Organizations International (FLO), Network of European Worldshops (NEWS!) and the European Fair Trade Association (EFTA)), as 'a trading partnership, based on dialogue, transparency and respect, that seeks greater equity in international trade. It contributes to sustainable development by offering better trading conditions to, and securing the rights of, marginalized producers and workers – especially in the South' (FINE, 2001).

The fair trade movement has existed in various forms since the 1960s when it developed as a campaign to supply fairly traded crafts and goods from the developing countries to Western markets. By the 1980s, a number of organisations had developed an international fair trade network, foremost of which was IFAT. In 1989, IFAT started engaging in the fair trade of food products and the first commodity traded was coffee (Moore *et al.*, 2006). Since then, this product has been joined by over 130 other food items, including tea, chocolate and cocoa. However, coffee has remained the main food product of the fair trade movement in

159

terms of both scale of sales and public understanding (Low & Davenport, 2005). The estimated overall value of fair trade coffee in the USA in 2006 was believed to be US$730 million (FLO, 2008). In 2007, fair trade coffee sales in the UK rose 24% to £117 million (FreshPlaza, 2008), this growth confirming consumer interest in the environment and social justice issues associated with fair trade. In 2007, fair trade global sales increased by 47%, which equates to the support of 1.5 million producers and workers in 58 developing countries (FLO, 2008). Although, as Rice (2001) notes, the development of fair trade food is just one dimension, along with organics, local foods, farmers markets and non-GE products, of the growth of ethical and conscious food consumption and production trends (see also Hall & Sharples, 2008).

However, as with other forms of ethical and environmental products, considerable concern is given to how labelling and branding is conducted and the extent to which the customer can be assured of the products validity. Globally, two main bodies lead the governance of fair trade and its accreditation. The WFTO, which is a global association of over 300 organisations in more than 60 countries, serves to link and network the fair trade producer cooperatives and associations, exporters, importers, retailers, national and regional fair trade networks and support organisations. As part of this process, the WFTO now registers fair trade organisations worldwide and allows them to use the FTO mark. By contrast, the FLO focuses on the certification of products. To ensure the transparency of the Fairtrade certification and labelling system, in January 2004 the FLO was split into two independent organisations: FLO International, which develops and reviews fair trade standards and assists producers in gaining and maintaining certification and developing market opportunities. FLO-CERT, which is an independent organisation, ensures that producers and traders comply with the FLO Fairtrade Standards and follows the international ISO standards for certification bodies (ISO 65).

In Australia and New Zealand, the lead organisation in the fair trade network is the not-for-profit association, Fair Trade Association of Australia and New Zealand (FTAANZ). Established in 2003, FTAANZ has developed a certification and accreditation programme, Fairtrade Labelling Australia and New Zealand (FLANZ) that can be employed on products, which is a guarantee to consumers that their purchases will benefit the producers, their families and the surrounding communities from the developing countries they originate from. The fair trade guarantee to consumers is backed by certification and trade audit systems that applies to all companies in the supply chain up to the point of final packaging. As a full member of the FLO, FLANZ has the sole right to license the use of the International Fairtrade Label in Australia and New Zealand and administers the Fairtrade Labelling scheme in Australia and New Zealand. In addition, FTAANZ acts to promote fair trade and fair trade products in Australia and New Zealand.

As of April 2008, 30 businesses in New Zealand had licenses to use the fair trade 'seal of approval' on products, with the majority of businesses engaged in coffee. Although separate figures for New Zealand are not available, the most recent publicly available annual report for FTAANZ suggested that approximately 320,000 kg of fair trade coffee was imported into Australia and New Zealand in 2006. The growth in the importation of fair trade coffee as well as the growing availability of fair trade labelled coffee in cafés, restaurants and retail supermarkets all highlight the extent to which a one-time 'alternative' product has now become 'mainstreamed' in consumer culture as well as the hospitality industry (Low & Davenport, 2005).

This chapter discusses some of the issues associated with the marketing and promotion of fair trade coffee in New Zealand's hospitality industry and particularly its perception and understanding by restaurants and cafés. Although previous international studies have investigated the perception of fair trade products and coffee by consumers and retailers, there has been a surprising absence of research on the role of the hospitality industry with respect to fair trade coffee. This chapter, therefore, first examines some of the general literature with respect to fair trade coffee before discussing the results of a study of New Zealand cafés' adoption of fair trade coffee products.

Promoting Fair Trade

As in other countries, the fair trade movement in New Zealand is undergoing a significant change in distribution channels. Once solely reliant on alternative distribution channels (bazaars, fairs, church groups, mail order, health food shops, student and political groups and membership lists), fair trade has emerged in commercial mainstream distribution channels (Low & Davenport, 2005). Examples include supermarket shelves, speciality and designer stores, retail-owned private-label initiatives and electronic mediums. Low and Davenport (2005) suggested that the dangers of mainstreaming include the potential loss of 'alternative' distribution channels, the focus on food products reduces emphasis on handcrafts, which as a consequence affects communities producing handcrafts, who have similar needs to those of food producers, and the ethical concerns attached to marketing the fair trade message via mainstream retail. By contrast, Moore *et al.* (2006) identified the positives of mainstreaming fair trade products in enabling significant increases in volume for producers, thus encouraging movement into channels previously untouched and, as a consequence, increasing markets, thereby reaching new customers who would ultimately become fair trade advocates and increasing awareness of the fair trade movement.

Fair trade coffee comes into New Zealand as either beans or instant coffee with each product having different distribution channels to end consumers. Organisations involved include importers, retailers, wholesalers, online and mail order retail, and cafés and restaurants. Cafés and restaurants can therefore purchase free trade coffee without necessarily being formally recognised by FTAANZ, although a number are also accredited outlets.

The notion of 'mainstreaming' is one that is usually associated with the selling of fair trade products in conventional supermarkets rather than cafés (Taylor, 2005; Weber, 2007). Moore *et al.* (2005) found that supermarkets were embracing the ethical certification of products not necessarily because of its fair trade principles, but because it was a way to extend the life cycle of product categories that had become mature and stagnant. Low and Davenport (2005) also argued that an issue with going mainstream was that the retailers did not always share the same attitudes towards fair trade, which was a potential disadvantage with respect to the overall promotion of fair trade ethics. Other disadvantages of placing fair trade products in supermarkets and other mainstream outlets were that there was a loss in product control, a potential loss in alternative distribution options and a 'watering down of the fair trade message' (Low & Davenport, 2005: 498). Indeed, Goldstein (2007: 2) observes that by choosing to go mainstream, fair trade has 'made the strategic choice to dance with the devil in the hopes of reforming him'.

In New Zealand, as in North America, arguably the most debated example of mainstreaming in terms of coffee shop outlets has been the adoption of fair trade or similar ethical coffee products by transnational restaurant companies such as McDonald's and Starbucks. Global coffee giant, Starbucks, offered one line of fair trade certified coffee through its 2300 US retail stores for the first time in October 2000 (TransFair USA, 2000). Fair trade coffee was first launched in Canadian stores in 2002 in partnership with TransFair Canada. The move saw Starbucks committed to sourcing, roasting and selling fair trade certified coffee to meet consumer demand, but also exhibiting stronger commitment to supporting corporate social and environmental responsibility goals (TransFair

USA, 2007). Although Starbucks has at times been criticised for the relatively small amount of fair trade coffee that it sells, this proportion has been gradually increasing over time (Starbucks, 2007). In New Zealand, two types of FLO certified coffee are sold through Starbuck's 45 stores.

Five years after Starbucks launched fair trade coffee, the fast-food multi-national, McDonald's, announced the regional launch of fair trade certified coffee in 658 outlets in New England and Albany, New York (TransFair USA, 2005). The move saw McDonald's converting all coffee products to Newman's Own Organics fair trade certified organic coffee, in a partnership with Green Mountain Coffee Roasters. The partnership between McDonald's, Green Mountain Coffee Roasters and Newman's Own Organics considerably raised the visibility of the fair trade movement in the USA. In a press release on 29 May 2008, McDonald's announced that all coffee served in its 141 New Zealand restaurants and cafés (McCafé and Espresso Pronto) will be purchased from Rainforest Alliance Certified farms (3 Media, 2008). Although the decision was also seen to be reflective of adapting to consumers evolving demands, it should be noted that the Rainforest Alliance certified farms, which also have a strong environmental dimension, are not FLO certified, although both the Rainforest Alliance and the FLO are full members of the International Social and Environmental Accreditation and Labeling (ISEAL) alliance.

The plethora of organisations and labelling schemes related to fair trade and ethical consumption has raised significant questions as to the mixed messages that may be promoted with respect to ethical consumption and sustainable development (e.g. Nicholls, 2002; Alexander & Nicholls, 2006; Moore *et al.*, 2006; Weber, 2007; Audebrand & Iacobus, 2008). For example, both Nicholls (2002) and Moore *et al.* (2006) raised concerns that these messages do not fit together, as pushing for more people to consume more fair trade products conflicts with the idea of consuming less in order to be more sustainable. Moore *et al.* (2006) also highlight the point that this message of ethical consumption conflicts with current public health messages that are being promoted. This includes messages about limiting the number of cups of coffee we drink and the amount of chocolate we eat. Both these products are very important to the fair trade movement. Moore *et al.* (2006) also question whether consumers are now missing the point of fair trade products and they are buying the product for the lifestyle image and not to help make the world more equal.

The definition of what fair trade actually means is also an area of debate. Audebrand and Iacobus (2008) raise concerns that there is a lot of misunderstanding among consumers and intermediaries as to what the fair trade principles are. They point out that there can be a big difference between how consumers of fair trade products interpret the fair trade message and how the producers do. Indeed, the confusion may, in part, be a product of the fair trade movement's own changing marketing and communication strategies.

Alexander and Nicholls (2006) point out that the fair trade message has moved from promoting the fair trade process to promoting the fair trade products to finally promoting the fair trade places. This shift has naturally led to confusion around what the fair trade brand is actually trying to promote or accomplish. Low and Davenport (2005) also acknowledge that this shift has been one of the consequences of going mainstream. They question what is fair trade's aim, is it to get their message about fairer trading systems across or is it about selling larger volumes of fair trade products? This perspective is also shared by Moore *et al.* (2006), who concluded that the fair trade movement needs to focus on just one primary goal, and by Nicholls (2006) who recommended much more cohesion among all fair trade campaigns.

Another recurring topic in the fair trade literature is the price of products and whether the premium price is beneficial to the cause or whether it is detrimental. The willingness to pay a price premium for an ethically labelled product appears to depend on the type of label, the credibility of the label and the strategies employed to distribute and promote the product in question. Maietta (2003) reinforced the importance overt labelling can have in purchasing decisions when they found that consumers were willing to pay a price premium of 9% for fair trade coffee and 25% for organic coffee. A further study in Belgium by De Pelsmacker *et al.* (2004, 2005) demonstrated that consumers perceive mass media advertising as less companionable with ethical products, suggesting the way in which ethical products such as fair trade coffee are promoted is highly important to the overall marketing strategy. Although, according to De Pelsmacker *et al.* (2005: 375), 'the appreciation for the fair trade attribute was not strong enough to support the actual price premium'. An issue that is also significant in many cafés that sell fair trade coffee given that it is sometimes available at a higher price than 'normal' coffee.

Case Study

In summer 2008/2009 in the southern hemisphere, a series of interviews were conducted with cafés in the city centre of Christchurch,

New Zealand. All cafés within a series of city blocks (45 in total) were invited to participate in a brief interview and answer a series of questions with respect to their use of and attitudes towards fair trade coffee. In addition, the servicescapes of the shops were also examined for fair trade signage and information.

Twenty-three cafés identified as selling fair trade coffee participated in the interviews (Table 10.1). Ethical concern was the primary reason given for selling fair trade coffee with customer demand, quality and good business practice regarded as significant reasons by just over half of respondents. Just over a quarter of respondents regarded taste as a reason for carrying fair trade coffee. Interestingly, no café reported that they were selling fair trade coffee as a competitive response to other cafés carrying it. Two cafés did not know the reasons why they carried it, but on further prompting it emerged that it was carried as it was provided by the roasters or suppliers from which they purchased their coffee range. Nine of the cafés only sold fair trade coffee with another two having more than 75% of their range available as fair trade coffee. One café had one fair trade coffee available as part of its range. The remainder were not able to state the proportion of coffee that was sold as fair trade, although one café noted that their standard blend was 80% fair trade.

Ten cafés who participated in the interviews did not sell fair trade coffee. Two of these stated that there was no customer demand with one claiming that they had tried to sell it but customers did not respond favourably. Interestingly, in terms of the role of the supply chain in promoting fair trade coffee, two cafés noted that they were happy with their existing suppliers and brands, which did not provide fair trade.

Table 10.1 Reasons given by Christchurch cafés for selling fair trade coffee

Reasons for selling fair trade coffee	Yes	No	Don't know
Customer demand	12	9	2
Ethical concern	16	5	2
Quality	12	9	2
Taste	6	15	2
Good business practice	12	9	2
Other cafés are selling it	0	21	2

Table 10.2 The fair trade servicescape of Christchurch fair trade coffee stores

Fair trade coffee stores	No. (30)	%
Fair trade sign/certificate	26	87
Fair trade coffee indicated on menu	14	47
Fair trade information available	6	20
Extra charge for fair trade coffee	3	10
Other forms of fair trade products advertised	5	17

The majority of respondents who did not sell fair trade coffee were not able to provide a reason why.

Although not all cafés participated in the interviews, all cafés were studied in terms of evidence of fair trade in their servicescape. McCafé did not want to participate in the interviews, though it should be noted that there was no evidence provided of the Rainforest Alliance coffee in the servicescape of the visited operation. Of the 30 cafés visited, 45 sold fair trade coffee (Table 10.2) with the majority providing signage or certificates, although less than half indicated the availability of fair trade coffee on menus. A total of 20% had information about fair trade coffee available (pamphlets or posters), while five stores also had other fair trade products available (primarily chocolate); 10% of cafés charged extra for fair trade coffee.

The Fair Trade Product: How Should it be Promoted?

As discussed above, there has been considerable debate as to what strategies should be used to market fair trade products and what attributes of the products should be promoted. The results of the Christchurch study of cafés and their adoption of and attitudes towards fair trade coffee suggests that there has been considerable advancement in the New Zealand hospitality industry towards Audebrand and Iacobus (2008) observation that the fair trade movement needed to translate the movement's principles into actual buying behaviour. This was also discussed by Nicholls (2002), who used Strong's (1997) marketing framework for converting the fair trade principles into purchase behaviours. This framework is modified in Table 10.3, which illustrates the connections between the marketing agendas of the fair trade movement to operational issues and solutions, as well as the operational situation in the context of Christchurch cafés.

Table 10.3 The translation of fair trade principles into purchase behaviours

Marketing agenda	Operational issues	Operational solutions	Operational situation
Getting fair trade products to cafés and restaurants	Lack of width and depth in available fair trade offer	1. Consumer-driven product development 2. Own brands	Significant level of adoption of fair trade products by cafés and perception of a reasonable degree of consumer demand. Some roasters provide 100% fair trade coffee under their own brands
Commitment of cafés to fair trade	Difficulty in establishing the direct benefit of fair trade to cafés	1. Explicitly link product and producer 2. Added benefits	Strong degree of ethical concern driving adoption, significant benefits perceived in terms of quality and good business practice
Consumer commitment to fair trade	Difficulty in establishing the direct benefit of fair trade to the consumer	1. Explicitly link product and producer 2. Added benefits	Perceived mixed consumer commitment to fair trade
Communication of human element of sustainability	Lack of consumer awareness/ understanding of fair trade	1. Brand building 2. Information dissemination	Substantial awareness of fair trade brand but limited dissemination of information

Source: Modified after Strong (1997) and Nicholls (2002)

Discussion and Conclusions

The availability of fair trade coffee in Christchurch cafés reflects the success of a strategy of mainstreaming fair trade products and building the fair trade brand (Moore *et al.*, 2006). This study has found that the ethical stance of cafés is an important dimension of the value chain for fair trade coffee. Many cafés also believe that they are responding to consumer demand for fair trade coffee products. The recognition by cafés that they are promoting a quality product may also support the arguments of Low and Davenport (2005) who proposed that the fair trade attribute of the product should be an additional marketing tool and not the main one that fair trade or retailers try to promote. This they argued because they felt that if the fair trade movement wants to convert more coffee drinkers to fair trade certified coffee, then the coffee is going to have to prove that it is as good a quality as non-fair trade coffee. They also found that promoting the quality of the product was much easier to get across to consumers rather than the fair trade message, which many consumers found too complex to fully appreciate what it meant (Low & Davenport, 2005).

The level of availability of fair trade coffee in cafés reflects the success of New Zealand Fair Trade coffee campaigns in encouraging retailers and the hospitality industry to stock more fair trade products, including coffee. But with regard to questions raised by Moore *et al.* (2006), is this because the fair trade movement in New Zealand wants to reform the conventional trading system from within? Nowhere on the FTAANZ website does it suggest that this is what they want to do. However, on the webpage entitled 'Vision and Mission', it does state that one of FTAANZ objectives is to 'Promote the concept of fair trade and increase awareness of its importance within Australia and New Zealand communities and one of its visions is to 'coordinate efforts to raise awareness and promote fair trade to the extent that fair trade alternatives are widely available and understood by consumers' (FTAANZ, 2008). Therefore, perhaps the reason why fair trade marketing campaigns push for the placement of their products (such as coffee) is because it is perceived as a way to make mainstream consumers more aware of the product and, as a consequence, it is way to make it more widely available to all consumers. Therefore, perhaps as Low and Davenport (2005) suggest, going mainstream is more about reaching new customers than giving up on the alternative trading message.

The actions of Christchurch cafés therefore reflect the fair trade coffee campaigns of New Zealand by organisations such as FTAANZ, where they do not just focus on promoting the 'fair-tradeness' of the coffee, but also the quality. For example, the media release for the 'Fair Trade Fortnight' campaign promotes both attributes of fair trade products in the one sentence and it is interesting to note that it states the good tasting attribute first: 'So "Check Out Fairtrade" and not only will you experience great tasting Fairtrade products but you will also be making a difference to the lives of millions of farmers, workers and their families' (Morrison, 2008).

This chapter has highlighted the extent to which fair trade coffee has become mainstreamed in the hospitality sector via the activities of cafés. It is also one of the first studies to examine the reasons why cafés have adopted fair trade product, as the majority of studies focus on the attitudes and behaviours of either supermarkets or consumers. Ethical reasons predominated, but quality of product, good business practice and a perception that there is significant customer demand were also important reasons for cafés to sell free trade coffee. However, a longer-term issue that remains to be resolved is the extent to which the purchase of free trade coffee is translated into a broader change in consumer purchasing patterns with respect to ethical products as well as a greater understanding of issues of sustainable consumption.

Acknowledgements

The author would like to thank Rebecca McNaughton, Fiona Crawford and Zainab Abdul-Razzaq for their assistance with the research project from which this chapter is derived and particularly Zee for her help in undertaking fieldwork. In addition, the ongoing contribution of C4 to the author's fair trade coffee experience is also gratefully acknowledged.

References

Alexander, A. and Nicholls, A. (2006) Rediscovering consumer-producer involvement – A network perspective on fair trade marketing. *European Journal of Marketing* 40 (11/12), 1236–1253.

Audebrand, L.K. and Iacobus, A. (2008) Avoiding potential traps in fair trade marketing: A social representation perspective. *Journal of Strategic Marketing* 16 (1), 3–19.

De Pelsmacker, P., Driesen, L. and Rayp, G. (2005) Do consumers care about ethics? Willingness to pay for fair-trade coffee. *Journal of Consumer Affairs* 39 (2), 363–386.

De Pelsmacker, P., Janssens, W., Sterckx, E. and Mielants, C. (2004) Consumer preferences for the marketing of ethically labelled coffee. *International Marketing Review* 22 (5), 512–530.

FINE [IFAT (International Fair Trade Association), FLO (Fair Trade Labeling Organizations International), NEWS! (Network of European Worldshops) and EFTA (European Fair Trade Association)] (2001) Fair trade definition and principles as agreed by FINE in December 2001.

FTAANZ (2008) *Vision & Mission.* Fair Trade Association of Australia and New Zealand Inc. On WWW at http://www.fta.org.au/FTAANZ/Vision. Accessed 1.4.09.

FTAANZ and FLANZ (2007) Annual Report 2006/07. Melbourne; FTAANZ and FLANZ. On WWW at http//:www.fairtrade.org.nz/FTAANZ/AnnualReport.

Fairtrade Labelling Organizations International (FLIO) (2008) *Global Fairtrade sales increase by 47%*. Fairtrade Labelling Organizations International. On WWW at http://www.fairtrade.net/single_view.html?&cHash=d6f2e27d2c &tx_ttnews[backPid]=104&tx_ttnews[tt_news]=41. Accessed 24.5.08.

FreshPlaza (2008) *UK: Fairtrade sales grow 81% in 2007 to £493 million*. FreshPlaza. On WWW at http://www.freshplaza.com/news_detail.asp?id=17328. Accessed 26.5.08.

Fridell, G. (2007) *Fair Trade Coffee: The Prospects and Pitfalls of Market-Driven Social Justice*. Toronto: University of Toronto Press.

Giovannucci, D. and Ponte, S. (2005) Standards as a new form of social contract? Sustainability initiatives in the coffee industry. *Food Policy* 30, 284–301.

Goldstein, E.R. (2007) Fair Trade. (Brewing Justice: Fair Trade Coffee, Sustainability, and Survival) (Book Review). *The Chronicle of Higher Education* 53 (47), 1–3.

Grankvist, G., Lekedal, H. and Marmendal, M. (2007) Values and eco-and fair-trade labelled products. *British Food Journal* 109 (2), 169–181.

Hall, C.M. and Sharples, L. (2008) Food events and the local food system: Marketing, management and planning issues. In C.M. Hall and L. Sharples (eds) *Food and Wine Festivals and Events Around the World: Development, Management and Markets* (pp. 23–46). Oxford: Butterworth Heinemann.

Jones, P., Comfort, D. and Hillier, D. (2003) Retailing fair trade products in the UK. *British Food Journal* 105 (11), 800–810.

Low, W. and Davenport, E. (2005) Has the medium (roast) become the message? The ethics of marketing fair trade in the mainstream. *International Marketing Review* 22 (5), 494–511.

McDonagh, P. (2002) Communicative campaigns to effect anti-slavery and fair trade. The cases of Rugmark and Cafédirect. *European Journal of Marketing* 36 (5/6), 642–666.

Moore, G., Gibbon, J. and Slack, R. (2006) The mainstreaming of fair trade: A macromarketing perspective. *Journal of Strategic Marketing* 14 (4), 329–352.

Morrison, R. (2008) Check Out Fairtrade! Fair Trade Fortnight (3–18 May), FTAANZ press release. On WWW at http://www.fairtrade.net/ftf08/ resources/press/NZ%20ftf%20press%20release.pdf. Accessed 14.5.08.

Muradian, R. and Pelupessy, W. (2005) Governing the coffee chain: The role of voluntary regulatory systems. *World Development* 33 (12), 2029–2044.

Nicholls, A.J. (2002) Strategic options in fair trade retailing. *International Journal of Retail & Distribution Management* 30 (1), 6–17.

Rice, A. (2001) Noble goals and challenging terrain: Organic and fair trade coffee movements in the global marketplace. *Journal of Agricultural and Environmental Ethics*, 14, 39–66.

Starbucks (2007) *Starbucks 2007 Corporate Social Responsibility Annual Report*. Seattle: Starbucks.

Strong, C. (1997) The problems of translating fair trade principles into consumer behaviour. *Marketing Intelligence & Planning* 15 (1), 32–37.

Taylor, P.T. (2005) In the market but not of it: Fair trade coffee and forest stewardship council certification as market-based social change. *World Development* 33 (1), 129–138.

TransFair USA (2000) *Starbucks Coffee Company Brings Fair Trade Certified Coffee to Retail Stores Through TransFair USA Alliance*. [Online press release.] TransFair

USA. On WWW at http://www.transfairusa.org/content/about/archives_pr/pr_000925.php. Accessed 24.5.08.

TransFair USA (2005) *McDonald's to Sell Fair Trade Certified™ Coffee; Commitment is a Step in the Right Direction, Says Oxfam.* [Online press release.] TransFair USA. On WWW at http://www.transfairusa.org/content/about/archives_pr/pr_051027_2.php. Accessed 25.5.08.

TransFair USA (2007) *Starbucks Celebrates Fair Trade Month, Reinforcing Its Commitment to Supporting Coffee Farming Communities.* [Online press release.] TransFair USA. On WWW at http://www.transfairusa.org/content/about/ppr/ppr_071002.php. Accessed 25.5.08.

Weber, J. (2007) Fair Trade coffee enthusiasts should confront reality. *The Cato Journal* 27 (1), 109–118.

Wright, C. (2004) Consuming lives, consuming landscapes: Interpreting advertisements for Cafédirect coffees. *Journal of International Development* 16 (5), 665–680.

3 Media Press Release (2008) *Coffee with a Conscience.* On WWW at www.3media.co.nz/foodnews/news.asp?ID=2691. Accessed 31.5.08.

Chapter 11

Canada's Just Us! Coffee Roasters Co-operative Coffee Tour Venture

NANCY CHESWORTH

This case study is about a coffee company with a mission. The founders, Jeff and Debra Moore together with three friends, found a mutually beneficial way to bridge the gap between the developed world and struggling farmers in less-developed countries. As the company has grown, new initiatives have developed that add depth and breadth to the founder's original mission of fair payment for a product, concern for the environment and the society that is dependent on the environment. This case illustrates how commercial enterprise, tourism and education can combine to create numerous benefits for both visitors and host communities. It also demonstrates the possibilities that can become realities when people who share a vision of a more just world make that aspiration a reality.

Since founding the Just Us! Coffee Roasters (JUCR) Co-operative, all their coffees have been certified fair trade and organic. Additional organic products have been added, including natural organic sugar crystals, herbal, black and green teas, and dark, milk and white chocolate. Retail operations began with a small coffee shop in New Minas, NS, which has since been closed. A kiosk is now open on the Halifax, NS, waterfront. Two other Halifax locations offer a variety of coffees and a limited menu. The main office, packaging facility and a coffee shop, gift shop and museum are located at Grand Pre, NS. A separate educational and development spin-off – the Just Us! Development and Education Society (JUDES) – was launched in 2006. A not-for-profit organization, JUDES works to facilitate education regarding fair trade. A coffee tour program was developed in 2008 with the aim of providing the tourist with a socially and environmentally sensitive tour of the coffee farms and communities involved in fair trade in Mexico.

The Beginning

In December 1995, Jeff Moore decided to act on his interest in the concept of fair trade. Finding little information on fair trade in Canada, he went to Mexico where he had heard there were organized coffee co-operatives and found his way to Chiapas, Mexico. He met with members of a co-operative of marginalized organic coffee growers, and learned that coffee grown high up in the mountains was grown organically, without the pesticides or chemicals commonly used in growing and processing the freshly picked beans. In addition, this superior, shade-grown coffee was harvested in the traditional manner, using hand labor, not machinery.

Returning to Canada, Jeff and his wife Debra took out a mortgage on their home to finance a shipment of ten thousand dollars worth of organic coffee beans, purchased from the co-operative in Mexico. They had no customers. Turning to local churches in the Annapolis Valley of Nova Scotia, they found that the congregations proved to be both sympathetic to the plight of the coffee growers and a responsive market (Debra Moore, personal communication, January 2009). The Moores sold the entire shipment and together with three friends, they incorporated JUCR as a worker-owned co-operative in March 1996, becoming the first fair trade coffee co-operative in Canada.

The rules governing co-operatives in the province of Nova Scotia require that all members of the co-op have equal voting rights. As more and more people expressed an interest in investing in JUCR, it became obvious that the workers were outnumbered by the number of investors. In practice, this meant that the workers would no longer have enough votes to control the day-to-day working and overall direction of the company. Concerns arose as to whether JUCR could still legally and practically function as a worker-owned co-operative. However, the province of Nova Scotia provides an alternate route for public funding. The Community Economic Development Fund Program allows the Equity Tax Credit program to promote public investment. A second co-operative, the Just Us! Fair Trade Investment Co-op (JUFTIC) was incorporated to enable investor owners to support the organization and benefit from a tax credit at the same time.

The two organizations work in tandem, with two of the members of the JUFTIC Board of Directors also sitting on the JUCR Board. Their mutual goal is to promote both the fair trade concept of doing business and JUCR as a business. This model appears to function well as reflected in the annual profit statement, which shows a growth rate of 25% per year for each year since inception, with the exception of 2008 when the rate was 20%. The obvious question is whether coffee drinkers will continue to support the slightly higher cost for fair trade coffee in difficult economic times.

Corporate Social Responsibility

Corporate social responsibility (CSR) or corporate social performance, are know by many names, including sustainable responsible business, corporate citizenship, among others (Wood, 1991). Ideally, CSR is meant to encourage businesses to include ethical, social and environmental accountability as a part of business planning and decision-making. The inclusion of CSR in a corporate strategy has led to a focus on the triple bottom line (TBL): people, planet, profit (Elkington, 1998). The JUCR Co-operative was founded on ethically and socially responsible principles from the beginning. The seriousness of their intent is reflected in the Co-operative's mission statement. It serves as an example of ethics put into action by the founders and their customers. Visitors to the Just Us! website are given a clear indication of the ethics of the business in the vision and mission statements found there. It provides web visitors with a clear understanding of the reasons Just Us! goes beyond a simplistic approach of paying a fair price for coffee and other products.

Their vision is to be a leading fair trade business that builds on quality, professionalism and innovation for the benefit of all their stakeholders. This is followed by the mission statement:

- To be a viable, progressive and leading Fair Trade business which serves as a model for worker (community) ownership and social and environmental responsibility.
- To serve our customers by giving them the best possible value, service and information.
- To serve the interests of Fair Trade producers by developing personal and long-term relationships that will adhere to the basic principles of Fair Trade, but more than that, will strive to help the indigenous communities move beyond the poverty level.
- To develop relationships among our co-op members, employees, business associates and the broader community based on honesty and respect and to maintain an ongoing commitment to education, innovation and collaboration. (Just Us! Coffee Co-operative, http://www.justuscoffee.com/2009.aspx. Accessed 4.6.09)

Why Fair Trade Coffee Costs More

The JUCR Co-operative was founded at a time when the price paid to farmers for a pound of coffee was in decline. In 2000, the price bottomed out at an average of US$0.50 per pound. By 2007, the world market price for coffee had risen from US$0.60 to US$0.70 per pound (Global Exchange, 2007). This price means that coffee sold to the major multi-national companies may often be below the cost of production.

Coffee is a commodity traded on the New York Stock Exchange. The value of coffee traded annually on the Exchange is seven times the value of the coffee itself, which demonstrates a high degree of speculation (Tom Walsh, personal communication, June 2009). In June 2009, coffee was being traded at US$1.20 per pound. The fair trade price at the same time was US$1.26 per pound. Coffee purchased by Just Us! averaged US$2.02 per pound, which included a US$0.20 organic premium and US$0.10 social premium, which goes directly to the community from which the coffee was purchased. The higher cost includes additional money paid for high-quality specialty coffee, which consists of 14% of total coffee production. The remaining production may be differentiated by location, type of bean or combination of beans. Just Us! also pays additional fees to ship coffee to Canada. Coffee beans purchased by Just Us! may in fact come from a wide variety of countries around the world, such as Mexico, Ethiopia, Guatemala and Colombia.

Because Just Us! is a small company, costs incurred in shipping, storage and packaging are higher than for large multi-national corporations, which realize cost savings due to economies of scale. The fees incurred by Just Us! include an average of $4000 CDN in customs fees applied to each shipment, storage at customs, transportation fees from the place of origin to Wolfville, NS, on-site storage, packaging and the cost of shipping the roasted coffee to retail customers. The company aims for a 7% profit, selling their packaged coffee to the wholesale market for an average of $5.65 CND per 12-ounce bag (Tom Walsh, personal communication, June 2009).

Fair Trade and Education, Just Us! Style

As discussed by Hall in Chapter 10, fair trade is not new. The spread of the fair trade concept, along with increased interest in organic products in general, has contributed to higher sales of fairly traded products. The Fairtrade Labelling Organization's International annual report of 2008 cites an increase in 2007 of fair trade coffee sales of 47%

over the previous year (FLO International Annual Report (2007) at http://www.fairtrade.net/343.html).

Increased public education and awareness regarding the ethical and environmental issues concerning the plight of farmers in less-developed countries is an important aspect of the Just Us! mission. As part of their efforts to educate the public and raise awareness of fair trade, the Just Us! website informs readers of the strategic intent of fair trade as being threefold:

- Deliberately work with marginalized producers and workers in order to help them move from a position of vulnerability to one of security and economic self sufficiency.
- To empower producers and workers as stakeholders in their own organizations.
- To actively play a wider role in the global arena to achieve greater equity in international trade. (Just Us! Coffee Co-operative website, http://www.justuscoffee.com/2009.aspx. Accessed 4.6.09)

Coffee is purchased twice a year at the end of the growing seasons, in November and March. To the grower, the benefit of working with fair trade buyers is that they receive direct payment through their own coffee co-operatives or collectives. In the case of Just Us!, the fair trade buyer, usually Jeff Moore or another Just Us! executive, purchases coffee where it is grown. Aside from the advantages of receiving a higher price and immediate payment, the farmers have the opportunity to talk directly to the buyers and learn the business side of coffee through discussions with the buyers. Representatives of Just Us! take this activity seriously, sometimes spending additional time with the coffee farmers and their families. Educating the farmers about the coffee business enables them to understand their role in this global business, and helps to strengthen coffee co-operatives and relationships among coffee growers.

Just Us! Development and Educational Society: The Educational Commitment

The commitment of the founders of JUCR, as stated in their vision and mission statements, is to work with and empower marginalized workers. This goal found a logical expression in the founding of Just Us! Development and Educational Society (JUDES). JUDES is a separate organization, with its own Board of Directors. According to Satya Ramen (personal communication, 21 July 2009) JUDES coordinator, 'JUDES raises public awareness of fair trade and responsible purchasing. By providing educational resources and facilitating partnerships, JUDES builds solidarity between consumers and small producers across the hemispheres with respect to social, environmental and economic justice'. Hoping to develop and solidify relations, as well as understanding between the consuming public and the products that they consume, JUDES is working to encourage partnerships and exchanges that provide the opportunity for those goals to become a reality.

One of the partnership ideas came from the members of the coffee co-operative 'Unión de Comunidades Indígenas de la Región del Istmo' or UCIRI (Union of the Indigenous Cooperatives of the Isthmus Region) in southern Mexico. UCIRI is a co-operative of 54 communities striving to support community economic development and diversification of income generators (Satya Ramen, personal communication, 21 July 2009). Two communities, Chayotepec and El Porvenir, view commu-nity-based tourism as a possible economic generator and a way to diversify their income base (Satya Ramen, personal communication, 21 July 2009). Through UCIRI, they requested help to develop a coffee tour product. Just Us! worked with UCIRI to secure a Canadian International Development Agency (CIDA) grant. The grant provided the seed money necessary to launch the program, which began in 2008 (Debra Moore, personal communication, January 2009). UCIRI undertook to raise funds to develop infrastructure to support tourism from Canada, Italy and France (Satya Ramen, personal communication, 21 July 2009).

In 2008, 10 people travelled with Just Us! to Chayotepec to pick coffee berries and learn about the community, their way of life, customs and traditions. This initial trip was deemed a success, prompting another tour in 2009 developed and managed by JUDES. This second group consisted of five employees of Just Us! and five interested individuals, some of whom were customers of the retail outlets. Originally, two tours were planned, but given a limited marketing budget and the economic downturn, only one group went to Oaxaca, Mexico. The participants made their own air travel arrangements. JUDES made ground travel arrangements as well as providing guiding. Monies received for the several days the group stayed in the community went directly to the community, providing a direct benefit from the tour, an important consideration for some members of the group. JUDES is committed to transparency regarding costs and fees. Part of the fee paid by participants goes toward carbon offsets in the hope of mitigating the impact of visitors on the host community and part goes to a 'reciprocity fund' aimed at developing sufficient funds to bring members of the Chayotepec community to Canada.

The tour consisted of a combination of sightseeing, visiting Zapotec ruins and natural limestone pools, cultural experiences such as visiting a Zapotec weaving co-operative, learning about local medicines, and a musical exchange. The group also learned about coffee, the co-operative, fair trade, and spent a day coffee picking. Opportunities were available for hiking in the local cloud forest (Satya Ramen, personal communication, 21 July 2009). Staying in the village in cottages built for visitors, the members of the tour group experienced the way of life of the village first hand. This on-site experience was for many members of the tour group a life-changing experience (Kathy Day, personal communication, 29 May 2009). The shade-grown, organic coffee is grown on steep hillsides, which prompted Trudie Richards, one of the participants, to reflect that she found the picking of coffee berries a mind-opening experience. She stated, 'I had no idea of the extent of the back-breaking labour that went into what seems a simple task – picking coffee. It really opened my eyes' (Trudie Richards, personal communication, 24 April 2009). While this coffee tour offered the participants the opportunity to learn about the culture of the area, it also offered a taste of a southern winter vacation for the Canadian northerners. At the end of their time in Chayotepec, participants spent two days on the Pacific coast before returning to Oaxaca City for the return flight.

A New Niche?

The type of tour offered by JUDES falls into the category of experiential tourism. The combination of experiences offered in this package: culture, heritage and learning, offers a variety not found in most tours. Niche market tours such as those focussed on genealogy, culture, archaeology, heritage and food and wine are designed to provide an in-depth experience, the basis of which is usually learning, or expanding one's knowledge. Volunteer tourism can be focused on scientific, medical, social or construction projects to name a few. This form of tourism can be found in a wide variety of locations worldwide. It aims at a collaborative effort on the part of the tourist and the community that benefits from the volunteers work. JUDES does not consider the day the visitors spent picking coffee to be volunteer tourism. Instead it is considered a paid educational experience. Satya Ramen said, 'When we, as tourists, come and they show us how to pick coffee, we are taking them away from their normal income. We replace that income with a daily wage that allows them to host us'. This raises several questions, such as: Do the coffee farmers earn more money picking coffee or hosting tourists? How much money is lost or gained by hosting tourists as opposed to picking coffee? If the farmers are losing money hosting tourists, is there any reason to continue to do so?

If a multi-faceted tour were offered by JUDES, combining many of the aspects of both niche and tightly focussed volunteer tourism, would the tour be more attractive to potential visitors? As a sort of sampler of a range of niches, a tour combining several forms of niche tourism could offer an unusually rich experience. As such, it could act as a catalyst or as a model for the development of similar tours.

This kind of tour structure could serve as a model for tour planners who are motivated to provide a benefit to the host community and to interest and encourage less committed tourists to sample a different culture. The opportunity to participate in some volunteer work, learn about the heritage of a culture with which they are unfamiliar could create a multi-faceted product appealing to those tired of the standard beach resort offering. To capture a wider market, a few days vacationing in a locally owned resort or hotel would increase appeal and potentially more visitors who wish to travel in a responsible and ethical manner.

The decline in interest in sightseeing tours by motor coaches and the trend toward greater consumer awareness of and participation in fair trade could set the stage for tours like the JUDES tours, which offer a wider range of experiences to the mass market tourist. The future of multi-niche tours and indeed, fair trade itself hinge on a combination of ethical consumer consciousness and genuine CSR. For their part, JUCR and JUDES are committed.

References

Baue, W. (2009) World's coffee traders agree to sustainability. Ethical Corporation. On WWW at http://www.ethicalcorp.com/content.asp?ContentID = 654. Accessed 25.4.09.

4c Coffee Association (2004) On WWW at www.4c-coffeeassociation.org/download/2004/world-bank-press-review_en.pdf. Accessed 16.4.09.

Elkington, J. (1998) *Cannibals with Forks*. Gabriola Island, Canada: New Society Publishers.

Fairtrade Labelling Organizations International Annual Report (2008) On WWW at http://www.fairtrade.net/343.html. Accessed 21.3.09.

Global Exchange (2007) Fair Trade Coffee. On WWW at http://www.globalexchange.org/campaigns/fairtrade/coffee/. Accessed 27.2.09.

Just Us! Coffee Roasters. On WWW at http://www.justuscoffee.com. Accessed 11.08.

Oxfam. On WWW at http://www.maketradefair.com/en/index.php?file = 12092003132827.htm. Accessed 11.08.

Wood, D. (1991) Corporate social performance revisited. *The Academy of Management Review* 16 (4), 691–699.

Chapter 12

Beyond Fair Trade: Enhancing the Livelihoods of Coffee Farmers in Tanzania

HAROLD GOODWIN and HARRO BOEKHOLD

This chapter profiles a project from Tanzania, East Africa, which is working with several coffee farmer communities to implement a sustainable form of coffee-related tourism. Working with a fair trade coffee co-operative located in the Kilimanjaro region of Tanzania, the Fair Tourism Project has developed locally managed and owned tours around their small-scale coffee farms that are now returning significant individual and collective benefits to the community.

The film, Black Gold, released in 2007 was made, according to the directors, as a response to the announcement of a further famine in Ethiopia, the birthplace of coffee, at the end of 2002. Marc and Nick Francis, the directors and producers of the movie, wanted to challenge audiences to 'wake up and smell the coffee', to recognise the inextricable connection between the daily habit of drinking coffee and the 'livelihoods of millions of people around the world who are struggling to survive'. As the producers of the movie point out on their website: 'As westerners revel in designer lattes and cappuccinos, impoverished Ethiopian coffee growers suffer the bitter taste of injustice. In this eye-opening expose of the multi-billion dollar industry, Black Gold traces one man's fight for a fair price'.[1]

As discussed by Hall in Chapter 10, retailers of fairly traded coffee are increasingly making the connection between the luxury experience of drinking coffee and the lives of those who grow it. For example, Union Hand-Roasted argue that their Union 'of founders and farmers, of countries and coffees, and of principles and processes – works in harmony to guarantee the most exceptional coffee experience for you and your customers'.[2] Tourism is another way in which coffee consumers in the world's tourism-originating markets can learn more about the production of coffee and come to understand the economics and the inequality and economic poverty inherent in the production process. This chapter presents a case study of a tourism project with a co-operative of coffee farmers in Tanzania that fulfils these goals.

Tanzania is the largest producer of Arabica coffee in Africa, exporting about 1% of world output. In Tanzania, coffee is the major source of revenue for approximately 400,000 low-income farming families and constitutes 20% of Tanzania's export earnings. In 2003, the Kilimanjaro Native Cooperative Union (KNCU) traded more than 5250 tons of Arabica coffee, about 11% of national production.[3]

Coffee has been grown on the slopes of Kilimanjaro in Tanzania since the late 1800s when European settlers began to develop commercial coffee production. The southern slopes of Mount Kilimanjaro have rich volcanic soils and enjoy relatively high precipitation, creating ideal conditions for growing quality coffee. Large areas of the southern slopes were developed for coffee production and coffee rapidly became the primary export crop in the region. The local population was initially excluded from coffee production, but by 1929 the local Bantu-speaking Chagga population formed the KNCU to market Kilimanjaro Arabica coffee; in doing so, it was the first co-operative to be legally registered in Tanzania in 1932. The Chagga have developed a farming system that combines the growing of food crops, including coffee, bananas and hardwood trees. The hardwoods and banana trees provide shade and wind protection for the coffee; this diversified livelihood strategy also reduces vulnerability to crop failure.

In Europe and America, Mount Kilimanjaro is famous as a tourism destination. Located only 3° south of the equator, Africa's highest mountain is snow capped, attracting travellers and holidaymakers in large numbers. Of Tanzania's holiday visitors, 25–30% is reckoned to arrive through Kilimanjaro International Airport (CHL, 2002: 11). Kilimanjaro is the gateway to the northern circuit, attracting game-viewing tourists and large numbers of trekkers seeking to climb Africa's highest mountain. Kilimanjaro is the highest mountain that can be trekked and scrambled up. The summit can be reached without professional climbing equipment, but altitude sickness, exhaustion and exposure prevent many from reaching the summit.

Moshi is the capital of the Kilimanjaro region and the gateway to climbing the mountain. There are no reliable figures on the total number of tourists who visit Moshi each year, but it is known that some 25,000 people climb Kilimanjaro each year, so there is a viable market from which to establish other tourist experiences. The industry is sufficiently large to support more than 150 official ground handlers or inbound operators and there are thought to be at least as many unofficial agencies handling incoming international tourists.

The KNCU is composed of 60 village co-operatives, called Rural Cooperative Societies, representing about 60,000 small-scale farmers (KNCU, 2007). The success of the KNCU in developing export markets for Kilimanjaro coffee has generated a local cash economy and brought relative prosperity. From the 1960s onward, the coffee trees began to age and became prone to coffee berry disease (CBD) and coffee leaf rust (CLR), resulting in very significant crop losses, which coincided with a major decline in the world market price for coffee. From 1972 to 1974, a severe local drought exacerbated these already serious difficulties, and then came the oil price shock of 1973 and Tanzania's war with Idi Amin's Uganda. In these circumstances, there was major harvesting of hard-woods and consequent deforestation, leading to widespread erosion and the loss of topsoil. The KNCU, in common with other co-operatives, was abolished by the Tanzanian government in 1976 and was only reinstated eight years later as the KNCU (1984) Ltd.

The International Coffee Organization, under the authority of the United Nations, from the early 1960s until 1989 successfully controlled the supply of coffee and maintained a stable price for it. The International Coffee Agreement limited excess supplies using a quota system, implemented price controls and promoted an increase in coffee consumption. When the USA pulled out in 1989, the quota system broke down and coffee prices plummeted. Vietnam became a major producer and supply outstripped demand. These international trends also impacted coffee prices in Tanzania and producers were impoverished.

In this context, it has been among the priorities of the KNCU to improve the livelihoods of the farmers and their families. The membership of the co-operative operates in a difficult international market place, one where the price of coffee has fallen due to increased production. The KNCU's objectives are to diversify farmers' incomes; to encourage them to look after their fields; to encourage people to both understand the coffee-growing process and to purchase fairly traded coffee from Kilimanjaro. The KNCU was certified by the Fairtrade Labelling Organisation (FLO) in 1993, which meant from that time onward its coffee could be sold under the fair trade label. The FLO is a group of 24 fair trade organisations that sets fair trade standards and promotes fair trade. Nowadays, the KNCU sells fair trade certified coffee to a range of buyers including Twin Trading, a producer-owned membership organisation that works to develop a fair trade supply chain, retailing through Café Direct, the UK's largest fair trade hot drinks company.

The KNCU has sought to diversify and improve the livelihoods of coffee farmers on the slopes of Kilimanjaro by enabling the farmers to secure an additional livelihood through engaging with tourism. The KNCU has worked with and through the NGOs with which it was already engaged in promoting the development and marketing of fairly traded coffee. Kahawa Shamba means coffee farm in Swahili and KNCU has used this Swahili name for a number of its tourism experiences. The KNCU Fair Tourism Project launched its own website in 2008 (www.kahawashamba.co.tz) and the KNCU is developing a form of tourism that provides a fair revenue for the coffee farmers who engage with it by applying the same principles that are applied to fairly traded coffee to tourism.

The Coffee Tour

The KNCU sought to use the tourism in the region to develop an additional livelihood for economically poor coffee farmers and their families and thought that the interest of tourists in the coffee farmers' farms might lead to a renewed interest in investing in farms and the planting of new coffee seedlings by the farmers. The KNCU approached the Dutch Green Development Foundation (GDF), with which they had worked to develop their coffee production, for assistance in developing a tourism product. GDF approached and involved Contour Projects, a Dutch tourism consultancy firm, who had the appropriate expertise to assist the KNCU.

Contour Projects then approached Sawadee Reizen,[4] a Dutch adventure and activity holiday company, with about 900 passengers on three types of itineraries passing near to the project in 2005. Sawadee Reizen committed to schedule one group a week if an appropriate product could be developed. Sawadee Reizen had groups arriving in Tanzania either through Kilimanjaro International Airport or from a combined trip within Kenya through Nairobi. From the outset, there was a defined market and a clear commitment from the operator to use the product if a suitable experience of appropriate quality and price could be developed.

Contour Projects worked along with the KNCU from July 2004 to define a 'Fair Tourism' product that the coffee farmers could engage with as an additional livelihood activity. The purpose of the intervention was to secure an additional supplementary livelihood activity for coffee farmers and their families, and to improve the livelihoods of coffee farmers rather than to turn coffee farmers into employees or entrepreneurs in tourism.

During the season from June to January each year, Sawadee Reizen was sending at least one group per week into the region through Kilimanjaro International Airport. These groups could therefore be expected to arrive at a regular time each week. The Coffee Tour product developed is both standardised and unique for the visitor, meeting the objectives of the KNCU and the farmers in securing a regular and reliable supplementary income with little or no risk.

The experience is a high-quality encounter for the tourists with a Tanzanian coffee farmer rather than a tourist guide, a very personal experience because the tour groups are broken into groups of between four and six participants to be shown around different farms by several farmers. The visit generally begins with lunch prepared by a group of farmers' wives and eaten outside one of the farmhouses. The tourists in the smaller groups then go with the farmer to visit the farmer's field where the farmer explains how he farms coffee and tells the history of some of his coffee plants, recounting the various problems they have each encountered and how he dealt with the infestation or blight.

This a very intimate series of encounters as the farmer explains the process of coffee farming from the planting of the seedlings to the harvesting and processing of the beans. The tourists are encouraged to pick the berries and to carry them back to the farm where they process them, separating the beans from the pulp, roasting the berries over a wood fire, grinding the roasted beans with a pestle and mortar and finally drinking the coffee that they have harvested with the farmer. The conversation begins around coffee, but soon expands into a personal encounter and conversation about school, children and football – with both the farmers and the tourists asking questions of the other. This is not a conventional tourist experience; it is much closer to the host and guest paradigm, one enhanced by the original encounter being over lunch and by the fact that the guide is not a professional tourist guide but rather a farmer who occasionally shows guests round his farm.[5]

The pleasure of drinking coffee with the farmer is an important part of the experience, but the farmer's home-roasted coffee does not taste as good as the roasted product sold in vacuum packs on the supermarket shelves in Europe. However, professionally roasted vacuum-packed coffee from the KNCU is available for purchase by the tourists at the end of their visit, in the same packs they will find on the supermarket shelves. This ensures that the connection with regular purchasing is made and that there is a meaningful discussion about organic coffee farming and the importance of fair trade. The tourists leave having enjoyed a meaningful social encounter with a Tanzanian coffee farmer, gained a practical understanding of the effort required to grow coffee and produce the beans, and a keen awareness of the difference in price at the farm gate and on the supermarket shelves. This is an understanding and experience that probably ensures that the tourists will go home and talk about the importance of buying fairly traded coffee.

The coffee tours were successfully piloted at Uru with Sawadee Reizen groups in the second half of 2004. Sawadee Reizen initially maintained detailed quality checks on the experience, asking its clients to fill in a separate customer satisfaction survey for the coffee experience. This was terminated after a few months because the coffee experience was consistently getting the highest possible scores across all elements of the experience.

Immediately before the first groups arrived, the training of the guides and cooks took place over an intensive one-week period and involved trainers contracted by Contour ensuring that the training was both practical and relevant, and that the trained guides and cooks were immediately able to practise and further develop their skills. The guides were selected after an application procedure by a committee of KNCU, village board members and the consultant from Contour. Out of 52 applications, initially only nine farmers were selected based upon three main criteria: ability to speak English, understanding service and hospitality and knowledge of the natural environment.

Campsite, additional tours and restaurant at Uru North Msuni

In 2005, after the pilot season of the Coffee Tours, a campsite was established at Uru North Msuni, 20 km north of Moshi. The campsite was built to provide accommodation for Sawadee, who had received many suggestions from their clients to spend more time in the Uru area rather than just a few hours for the tour. An area of communally owned land was cleared 1,800masl and a basic facilities block was constructed with toilets and two hot showers, with investment from Sawadee (25%), KNCU contributed from tourism revenues from the previous year (25%) and additional funding from GDF (50%). This was a very low-risk way for the village to be able to provide accommodation and one with low maintenance overheads. The Kahawa Shamba Campsite is a joint venture on communally owned land.

After one year of Coffee Tours with some groups staying overnight on the campsite, Sawadee asked about the possibility of staying two nights on the Kahawa Shamba campsite from 2006 onward. This required the development of additional products for groups that would stay two nights with one full day to spend in the Uru area. Therefore, additional tours were created; the Chagga History Hike, the Cultural Village Walk, the Nature Walk and the Mongyoni Falls Adventure were developed with technical support from Contour Projects and funding from GDF.

In 2006, additional tour operators[6] were seeking contracts for the Coffee Tour, which resulted in the decision to expand into the Hai district to involve and train more farmers from Rural Cooperative Societies. This was to ensure that as many farmers as possible were able to benefit from the tourism project and to avoid congestion and dependency in the Uru area. Since 2006, several Dutch and Spanish outbound and several inbound tour operators have engaged in the Coffee Tour program, and the Chagga History Hike has became a popular day activity.

Again based on expressed demand from Sawadee, a small local-style restaurant, with modern facilities, was built on an adjacent piece of land to the campsite in Uru early in 2007. Sawadee decided to change their itinerary so that Uru became the last stop before flying to Zanzibar for the last three days of the tour. This meant that upon arrival in Uru, their safari trucks including the drivers and cooks could go home, which created the opportunity for the local women's groups to provide all the meals to the tourist groups rather than just one lunch during the Coffee Tour. After one week of intensive training with crew from Contour, the women were able to provide meals sold buffet style for a fixed price.

By 2007, coffee tours were being provided in Uru, Hai and Lyamungo, the campsite was being used for up to two nights and providing food, additional tours were being offered in Uru and the product was being included in itineraries and sold by an increasing number of tour operators.[7]

Financial Performance

The rationale behind the KNCU's Fair Tourism Project is that the local farmers should reap the majority of the financial benefits from the tourism products, either directly as tour guide, cook or campsite manager or indirectly through the Community Development Fund (CDF). A fixed amount per tourist is set aside to support community projects, which are funded with the CDF money. The objective is that 70% of the total income accrues to the local communities involved in the project, whereas 30% remains behind to cover the operational costs of the KNCU tourism office.

The results of the tourism project have been exceptionally good with earnings in the first half year of operation amounting to one third of the consultancy costs expended. In the first six months of operation, there were total sales revenues of US$10,626 (Goodwin, 2006: 70–71). The initial investment was about US$35,500 in consultancy costs, plus some contributions in kind from Sawadee Reizen.[8] The development of the coffee tours and the campsite at Uru North Msuni was a remarkably effective development initiative. The project earned back one third of the investment in the first six months of operation and the community investment was limited and focussed into a few months of preparation and training.

The Coffee Tour was designed as the signature product, which means that the marketing efforts are directed at selling the coffee tour. The campsite functions as a side-product. It is no less important as a source of revenue, but it is much harder to market accommodation in the competitive tourism industry. Table 12.1 provides details of total sales in the three years from 2006 to 2008.

Over the three seasons (2006–2008), the tourism products had a total sales value of nearly US$87,000. The signature product, the coffee tours, was the largest source of revenue with a sales value of almost US$45,000, forming 52% of the total sales. The additional tours earned nearly US$12,000, meaning that the guided tours accounted for more than two thirds of the income, 65% of total sales over the three years (2006–2008). In this same period, the campsite earned only US$12,800, securing the slowest return on the initial investment. By comparison, the restaurant took in over US$17,000 in two years, although these are sales values, there are significant consumables in the restaurant. Other than time there are almost no costs associated with the guiding, making this the most lucrative form of tourism for the community to engage in.

The plan was for no farmer to guide on more than one day per week during the season. This was for two reasons. First, to ensure that the experience remained that of being shown round by a coffee farmer rather than a tourist guide, this required that the farmer was only an occasional guide. Second, because the plan was to extend the opportunity to other farmers as demand grew. However, in the short term, with sometimes as many as nine tourist groups arriving on one day, some of the coffee tour guides were employed several times a week.

From the outset, detailed records of earnings have been maintained by the KNCU Tourism Office. These records include details of the

Table 12.1 Volume of business and income KNCU Tourism Project 2006–2008

	2006			2007			2008			Total		
	No.		*Income (US$)*	*No.*		*Income (US$)*	*No.*		*Income (US$)*	*No.*	*Income*	*%*
Coffee tour	672	Pax	10,080	1191	Pax	18,314	1162	Pax	16,570	3025	44,964	51.8
Additional tours	189	Pax	1,415	783	Pax	7,500	331	Pax	2,980	1303	11,895	13.7
Campsite	436	Nights	2,180	1345	Nights	7,522	622	Nights	3,104	2403	12,806	14.7
Restaurant	–	Meals	–	2397	Meals	10,855	1361	Meals	6,312	3758	17,167	19.8
Totals			13,675			44,191			28,966		86,832	100

Source: Local project records, 2008

distribution of revenues (Table 12.2). Of the total sales value from tourism, 70% was distributed locally. Of the revenues, 30% were retained to run the KNCU tourism office and to meet costs associated with establishing the initiatives. Individuals earned as farmers for permitting visitors (2% of total sales), tour guides (10%) or cooks (14%, but this revenue had also to cover consumables). The camp security earnings went to two elderly men in the village and might be more accurately seen as pensions (3% of sales value).

Table 12.3 presents estimates of net income (income less direct costs) for each of the groups of individuals involved in the tourism initiative at Uru. This is significant additional income and supplements the household incomes of coffee farmers. For example, the eight tour guides

Table 12.2 Distribution of revenues 2008 on local level, Uru site

	Total earnings (US$)	%
Tour guides (farmers)	2,056	10
Women groups (cooks)	2,878	14
Women projects	3,701	18
Community Development Fund	4,523	22
Food purchase	2,673	13
Farmer families (for visiting their plot)	412	2
Campsite maintenance	1,439	7
Local administration	412	2
Campsite security	617	3
Campsite officer	206	1
Restaurant maintenance	617	3
Gas, water, electricity	412	2
Hut owner	206	1
Cave owner	206	1
School	206	1
Total distributed	20,560	100

Source: Local project records (2008)

Table 12.3 Estimate of net income accruing to individuals by group 2008, Uru site

	Beneficiaries	*Net earnings/ individual in US$*	*Total individual net earnings*
Tour guides (coffee farmers)	8	257	2056
Women (for food preparation)	22	137	2878
Campsite officer	1	206	206
Campsite security	3	206	617
Farmers (for visits to their land)	52	8	412
Total	86		6169

Source: Estimates based on local project records (2008)

earned in total US$2056, or US$257 per guide and, overall, 86 individual beneficiaries earned US$6619 between them, an average of US$72.

The farming plots are very small due to subdivision at inheritance; plots are between 01.5 and 1.5 acres per household of between five and seven persons. Each household produces between 20 and 100 kg of coffee per year. These tourism earnings compare very favourably with those from coffee farming, when the average-sized farmers' plot of one hectare produced two bags of coffee worth US$160–200. Coffee farming produced an annual income of around US$180 – an income of 50¢ per day for farming coffee. By contrast, tour guides were earning an additional US$257 from a season's guiding. While the poorest cannot engage in the project, the marginally less poor can. The coffee is worth 80¢ per kilo at the farm gate unprocessed, the same amount of coffee sells for US$20 per kilo roasted (250 g – US$5) to a tourist (Goodwin, 2007: 70).

As an additional source of income, the intervention had high net benefits both for the community and for the individuals who secured additional earnings through the initiative.

In Hai District, all the tourists continue to arrive on booked tours through tour operators. However, in Uru District there are increasing numbers of tourists arriving independently – 4% in 2006 and 2007, but 16% in 2008. The arrival of independent tourists in larger numbers may result in some farmers becoming more engaged in and dependent upon tourism, this may also change the character of the experience for the tourists who may encounter guides who are more engaged in the tourism industry than in coffee farming.

The data on farmers' incomes from local records (Table 12.4) demonstrates that the earnings from tourism, limited though that engagement is, are very significant. In Uru, coffee tours have increased the incomes of those farmers who participate by 36% and in Hai by 20%. Table 12.5 demonstrates that the women engaged in providing meals for the tourists have also increased their earnings significantly by engaging with tourism.

Table 12.6 estimates the value of tourism as a proportion of the total income of farmers in Uru (9%) and Hai (4%, one year less). The benefits of engaging with tourism for individual farmers are significant and it is noticeable at the community level. But, as is demonstrated by the estimates reported in Table 12.7, it is the scale of the tourism contribution to the CDFs used to provide local services and a nursery for coffee seedlings that is so significant.

The CDF contributions are significant in all years. They are erratic because they depend on tourism revenues, but also because the proportion varies relative to other sources of CDF money in any give year in the local co-operative areas.

Table 12.4 Income from coffee tours as a percentage of total income farmer tour guides 2005–2008

Tour guides	Uru (%)	Hai (%)
Income from coffee farming	30	38
Income from coffee tours	36	20
Other activities	34	42

Source: Estimates based on local project records (2008)

Table 12.5 Income from meals as a percentage of total income of cooks 2005–2008

Women groups	Uru (%)	Hai (%)
Income from cooking for tourists	41	22
Other activities	59	78

Source: Estimates based on local project records (2008)

Table 12.6 Income from the tourism project as a percentage of total income farmers 2005–2008

Farmers	Uru (%)	Hai (%)
Income from farming	35	26
Income from tourism	9	4
Other activities	56	70

Source: Estimates based on local project records (2008)

Table 12.7 Community Development Fund income (US$) 2005–2008

	Uru (%)	Hai (%)
2005	45	–
2006	45	34
2007	24	25
2008	21	20

Source: Estimates based on local project records (2008)

Table 12.8 reanalyses the data presented in Table 12.2 to demonstrate that in 2008 in Uru, one third of the sales value went to individuals, a quarter was used to meet costs and over 40%, US$8430, was used to fund community projects.

The ecological and social impacts have been monitored throughout the three years. Additional firewood has been used for cooking, but there was no reported damage to plants and trees, no increase in water consumption and no increase in rubbish or littering. There were no signs of negative behaviour by children, e.g. begging, shouting or throwing stones at tourists (Hewett, 2008).

Paseo

Contour Projects was centrally involved in the creation of the coffee tours, the campsite, the additional tours and the restaurant at Uru-North. Recognising that the tourism industry is an experience and service industry and convinced that socially and environmentally responsible development adds value to the industry, a Fair Tourism Program was established as a response to meet the demand among tour operators for

Table 12.8 Revenue distribution by function 2008 at Uru site

	Total earnings (US$)	%
Tour guides (farmers)	2,056	10
Women groups (cooks)	2,878	14
Farmer families (for visiting their plot)	412	2
Local administration	412	2
Campsite security	617	3
Campsite officer	206	1
Hut owner	206	1
Cave owner	206	1
Individual beneficiaries	6,993	34
Food purchase	2,673	13
Campsite maintenance	1,439	7
Restaurant maintenance	617	3
Gas, water, electricity	412	2
Costs incurred	5,141	25
Women projects	3,701	18
Community Development Fund	4,523	22
School	206	1
Community funds	8,430	41
Total distributed	20,560	100

Source: Local project records (2008)

these kinds of tourism experiences. Within the framework of this programme, Contour Projects has worked with the tourism industry, NGOs and government agencies to develop similar projects based on fair trade oranges in South Africa, fair trade bananas in Ecuador and fair trade cacao in the Dominican Republic.[9] In order to avoid confusion with terms such as eco, pro poor, community based and sustainable, the name of the programme was not used to market the products in the tourism industry. Instead, one clear brand name was developed: Paseo.[10] The

Paseo website and logo is used to provide information to tour operators about high-quality experiences of the daily lives of local farmers and their families who produce coffee, cacao and fruit with a fair trade character, some of which are also organic.

This approach to product development and marketing with economically poor coffee producers in Tanzania has a number of benefits. It has provided significant additional income at individual, household and community levels and has encouraged farmers to reinvest in their coffee fields. This has been achieved at a very reasonable cost and with considerable efficiency; the return on investment has been excellent and the community has not been encouraged to take risk. The income is additional, existing livelihood strategies have been maintained and individuals and households have not incurred debt. Engaging the tour operator in the design, development and marketing of the complementary product ensured that there was a viable income stream to support the initiative from inception. The model is replicable with other producer co-operatives and Contour is replicating the concept, developing and marketing the Paseo range of experiences.

The coffee tour provides a high-quality experience for holidaymakers and travellers, evidenced by the growth of the experience and resulting in the extended length of stay. Linking the tourism experience with the production of fairly traded coffee provides a deeper understanding for consumers, gained in the context of a great holiday experience. The Kahawa Shamba coffee tours provide a real opportunity to 'wake up and smell the coffee'.

Notes

1. On WWW at www.blackgoldmovie.com. Accessed 10.5.09.
2. On WWW at www.unionroasted.com. Accessed 10.5.09.
3. KNCU (2003) Kilimanjaro Native Co-Operative Union EPOPA. On WWW at http://www.grolink.se/epopa/Publications/Proj-folders/KNCU.pdf.
4. On WWW at www.sawadee.nl.
5. For more detail on the experience, see www.kahawashamba.co.tz and www.trees4africa.org/Fair_Trade_Coffee_Tour.pdf.
6. Baobab and Tanzania Journeys.
7. Sawadee, Baobab, Tanzania Journeys, Tanzatrail, SNP Naturreizen and others.
8. Unpublished project evaluation undertaken for the PSO – association that consists of 50 Dutch development organisations – focusing on capacity development in developing countries' civil society organisations. On WWW at www.pso.nl.
9. For details, see www.contour-projects.com/en/what_we_do/products/product_development.html.
10. On WWW at www.paseo.nu.

References

CHL Consulting Group (2002) Tourism master plan strategy and actions. Ministry of Natural Resources and Tourism, Tanzania. On WWW at www.tzonline.org/pdf/tourismmasterplan.pdf.

Goodwin, H. (2006) Measuring and reporting the impact of tourism on poverty. Proceedings Cutting Edge Research in Tourism New Directions, Challenges and Applications, School of Management, University of Surrey.

Goodwin, H. (2007) Measuring and reporting the impact of tourism on poverty. In D. Airey and J. Tribe (eds) *Tourism Research: New Directions, Challenges and Applications* (pp. 63–75). London: Elsevier.

Hewett, B. (2008) The story of the Kilimanjaro Native Co-operative Union: Strengthening community involvement. Unpublished manuscript.

KNCU (2003) Kilimanjaro Native Co-Operative Union EPOPA.

Ocon, K. (2008) Designing a monitoring tool for the KNCU fair tourism project, Tanzania. Unpublished Master's thesis, NHTV University of Applied Sciences, International Tourism Management & Consultancy Degree Program.

Chapter 13

La Ruta del Café and Los Santos Coffee Tourism: A Central America Project to Develop Coffee-related Tourism to Augment Coffee Families' Incomes

BOB HARVEY and DIANE KELSAY

In the late 1990s, as consultants we were approached on behalf of the Organization of American States (OAS) for a series of discussions on the coffee crisis in Central America that evolved into the challenge outlined below.

The Problem

Two key trends were impacting the coffee-growing communities of Central America, those of world coffee prices and shrinking farm size.

In the 1990s, Vietnam coffee production soared, almost tripling between 1995 and 2000. With aid from the USA and Canada, Vietnam reinvigorated an old coffee-growing region, cleared thousands of hectares of forest land, brought thousands of new farming families into the Dac Lak Province, and began to flood the world coffee market with low quality, low-priced beans. That move (and other world coffee events of lesser nature) began to drive down world coffee prices.

In Central America, most of the coffee farming communities have their roots in Spain or Italy, and have traditionally divided a family's land among all the sons as they grew up. In those areas where coffee plantations are family owned, the plantations have continued to shrink as generation after generation has divided the land.

Those two trends began to combine in the late 1990s, threatening to make it impossible for small farmers to earn a living raising coffee. As the

OAS explained, farmers were getting less for a sack of processed unroasted coffee than Starbucks was getting for a cappuccino.

The Question

The OAS asked us as consultants, in light of our agritourism experience (wine tourism, ranch tourism) and our history of understanding Central American tourism (helping set up the Belize tourism economy, guiding the recovery of Honduras tourism after Hurricane Mitch), to see if coffee tourism was a viable concept, and, if so, could it be engineered to augment the income of Central American coffee communities? Furthermore, could that tourism be engineered to channel dollars to those farmers growing coffee on small tracts?

The Challenge

If, abstractly, coffee tourism had the potential to bring a supporting line of income into small coffee-producing families in Central America, could we design a project, within an economic range the OAS could handle, that would enable coffee-producing communities in Central America to launch appropriately scaled and beneficially engineered tourism economies? Moreover, would we believe in our planning strongly enough to lead such a project?

To answer the questions, the OAS set up a series of cautious steps in the form of a pilot project. Their goal was to avoid making promises they couldn't deliver on and to be as frugal as possible, especially until there was solid evidence that investment would yield results – and that those results could be self-sustaining.

Organizing the Project: Testing a Target Community

Using a guarded approach, the OAS, with input from Antonio Arreaga (Grulex, Vancouver, British Columbia) and David Russell (DM Russell Consulting), chose the Los Santos valley of southern Costa Rica as a target community in which to assess possibilities and possibly build a small pilot project to test the viability of tourism as a way of augmenting coffee farmer income. Plate 13.1 shows the view from a coffee plantation (finca) down into San Marcos de Tarrazú, one of the communities of Los Santos, Costa Rica. The hills beyond the town are covered with small fincas, growing coffee.

Los Santos itself is a complex geographical arrangement as several small streams pour down from the steep crest that navigates down the

Plate 13.1 View from a coffee plantation (finca) down into San Marcos de Tarrazú, Costa Rica (Source: Diane Kelsay)

isthmus that is Costa Rica, between the Caribbean and the Pacific. In many places here, the distance between the two seas is less than 30 miles and the elevation of the crest is as high as 11,000 feet. These streams have carved a network of narrow connecting valleys that are home to the communities that make up Los Santos. At high elevations, farmers raise potatoes, onions, strawberries and members of the cabbage family. Progressing downward toward the Pacific, one moves through zones of apples and then down to bananas and citrus and avocados. Finally, below the area known as Los Santos, it is warm enough to produce pineapple.

The original settlers cleared the valley floor to build small communities. When coffee became a serious economic possibility, more people moved to the valley and more land was cleared for coffee culture. In many cases, steep hillsides were totally cleared and coffee was planted on slopes that one might not think could support agriculture.

Beyond the valleys is a dense forest. In the lower zones, it is a lush deciduous forest. Higher up, it is an oak-dominated cloud forest. Some of the forested lands have been grazed. Others have been raided for firewood. But most of the forest lands are in relatively pristine condition. Additionally, at the time this project began, many of those lands were protected in forest reserves. Under that forest reserve system, some private ownership is included and some carefully managed use is allowed on those lands. Riparian zones are protected.

These forests are home to a diversity of flora and fauna, notably including the resplendent quetzal, arguably the most impressive bird of the Americas. The quetzal has been a big hit in other parts of Costa Rica among those visiting the country for nature tourism. In fact, the quetzal, a shy and elusive forest bird, has been declining in numbers in the heavily visited iconic national parks of Costa Rica – a cause of some concern to the nation.

Los Santos is a group of several towns, most notably named after Catholic saints, on the Pacific facing slope of southern Costa Rica. The area has been growing coffee for over a hundred years – and most of the coffee is grown on small privately held tracts. Los Santos grows about 6.5% of Costa Rica's coffee production, but has about 30% of Costa Rica's small coffee producers. A majority of the farmers belongs to one of two strong cooperatives, which process and market their coffee. The farms have decreased in size over the generations as families have split the land among offspring. At this point, most of the coffee in Los Santos is grown on plots that average five acres in size.

It is best to characterize the farmers of Los Santos as hard-working, middle-class farmers. They take education and farming seriously. They live in houses with electricity and indoor plumbing and drive well-maintained vehicles. This hard-working, close-knit set of communities is very much focused on being successful at the business of growing coffee.

The region's coffee, known as Tarrazú, is among the finest coffees in the world (Thorn, 2006). Historically it has brought higher than normal prices in wholesale markets and has been used to bring up the quality of coffee blends. While Tarrazú is known to serious coffee aficionados and throughout the industry (Davids, 2001), it has not become a serious name with consumers; until recently, it was tough to get single origin Tarrazú coffee as whole beans at the consumer level.

The two cooperatives have taken markedly different paths. One follows the traditional Costa Rica model, receiving coffee from members, processing that coffee in traditional ways, and working with wholesale buyers of that coffee. As a cooperative, it has also invested in a grocery store and a fuel station. It works directly to influence the well being of the communities where its members work and live.

The second cooperative is very progressive. It has (since this project started) made huge steps to be more environmentally friendly. It has virtually eliminated water and air pollution. It has reduced (almost to nothing) the need to burn wood (harvested from nearby forests) to dry coffee. It is now composting its waste to make soil amendments, enabling its members to reduce dependence on chemical fertilizers. It actively works with members to help them manage their use of and exposure to agrichemicals. It has undertaken a comprehensive effort to raise the value of its coffee by refining its processing techniques, by creating its own domestic and export brands of roasted coffee and by working more closely with international coffee buyers. It has, with this project, begun to offer coffee plant tours, hired a bilingual guide, invested in headsets for communication with visitors to the factory floor, developed a cooperative retail center and built a café where a fully trained barista prepares a variety of coffee drinks for the public.

While Costa Rica embraced nature tourism as a national economic strategy (Whelan, 1991; Dasenbrock, 2002), using it to attract both outside investment and the flow of tourism dollars into the country, Los Santos has, until recently, focused on the growing, processing and sales of its very fine coffee. At the point when this community was targeted for the pilot project, there was only one small family-owned nature lodge aimed at international visitors – and that was in its infancy as a business.

The progressive cooperative, along with other key Los Santos leaders, supported the idea of bringing visitors to the valley – so long as tourism was managed on the terms of the residents and did not interfere with the social and economic lifestyles of the valley. It was keenly interested in the idea that tourism could be managed in a way that could result in revenues that were shared by the residents of the valley, and perhaps even distributed through the cooperative. The traditional cooperative was supportive, but not enthusiastic, about the 'tourism experiment'. Some of the private coffee processors were also supportive, perhaps more so than the traditional cooperative.

The government of Costa Rica, as expressed through the Ministry of Tourism, supported the concept of using tourism to enhance the economic status of small farmers. Other institutions in Costa Rica were brought into the partnership to examine the concept of the tourism experiment. Those included ICAFE, the national coffee cooperative (cooperative of coffee cooperatives), which focused on raising the value of Costa Rica's coffee and lobbying government on behalf of the industry, financial institutions and the country's electrical cooperative.

There were two other key factors in looking at Los Santos as the 'test site'. First, Costa Rica, at the inception of this project, was 15 years into an intensive effort to grow its nature tourism infrastructure, patronage, image and revenues. It was (and is) focused on being a world leader in nature tourism and on using that position to drive a substantial nature tourism economy (Whelan, 1991; Dasenbrock, 2002). Second, Antonio Arreaga (Grulex) was (and is) well connected in Los Santos with key coffee and community leaders. Don Antonio was the persistent force that called the attention of the OAS to the plight of Central America's coffee producers – and drove the process that led to this project.

Building a Concept for Developing and Managing Coffee Tourism for the Benefit of Host Communities

As consultants, we came to this project with a broad experience in agritourism, nature tourism and rural tourism in general. We had worked with wine tourism in the Pacific Northwest, with ranch-based tourism in Wyoming, with small-scale agritourism in both the USA and Central America and with tea tourism in Sichuan, China.

We were aware that some locations in Costa Rica were giving coffee demonstrations to visitors, especially big bus groups from cruise ships. We researched the relationship of tourism to coffee in Jamaica, Hawaii and some locations in Costa Rica. We had even, while working on the recovery of tourism in Honduras after Hurricane Mitch, visited a small, private, coffee processing plant and had suggested to Norman Garcia, the Honduras Minister of Tourism that small-scale coffee production had potential as a tourism experience (Harvey & Kelsay, 1999).

We were aware that coffee, like wine, differs in each location where it is grown. We were cognizant that various approaches to coffee growing (some focusing on volume, others on quality, shade, chemical, etc.) impact the taste of the resulting product. We had some knowledge that processing differences could yield changes in taste.

What we were unsure of, though, was whether one could build a set of experiences around visiting a coffee-producing area and couple that with tasting coffee to create a tourism product that had enough substance to engage visitors for longer than a quick tour. And it was unclear to us whether there were enough differences among coffees within a region, or among a set of regions, to justify a style of tourism akin to a journey to wine country.

The visitor experience was one challenge to unravel. The second was how, if such tourism were to be developed, could visitor revenues end up spread out among the families of a coffee-producing area? And how, in coffee-producing regions that were dominated by small farming families that valued their traditions and privacy, could the social impacts of such tourism be managed?

In theory, if tourism could be designed to draw people to the cooperatives, money spent there could be disbursed among the membership, effectively spread among the coffee growers needing support. There would still be room, in such a scenario, for some individual families to decide to move more aggressively into tourism, offering guided tours, farm tours or designing crafts for sale.

Further, since the region was lacking in lodging, if the cooperatives could become investment partners in lodging operations, then more revenue could be distributed among the coffee farming families. Lodging operations would also present employment opportunities, enabling some of those families to augment their income. Similarly, lodging operations would enable visitors to spend longer in the valley, buying more meals, taking tours based from the valley and leaving more tourism revenue behind.

Longer stays, from a local lodging base, would also enable the valley to build relationships with patrons, rather than serving day visitors who don't really have time to get more than a shallow impression of the area. These relationships, plus quality experiences, would have the potential to build a constituency for the valley, a cadre of patrons that repeat and refer.

Because of its location, and the distance from ample lodging, Los Santos does not have an issue with volume. It is simply not on the path, nor near an easy source of volume visitors.

As long as this condition continues, and given the close-knit nature of the communities, tourism does not pose a significant threat to social structure. If tourism were to grow significantly, that issue might require rethinking.

In many ways, the shrinking farm size generates a bigger threat – as there is the temptation to sell a small farm that is unable to support a family to wealthy urbanites (mostly from the San Jose area) and to take work in the city. In that respect, tourism that would generate distributable revenue and local job opportunities could be construed as contributing to the health of the local social structure.

Assessment

In January 2003, the OAS, with economic support from the Costa Rica Ministry of Tourism, the government of Los Santos and local businesses, contracted Egret Communications and Grulex to conduct an assessment of the potential to develop tourism to augment incomes for coffee farmers in Los Santos, Costa Rica (Harvey & Kelsay, 2003).

The assessment team toured and evaluated coffee businesses and cooperatives, tourism businesses (both lodging and guided), coffee farms, dining options, retail offerings and basic visitor infrastructure. The team looked closely at local aptitudes related to hosting visitors. The team also examined Costa Rica coffee experiences designed for cruise ship and bus tour business in the San Jose area and met with (visited and toured) coffee processing plants outside the target region to assess competition, partnership and visitor count projections. Señor Areaga met with national coffee leaders and with potential airline and lodging partners (in San Jose).

The team found some existing tourism in the Los Santos coffee-producing region, including about 1000 visitors per year to Coopedota (the progressive coffee cooperative beneficio (coffee mill)) and La Familia (a private coffee beneficio). For the most part, these visitors were brought to Los Santos by tour operators and lodges from the south, who are hosting nature travelers. While the traveler was experiencing a day-long trip (traveling two hours each way) and passing among the coffee farms with in-vehicle interpretation, the out-of-vehicle tours were lasting one hour at the coffee mills, including a tasting. The team found that the mills were not charging for the tours, but were making some revenue from direct coffee sales.

The project team found only one viable lodge in the coffee-producing area, capable of delivering an experience up to international tourism standards. El Toucanet was a small, family-owned, nature lodge focused on hosting birders and other nature travelers. At the time of the assessment, the lodge was just beginning to come on the radars of its target market, and did not have the capacity to serve more than small groups. Other small lodging facilities are set up to serve in-country weekend getaways and regional business travel. The team also found that the more adventurous coffee buyers were being hosted by local coffee-growing families. Other buyers were coming on day trips from San Jose – local lodgings were deemed not suitable for hosting these important guests of the region.

Visitors to Los Santos, at the time of assessment, had opportunities to dine alongside locals in restaurants catering to residents. Several of those would provide a very valid cultural experience, but require the visitor to speak Spanish (or have a guide). The assessment found no dining facilities set up with international visitors in mind, in terms of facility design, menu offerings, or wait staff prepared to serve international patrons.

One local businessman had recently opened a café, a place where local coffees were served in a gourmet style very similar to that served in a fine coffee house in Europe or the USA. His intentions were to serve both visitors and locals, showcasing the quality of the local coffee. As observed by Goodwin and Boekhold in the case from Tanzania in Chapter 12, it should be noted that local farmers in Costa Rica, while growing some of the best coffee in the world, do not for the most part consume that coffee prepared in a manner that brings out its qualities.

The team examined the potential of nature tourism, using the valley as a base for exploration. There are countless opportunities in this region to experience nature at its best, including waterfalls, cloud forests, birds (especially the resplendent quetzal), horseback riding and mountain biking. The assessment noted extensive forest reserves and the proximity of national parks. White water rafting is available within the range of a day trip from Los Santos. And there are reputed to be some impressive caves in the area, but those were not, at the time of assessment, within reasonable range of visitors. Day trips to Manuel Antonio National Park (beaches and rainforest) are also within range of the valley.

Costa Rica has been very successful at developing a steady flow of nature tourism to the nation and in attracting both national and international investment in its nature tourism infrastructure (Whelan, 1991; Dasenbrock, 2002). It also has a good flow of adventure tourism in which visitors test themselves by rafting, ziplining, orienteering, climbing, caving and other ventures into the wilds. The team found that almost no visitors arriving in Costa Rica were driven by the patrons' intentions of seeing and experiencing coffee growing and production. It found that coffee experiences were 'tacked onto' tourism itineraries that were primarily focused on nature and to a lesser extent adventure.

The team evaluated the tourism potential related to the coffee harvest, processing at the mill, tasting and other related experiences. The coffee harvest is actually a very exciting experience – to a select market. Both locals and indigenous immigrant labor, primarily from Panama, pick the cranberry-sized coffee fruits by hand from bushes that are four to eight feet tall. Whole families come out to pick. Schools are closed for the season. The weather is typically dry, sunny and comfortable. Harvest time is almost festive, with friends and families chattering with each other as they pick.

Pickers have traditional woven baskets (or modern plastic baskets) tied around their waists to free both hands for picking. There is an elaborate system for measuring each picker's results, after burlap bags of coffee fruit are carried up or down steep slopes to waiting trucks. Then the trucks, usually meticulously cared for, are driven to the coffee mills, where the harvest is again measured and recorded farm by farm.

Following the fruit into the mill, watching as the beans are extracted from the fruit and cleaned, and then learning about sun or heat drying and resting is a very fascinating process. There is also a great deal of interpretive opportunity related to quality of beans, pea beans, and the history of how coffee was processed and then transported to the Pacific coastal ports in oxcarts. Touring the coffee mill has some challenges related to noise levels and, potentially, safety issues.

The team had the unique opportunity to observe an international expert taste testing coffee at one of the beneficios (coffee mills). The process of preparing and conducting the taste test is fascinating – and somewhat ritualistic. It is much more elaborate than a typical consumer wine tasting – and holds great potential for both interpretation and visitor participation. It really introduces a new level of knowledge about coffee and the nuances that distinguish great coffees from each other and various roasting procedures.

There are potential tourism opportunities in having visitors partici-pate in harvest, oxcart rides among the coffee plantations, mill tours and tastings. There are retail opportunities related to coffee, including coffee itself, items with coffee mills' logos and re-creations of historical coffee paraphernalia (traditional drippers, coffee picking baskets, etc.).

Having determined that, depending on a visitor's interests, there are experiences related to coffee culture, processing, roasting and tasting that are both rewarding and marketable, the team looked closely at who might be recruited as patrons for these products. Three key themes were dominant in their conclusions: (1) Costa Rica has a significant flow of nature and adventure tourism, but no flow of visitors for whom coffee is the primary motivator; (2) the Los Santos coffee-growing area did not have enough of a lodging base to support a substantial flow of overnight visitors to the region; and (3) while Tarrazú coffee was internationally recognized for its superiority by serious coffee experts, consumers had little or no knowledge of this unique coffee.

Looking at the long-range goals of La Ruta del Café, of establishing a viable flow of visitors seeking a coffee experience in the coffee-producing regions of Central America, it would have been nice to conclude that Los Santo could easily step into an existing demand for coffee-related experiences. Without penetration of the Tarrazú brand to consumer level, there was simply no mechanism to focus those with an interest in fine coffees to travel to Los Santos. With no significant flow of coffee-driven tourism to Costa Rica, there was no demand to market into – no share of the market to capture. With no lodging base, Los Santos could not achieve return on investment (ROI) on the marketing costs related to creating a demand for Tarrazú coffee experiences. Los Santos would have to base its short-term tourism hopes on visitors coming to Costa Rica for other purposes and work to develop capacity, brand recognition and market opportunities for coffee-driven tourism over time.

It was concluded that nature tourism held the most potential to bring visitors to the region who might also be interested in a coffee experience. In other regions of the world (and in Costa Rica), nature visitors have shown strong interest in both cultural and heritage tourism and also agritourism. The team noted that there was reasonable potential, especially as Costa Rica tourism patterns began to include more southern itineraries, that tour operators might be convinced to include a day in an itinerary to explore coffee in Los Santos. The existence of nature tour opportunities in the region augmented that possibility. The lack of lodging was seen as a restraint or a barrier, depending on the style of tour operation examined.

The profiles of adventure tourism patrons led the team to conclude that while these visitors might have an interest, they probably would not have the patience for a day-long deviation from adventure to navigate the distances and realize the coffee experiences in Los Santos. That would change if adventures were set up in the region. However, these patrons were less likely to be excited about coffee tourism than nature travelers were.

While many potential coffee tourism experiences were outlined, the key element that had to be addressed was the creation of lodging in Los Santos. There was a strong need for the development of one or more lodges that could cater to international visitors and provide the base for coffee tourism experiences. Because there was an existing flow of nature travel and the opportunities to provide nature travel experiences in Los Santos, it was concluded that lodgings should be compatible with the styles and needs of nature travel, while also reflecting the coffee culture of Los Santos. Further, these lodgings (and associated dining developed to international standards and styles) could serve to host international coffee buyers, raising the quality of experience related to buying trips in Los Santos.

Once lodgings were available, the door would open to Los Santos-based tours. Tours could be offered as a part of any lodging business, but could also be developed and offered by enterprising coffee-growing family. Lodging would also create opportunities to take visitors on oxcart rides, out picking in the fields, on nature tours, birding and more. It could also open the opportunity to bring visitors to the valley when the coffee harvest was not underway, particularly when coffee was in bloom, or when key nesting seasons made birds easy to find.

Further, lodging would bring visitors into the valley for longer periods of time, generating a greater flow of visitors into local restaurants and retail stores. It would create opportunities for visitors to develop relationships with the valley, finding its quaint and peaceful nature attractive enough to come back and to send friends. Lodging and locally guided tours, together, presented an opportunity to shape tourism patterns in ways that were economically and socially beneficial to Los Santos, while also managing social impacts. Finally, if the cooperatives were involved in lodging development, there was a way to distribute earnings to the majority of the residents in Los Santos.

The assessment concluded that there were substantial opportunities to develop both coffee and nature tourism in Los Santos, that the development could be engineered to economically benefit the small-scale coffee-farming families, that social impacts could be managed. The assessment pointed out that the length of time a visitor stayed in the valley directly impacted the benefits they would leave behind and that local lodgings were key in both keeping visitors longer and managing their economic and social benefits (and negative impacts). The assessment pointed out a number of small-scale tourism enterprises that could be developed relative to coffee tourism, but noted that the viability of many of those opportunities would depend on visitors being able to base within Los Santos.

The appraisal challenged the region to accomplish hospitality training, to train more frontline employees in English as well as Spanish, to train a cadre of potential tour guides, to upgrade the visitor experiences at the beneficios, to develop handicrafts for tourism retail and to develop more retail opportunities for visitors.

The Year after the Assessment

In the year after the January 2003 Assessment in Los Santos, there was a lot of activity relative to both the target site and the broad concept of La Ruta del Café. A momentum was building!

The communities of Los Santos requested and received training support – and a first round of potential tour guides were trained. At the end of that year, another round of students had lined up to take the training. The communities had sought support from Canada and were in the process of bringing in English teachers to prepare residents, especially frontliners, to interact with English-speaking visitors. The Canadians had also sponsored a consultant to examine the feasibility of a hotel development. That project was already underway.

Both cooperatives had begun to upgrade their visitor experiences. Coopedota refined its tour and developed a set of coffee-related retail items for sale (at the conclusion of its tour). Coopetarrazú upgraded its visitor reception area. Coopedota coordinated with the lodge in Los Santos and with one outside to bring in more coffee tours – and began charging for those tours (Plate 13.2). Revenues from those tours began to show as a separate item in their accounting and a line of return for members. All proceeds (tour, tips, coffee purchases) go into a special account that is distributed to coop members.

Rodrigo Jimenez opened his second coffee shop at the intersection on the Pan American highway where one would turn to visit Los Santos. He

Plate 13.2 Bilingual guide conducts coffee tour at Coopedota, Los Santos, Costa Rica (Source: Diane Kelsay)

expanded the number of local coffees he was showcasing and had available for sale. His shop in San Marcos was drawing more local interest and patronage and local coffee was becoming more of a point of pride.

Egret Communications (without economic support) conducted a feasibility study relative to developing a coffee lodge that would also serve nature travelers, and have its own in-house tour company. The goal was to engineer most of the jobs in the lodge and most of the profits from the lodge into the local community.

Coopedota's board charged its general manager to study the potential of having the cooperative build or invest in a lodging facility. Los Santos set up a working group to examine lodging initiatives to make sure they fit the tourism development intentions of Los Santos.

Egret Communications (without economic support) designed and marketed a pilot tour to test the theory that nature travelers would also find coffee tourism experiences rewarding (Plate 13.3). That tour was conducted one year after the assessment, creating lodging, dining, retail, coffee shop and coffee tour revenues in Los Santos.

Plate 13.3 Pilot tour visitor picks coffee cherries at Los Santos, Costa Rica (Source: Diane Kelsay)

The broader project moved forward as well. Leaders from the OAS, pushed by Antonio Arreaga and the coffee-growing communities of Central America, began to build a model to develop La Ruta del Café. Under this model, assessments would be conducted on a number of sites around Central America, while the target site of Los Santos would be supported as it continued to move toward the development of a sustainable and appropriately scaled flow of coffee-related tourism. There was much debate about when to move into market introduction related to the concept of La Ruta del Café – and there was more discussion on the question of whether to configure this tourism so that a given visitor would be encouraged to visit multiple countries (and coffee-producing areas) on one trip, or whether to design things so that repeating visitors might choose other coffee-growing regions on subsequent trips. To test the resolve of the coffee-growing communities to develop coffee-related tourism, and to give them the opportunity to see the post-assessment progress in Los Santos, the OAS sponsored a coffee tourism event, Primer Encuentro do Responsables del Proyecto Regional La Ruta del Café, in Los Santos one year after the assessment, in January 2004 (Harvey & Kelsay, 2004).

Primer Encuentro de Responsables del Proyecto Regional La Ruta del Café

Organized by Antonio Arreaga and sponsored by the OAS, El Primer Encuentro do Responsables del Proyecto Regional La Ruta del Café was the first gathering of its kind. Representatives of coffee-growing regions from Guatemala to Panama met at a resort on the outskirts of Los Santos to collaborate with the OAS and key consultants on the viability of and strategies for the development of a Central American coffee tourism.

Egret Communications presented a summary of the assessment, and various representatives from Los Santos spoke of the progress made in Los Santos during the year following the assessment. Attendees took a tour of Coopedota to see how visitors would be led through the plant and to observe its progressive actions to reduce environmental impacts. Egret and Antonio Arreaga spoke of the process of performing assessments in each location and then the process of addressing each region's challenges to the development of coffee tourism.

One of the most important parts of this discussion was that the ramp up of coffee tourism was not to follow a 'cookie cutter' process. Egret pointed out that there were key differences among the coffee-growing regions that required individual strategies for each region, including culture, land ownership patterns, variations in coffee and coffee culture, sizes of communities and local capacity for investment. Further, some coffee regions already had an existing flow of visitors that might be tapped into, had tourism infrastructure including hotels and dining facilities, had more bilingual residents etc. There were also distinct differences in the way tourism could be engineered to put revenues into the hands of coffee-growing families, especially in regions dominated by larger growers with many hired workers.

Some areas, particularly in Panama and Guatemala, had been following the progress in Los Santos quite closely and were already in the process of raising their own capacity to enter a tourism economy.

There was further discussion related to travel patterns. Egret maintained that evolving tourism patterns supported, at least in the initial years, a pattern of mixing coffee, nature and culture into a single country trip design. Some participants were eager to see the day when visitors would take longer trips focused only on coffee, visiting coffee-growing areas in several countries on a single trip.

There was strong agreement on the need to establish La Ruta del Café as a brand, and for each coffee-growing area to showcase the coffees of all Central America to incoming visitors. There was substantial discussion about the possibility of using tourism to support the development of direct marketing of Central American coffee to consumers, again raising the value of coffee produced in each region and channeling revenues to coffee-growing communities.

Egret also spoke of a need to move the concept of La Ruta del Café from an idea supported by international grants to an organization that would have the capacity to self-fund in the future. The OAS endorsed the need for the project to 'grow its own legs' because long-term international underwriting was not going to be forthcoming. Cecil Miller, Director of the Intersectoral Unit on Tourism at the OAS, maintained that unless the OAS could see a path to self-sufficiency, it simply could not fund the development.

The Encuentro ended with the following intentions:

- Develop a strategy to incorporate La Ruta del Café, probably as an international NGO.
- Develop a full-blown plan for ramping up La Ruta del Café, including:
  - Assessments.
  - Capacity raising.

- Training.
- Marketing.
- Building mechanisms for self-perpetuation.

Testing the Market: Bringing a Representative Audience

Egret brought a pilot tour to Los Santos in January 2004 (Plate 13.4). Drawing on a group of people that met specific demographic and experiential needs, Egret put together a custom tour that wove together the Los Santos coffee experience with local nature and another popular Costa Rica nature tour destination. The pilot was funded by the participants, with support from El Toucanet lodge (lower rates), Coopedota (free tours) and Rodrigo Jimenez (free visits to the coffee shop).

The participants included one couple from California's wine country (who have first-hand knowledge of winery operation and wine tourism) and a cranberry farmer who was looking at agritourism opportunities. All were from the USA (coast to coast) – none spoke significant Spanish.

Plate 13.4 Coopedota staffer instructs pilot tour participant on coffee-picking procedures, Los Santos, Costa Rica (Source: Diane Kelsay)

Several had serious interests in nature photography. Most had participated in international nature or culture tourism in the past. Some were in very good physical condition and used to outdoor activities, while others had limited physical abilities. None were serious coffee aficionados – in fact none had a real sense of how coffee is grown or processed, or what factors contribute to quality coffee.

The group lodged at El Toucanet for its stay in Los Santos and took several days to explore both nature and coffee. They picked coffee, watched as coffee was delivered to the mill, followed it through processing (see Plates 13.5 and 13.6), participated in sun drying, had a tasting experience and discussion with the manager of the cooperative, and took huge quantities of coffee home with them. They created countless photographic images of coffee farming and harvest, and of the processes at the mill. They delighted in the coffee drinks at the coffee shop.

The group both saw and photographed resplendent quetzals, had experiences in the cloud forest and marveled at nearby paramo habitat. They were fascinated with the setting at El Toucanet and were captivated with photographing the hummingbirds and other birds at the lodge. The pilot tour then moved to Arenal Volcano to explore the volcano, the rainforest canopy and experience a zipline. The resort atmosphere was certainly more sophisticated and the volcano and rainforest experiences were much appreciated.

As a whole, the group thought that the Los Santos experience was superior to the Arenal experience because they appreciated the sense of getting to know Costa Rica – and felt they were treated as individuals

Plate 13.5 Washing coffee cherries in Coopedota's micro lots processing facility, Los Santos, Costa Rica (Source: Diane Kelsay)

Plate 13.6 Cherries are fed into Coopedota's sorter before fermentation, Los Santos, Costa Rica (Source: Bob Harvey)

rather than processed as a group. They all valued their coffee experience and intended to advise others to try a similar experience. They all intended to go home and buy coffee from Coopedota in the future. They reported noise-level concerns on the tour through the coffee mill and had some advice on the organization of the tour.

Egret, after watching the group throughout the pilot tour, interviewing participants along the way and conducting post-tour interviews concluded:

- The mix of nature tourism and coffee tourism works well. Visitors had a clear set of expectations of Costa Rica's nature tourism products and were willing to add coffee tourism (about which they had little preconceptions).
- Los Santos is an excellent place to learn about coffee tourism – and visitors went away with strongly positive views on their experience and on the community.
- Los Santos is an excellent place to deliver nature tourism experiences.

- The small-scale design of this tour (10 participants) enabled visitors and hosts to feel satisfaction with the encounters. Note that the tour group expressed concern that if tourism was developed on the scale that they saw in Arenal, then there would be negative consequences for both host communities and the quality of the tour experience.
- The group expressed great pleasure in having their guide know the coffee farmers by name – and really enjoyed passing questions and answers back and forth through the guide/interpreter.
- These visitors strongly expressed that they thought the experience in Los Santos allowed them to see and understand the 'real' Costa Rica and not a 'prepared-for-visitors' tourism product. They valued this.

Spring 2004

Following el Encuentro and the Pilot Tour, things were on a roll. Egret, Grulex and the OAS were in frequent contact. Los Santos was buzzing with enthusiasm and actively taking steps to get ready for tourism. And communities up and down Central America were preparing to be spun into La Ruta del Café and expecting to both realize tourism revenues and raise the value of their coffees.

Egret and the OAS shared a concern. There was, in our minds, a real need to set this project in motion in a way that actually achieved results, rather than spending money. We were strongly focused on the need to create and institutionalize mechanisms to perpetuate La Ruta del Café with the knowledge that outside support would go away sooner rather than later. We were concerned that while the coffee-growing communities were strongly embracing the concept of La Ruta del Café, there was a need for those communities to unite that energy under the roof of a single multinational organization (either for profit or not for profit).

Telephone calls and emails flew back and forth between Egret, Grulex and Cecil Miller at the OAS in a frenzy of activity. Between February and early April, we all suggested and then tested scenarios to ramp up the program while building in mechanisms to manage it and secure self-funding for the long term. We looked at self-imposed taxes on rooms, on retail in target zones, on lodging and on coffee itself. We looked at how to phase training, infrastructure development and startup and when and how to initiate marketing. And we looked at strategies for disengaging international economic assistance and project dependence on outside leadership.

By early April 2004, we had a project design that was endorsed on all sides (Miller *et al.*, 2004). It would, over three years, bring all targets through assessment, training and begin to address infrastructure needs. It would build and set free an international organization owned by the coffee-growing communities. It would research and then settle on a set of mechanisms to constantly reprime the organization economically. It would set standards for products within La Ruta del Café, to protect the quality of the brand. It would bring in a set of tourism and coffee partners to strengthen the alliance. And, it would launch La Ruta del Café in a way that set the effort up for success. The project had a lean and efficient budget and plenty of safeguards to protect both the recipients and the OAS.

Then all hell broke loose. The Bush administration, in Washington DC, announced it would default on the USA commitments to the project in order to use those funds to continue prosecuting its war with Iraq. Within days, the OAS had reduced its operations. The Intersectoral Unit for Tourism was disbanded and the few remaining functions were folded into other portfolios. Cecil Miller was gone from the OAS. And so were the promises to the coffee-growing communities in Central America.

The Next Stage

Following the collapse of the OAS support for La Ruta del Café, there was a deafening silence. No one knew what to say or do. Everyone involved in the project was in shock. The people of Los Santos had come the furthest, had the most invested and had really begun to imagine an appropriately scaled and locally controlled tourism economy that they intended to be a part of. Where to go from here?

The situation demonstrated that one of the hardest things to deal with in planning rural tourism is the time between when a host community begins to believe that something will happen and having that something happen. The promise is on the table. People begin making life decisions, whether those decisions are appropriate or not. Skepticism has become hope. Trust makes people and communities vulnerable. There is a responsibility on the part of those involved, once that corner has been turned, to go the rest of the way.

Egret, using its own resources and working with leaders in Los Santos, began to plan a repeat of the pilot trip and to think through how we might connect them with international investors to support the development of that coffee lodge we had all looked at. Egret began distance coaching the evolution of tourism in Los Santos, using annual pilot tours to fund some time in the region.

Slowly, things began to evolve in Los Santos. The key to capturing at least some of the coffee tourism revenues and spreading it out among the people of the valley turned out to be the progressive cooperative. Coopedota was interested in tourism and willing to approach it in a way that both captured visitor revenues and distributed them among members. The cooperative was willing to learn to roast coffee and create products that it could retail to visitors. It began the process of designing tours – and was willing to refine and refine until those tours resonated among visitors. It hired a bilingual guide and taught her the nuances of coffee production, roasting and preparation. It began charging for the tours, selling both coffee and related retail, developed a 'tasting' portion to the tour, and opened a retail café. All revenue, including the guide tips, was put into a fund for general distribution to membership.

Los Santos is a substantial drive from any place with adequate tourism lodging. Some visitors lodge in a valley further south. There is a substantial tourism zone west, along the Pacific Coast, but roads are poor and frequently impassible. Visitors to San Jose (big population center but also a place most visitors move away from into areas along the coast or near national parks) have a two hour drive along a challenging section of the Pan American Highway to reach the turnoff to this tranquil region – and they have alternative opportunities to visit coffee farms prepared for the bus tourism along the route between San Jose and the Pacific cruise ship terminal.

Those distances from lodging mean that most visitors to Los Santos are day visitors, leaving key lodging and dining revenues outside the region. The lack of lodging has kept visitor counts to the region low. The lodges to the south have built some day tours to the valley – most of those stop only at Coopedota. Guided tourism, in this case, has been pretty good at limiting impacts. Tours have primarily stopped where people are working (primarily picking) in the coffee fincas (farms). Self-guided tourism, at this point, has not presented a significant volume, nor generated many social impacts.

Given the driving distances, tourism cannot grow appreciably without a significant lodging component. And, if it were to grow, the region, because it would only be serving day visitors, would receive only a small stream of revenue. Growing revenue substantially in this scenario means growing visitor counts. Growing visitor counts substantially would be both difficult – and prone to creating social impacts.

El Toucanet gradually bootstrapped its way to a bigger lodge, with better amenities. They built a reputation for birding that began to send a steady stream of visitors their way from both North America and Europe. They have an additional flow of national patrons, who are less interested in nature but add to the bottom line. El Toucanet does take as many guests to Coopedota for the coffee tour as they can interest.

Egret, Coopedota, Antonio Arreaga and Rodrigo Jimenez have continued to explore the concept of a coffee lodge. Egret, with input from the others, worked to engineer a lodge operational design that would be beneficial to Los Santos while profitable for investors. Models were tested and adjusted. Sites were explored. The cooperative board endorsed the concept of Coopedota as a partner, an investor in a lodge. Potential investors looked at the project. Some were ready to go, while others wanted to wait. Some potential investors were not a good match for the valley. One set of investors had to be turned away because their intentions were clearly not a match for the project. Each experience helped refine the concept – but time has also worked to erode the confidence of the people of Los Santos in the likelihood that tourism will become their tool to address their needs.

In May 2009, Egret brought a financial expert to Los Santos to revise the coffee lodge construction and operation design to make it more attractive to investors. A revised coffee resort and tour company concept will be presented to investors in the fall of 2009. The development of the resort and tour company would go a long way to creating a critical mass of coffee-related visitors to Los Santos and begin to leverage some measureable gains into coffee growers' bottom lines.

Summary

Coffee tourism, in and of itself, is viable. The processes of raising and processing coffee, especially on a small scale, are fascinating and resonate well with visitors who are interested in learning about the places they visit. Tasting coffee in the manner that professionals evaluate coffee for purchase is sophisticated and quite ritualistic – and very engaging. The whole coffee raising/processing/roasting/tasting scene is both educational and captivating. And, coffee tourism lends itself to retail spending.

Engineering coffee tourism to benefit those economically small family operations that produce coffee was challenging. In Costa Rica, the presence of strong and effective cooperatives presented a viable path for the flow of those economic benefits. Further, while coffee is labor intensive, particularly during harvest, coffee-growing families often have some ability to become at least part-time employees or entrepreneurs in a tourism environment.

The development of coffee tourism in an environment where there are larger plantations owned by fewer (and larger) operations promises to be an easier enterprise. The difficulty in that situation is related to ensuring that the benefits of such tourism reach the levels of the community that need it most.

It is always difficult to enable investment in a struggling economy, especially when that investment is intended to be profitable to the investors and to function within social limits in the target economy. While the path to building a viable tourism economy in Los Santos has been complicated by the consequences of the war in Iraq and the economic downturn of 2008, this team remains convinced that 'the numbers are there' for both investors and Los Santos.

References

Dasenbrock, J. (2002) *The Pros and Cons of Ecotourism in Costa Rica*. Trade and Environmental Data Base Case Study.

Davids, K. (1979) *Coffee: A Guide to Brewing and Enjoying Coffee*. San Francisco: 101 Productions.

Harvey, R. and Kelsay, D. (1999) *Tourism Options for Honduras in the Wake of Hurricane Mitch*. Report to Norman Garcia, Ministry of Tourism, Honduras.

Harvey, R. and Kelsay, D. (2003) *Los Santos: Assessment for Coffee Tourism Pilot Program*. Report to Organization of American States. Egret Communications.

Harvey, R. and Kelsay, D. (2004) *Tourism and Coffee in Central America, La Ruta del Café*. Report to First Encuentra on La Ruta del Café. Egret Communications.

Miller, C., Harvey, R. and Kelsay, D. (2004) *Budgetary Considerations for the Sustainable Implementation of La Ruta del Café*. Collaborative planning document between Organization of American States and Egret Communications.

Thorn, J. (2006) *The Coffee Companion: A Connoisseur's Guide*. Philadelphia, PA: Quintet Publishing Limited.

Whelen, T. (1991) *Nature Tourism: Managing for the Environment*. Washington, DC: Island Press.

Part 5

Conclusion

Chapter 14
Coffee and Tourism Research Directions

LEE JOLLIFFE

While coffee is pervasive in everyday life as a beverage, the value of coffee-related tourism as explored through this book is seen as primarily relating to the use of coffee culture for tourism, destination development and place-related experiences, and coffee tourism projects aimed at improving the livelihoods of coffee farmers in producing countries. This concluding chapter reviews these core themes exhibited by the book chapters, linking into existing research traditions in the history and sociology of food, the study of culinary tourism experiences, food and beverage in hospitality management and fair trade tourism, while suggesting considerable scope for future research.

Coffee culture provided a context for this research. This culture is a powerful force in modern society, as illustrated by the global rise of Starbucks (Clark, 2007). Consumers are exposed to coffee from around the world, both at their local café and during travel. Coffee culture has been globalized with the local café, and café districts have evolved from the historical roots of coffee houses (Pendergast, 2001) into social spaces (Boniface, 2003) where coffee is consumed. Café culture is designed in terms of a service environment (see Chapter 2). Coffee culture becomes part of the urban tourism experience as documented (see Chapter 3) and is also an event (see Chapter 5).

There is a rich culture of artifacts associated with coffee in terms of the equipment used for production, processing, roasting, preparation and serving. This evidence is found in operating contexts, in museums, in the commercial café and also in home settings, as noted by White (Chapter 4) in the case of Australia. There is the possibility for some artifacts related to coffee and for coffee beans to be purchased as souvenir reminders and memories of the coffee experience.

Coffee is place related in many complex and interrelated aspects, be it the place where it is consumed or the place where it is originally produced and this aspect has potential for cross-branding of the coffee product with related coffee destinations and experiences. At the point of consumption, coffee culture exhibited through cafés is a resource for the development of coffee-related tourism experiences. Clustered together in districts, cafés can be a powerful force in developing destinations. This has been amply demonstrated in the book with the development of café districts in Wellington, New Zealand (see Chapter 3) and Melbourne, Australia (see Chapter 7). Clustering encourages the development of cultural and arts districts and in some cases these café districts become ingrained as part of the destination image (Chapter 7). In another example, Toronto, Canada's Art and Design District (see Chapter 1) is nurturing café development as the café form reinvents itself in the context of such a district, as is evidenced by the Café Patio of the Drake Hotel and the Ballroom Café of the Gladstone Hotel.

As discussed throughout the book, coffee is inextricably linked with hospitality and tourism. Coffee is an integral and pervasive aspect of hospitality and is a part of many if not most travel and tourism experiences. In the hospitality setting, coffee can act as an attraction, when coffee cultures in café settings are featured. The traditional café environment, in an original or commoditized form, can serve to attract tourists, enabling them to have a coffee experience perceived of as being local and authentic even if it is not, as exhibited by the case of the transformation of the traditional *kafeneion* coffee houses of Cyprus for the purpose of tourism (see Chapter 5).

As with tea tourism (Jolliffe, 2007), coffee-related tourism can be viewed as a special interest or niche tourism activity of the type described by Novelli (2005) and a subset of culinary tourism. On the other hand, as indicated in Chapter 1, while many tourists will experience some aspects of coffee and coffee culture during their travels, only a few will dedicate their travels to coffee tourism. Those very few might perhaps be identified as dedicated coffee enthusiasts, and if viewed from a tourism perspective, as dedicated coffee tourists.

Given the popularity of coffee as a beverage, there is capacity to develop a variety of coffee tourism experiences as a tourism product. For example, in New York City, coffee-tasting (cupping) sessions have become a popular activity at independent cafés, with willing participants paying $20 each to taste coffee from three origins (Wallace, 2008); this type of activity would appeal to culinary tourists. In Italy, the Illy-sponsored University of Coffee offers programs for professionals, coffee lovers and producers, franchising these programs to other countries, including Brazil, the USA and the UK. When offered to tourists, such coffee education opportunities could easily be seen as part of a culinary-focused coffee tourism. However, for coffee-related tourism to be more than just an activity for a few enthusiasts, such opportunities would need to be assembled and formally packaged into dedicated coffee tourism products.

Tourism to coffee-producing locations has emerged as a tool for educating coffee consumers, as in the case of Canada's Just Us! Coffee's foray into coffee tours (see Chapter 11), as well as for diversifying and enhancing the livelihoods of coffee farmers and their communities, as in the case of local coffee tours in Tanzania (see Chapter 12) and Costa Rica (see Chapter 13). These case examples demonstrate that coffee-related tourism holds considerable promise for adding value to coffee production in producing countries. In Hawai'i, coffee-related tourism is also providing a viable alternative for coffee farmers to augment incomes derived from coffee farming (see Chapter 8). In the case of Papua New Guinea (see Chapter 9), while coffee tourism has not so far emerged as a method to improve the livelihood of coffee farmers, this could happen on a small scale in the future (if even through business travel) should the security position improve.

Project case studies such as those presented in this volume need to be disseminated as 'best practice' approaches for developing the type of coffee-related tourism discussed here, in coffee-producing countries around the globe. As pointed out in the case of Costa Rica (see Chapter 13), engineering coffee tourism for the economic benefit of small-scale coffee producers is challenging. Therefore, it is suggested that a methodical approach needs to be taken to documentation on coffee-related tourism development projects (see, in particular, Chapters 11–13), and that such work needs to be widely discussed and distributed.

In the case of these responsible tourism coffee projects, those participating in such coffee-related tourism, defined earlier in this volume as 'related to the consumption of the coffee, history, traditions, products and culture of a destination' (Jolliffe & Bui, 2006), can become informed consumers, returning home with new insights into coffee production and the livelihoods of the producers. By participating in the purchase of fair trade coffees (see Chapters 5, 10 and 11), these consumers also have an opportunity to support the improvement of coffee farmer livelihoods, without leaving home.

Research Frameworks

In a previous paper, Jolliffe (2007) identified three assumptions to frame research on tourism related to coffee:

- That coffee tourism may be a potential niche or special interest area of tourism.
- That the demographics of coffee consumption inform the potential profile of the coffee tourist.
- That coffee tourism at producing locations has potential for community tourism projects that have the ability to impact positively on the quality of life of the local population through poverty reduction.

This book has further illuminated, illustrated and discussed these assumptions, identifying the coffee tourism niche as being small but apparent (see Chapters 8 and 9); looking at the demographics of coffee drinkers' experiences as international coffee tourists (see Chapter 6) and exhibiting cases of the possible benefits of community tourism projects in coffee-producing countries (see Chapters 11–13).

This volume has also uncovered other perspectives of coffee-related tourism, identifying four key areas and providing a framework for further research on tourism related to coffee:

- The history and sociology of food.
- The study of culinary tourism destinations and experiences.
- The area of food and beverage management within hospitality management.
- The subject of fair trade and tourism.

Studies in the history and sociology of food area usually mention coffee, briefly providing some context for understanding both the coffee context and the development of tourism related to coffee (see Tannahill, 1973; Telfer, 1996). For example, from a historical perspective, Montanari (1994: 167) notes the value attributed to coffee in the 18th century 'represented as the drink of intelligence and efficiency in contrast to traditional aristocratic idleness and dullness'.

According to Wood (2007), significant research on touristic experiences of food and its geographic contexts comes from geographers (such as Boniface, 2003; Hall *et al.*, 2003). Culinary tourism researchers have documented culinary tourism experiences, Long (1994) being recognized as the first to discuss 'culinary tourism' in terms of the idea of experiencing other cultures through food. Researchers such as Hjalager (2003) have also offered a model of culinary tourism experiences, depicting food and beverage preferences according to the categories of recreational, existential, diversionary and experimental gastronomy tourists. Other researchers, such as Kivela and Crotts (2006), have explored the influence of gastronomy on how tourists experience a destination. Coffee, with its rich variations and different preparations could definitely be further explored as tourism destination experiences within the culinary and gastronomic tourism study frameworks mentioned here.

Wood (2007) examines the future of food and beverage research, noting that within hospitality management this subject is drastically underresearched. The food and beverage literature has included gastronomic comments on food and beverage as well as formal texts on the history, philosophy, culture and sociology of food and eating (e.g. Tannahill, 1973; Telfer, 1996), providing a context for future research on coffee within the food and beverage research subject area.

At the local level, fair trade coffee has been incorporated as a way to connect local consumers with coffee producers and their locations, as outlined by Hall (see Chapter 10) and Chesworth (see Chapter 11). As Know and Huffaker (1997: 163–164) observe: 'A relationship with coffee allows us to travel vicariously to intriguing parts of the developing world; accompanying the excitement of this kind of exploration is a responsibility to try and see coffee through the eyes of the people who grow it'.

The global coffee giant, Starbucks, initially resistant to the concept of fair trade, adopted selling fair trade coffee in 2000 and has since used this as a social action marketing tactic (Jaffee, 2007). This fair trade concept, originally applied to the production of goods, has evolved into fair trade forms of tourism, and likewise fair trade coffee has in some cases morphed into fair trade coffee tourism projects.

Future Research

Each chapter in the book has provided a different view of the connection of coffee to tourism, from the diverse perspectives of different disciplines and varied coffee contexts that include the café, café districts, coffee events, coffee destinations, coffee tourism experiences (both planned and serendipitous), coffee tours and other forms of coffee tourism at producing locations.

Drawing from the analysis in this volume, some topics for future research on coffee and tourism may include:

- Studies of the history and sociology of coffee consumption.
- Identification of elements and stages in development of café districts, coffee tours and events.

- Proposal of coffee destination experience typologies.
- Studies of coffee beverage management in a hospitality context.
- Participatory research with coffee-related tourism development projects in producing countries.

This book is the first to specifically broadly explore the relationship between coffee culture, destinations and tourism, setting the foundation for continued research. Areas for future research are many, as identified above. More needs to be known about the motivations of tourists in terms of coffee – do tourists indeed want to experience more about coffee than just beverage consumption as they travel? – and this could be a rich area for prospective research. There is also potential for more dedicated research into the use of coffee tourism as a development tool at coffee-producing locations, harnessing the power of tourism at the grass roots to improve the livelihoods of the farmers who produce the beans for our daily cup of coffee.

Conclusion

Rather than arguing for the establishment of coffee tourism as a niche type of tourism worthy of study, this volume has instead taken a broad based view of the myriad connections between coffee culture, hospitality and tourism, sketching out the import of the relationships and providing perspectives of the current study of coffee culture in relation to destinations and the broader phenomenon of tourism. The volume nonetheless advocates that there should be further study of this connection between coffee and tourism, particularly with respect to the dynamic coffee cultures around the world, investigating how both café enterprises and destinations are capitalizing on the power of such culture, for branding, marketing and creating experiences for locals and tourists. Of no less importance is the value of coffee tourism as a tool for improving the livelihoods of coffee farmers and their communities, possibly alleviating some of the adversity caused by the global coffee crisis. For students of tourism, academics, destination managers and tourism development specialists, their next cup of coffee may therefore offer a window on the world of possibilities for positive cultural change when coffee and tourism are connected under a cultural and socially responsible lens.

References

Boniface, P. (2003) *Tasting Tourism: Travelling for Food and Drink*. Aldershot: Ashgate.

Clark, T. (2007) *Starbucked: A Double Tall Tale of Caffeine, Commerce and Culture*. New York: Little, Brown and Company.

Hall, C.M., and Sharples, E. (2003) The consumption of experiences or the experience of consumption?: An introduction to the tourism of taste. In C.M. Hall, E. Sharples, B. Camborne, N. Macionis and R. Mitchell (eds) *Food Tourism Around the World: Development, Management and Markets* (pp. 1–24). London: Butterworth-Heinemann.

Illy University. On WWW at http://www.illy.com/wps/wcm/connect/us/illy/the-world-of-coffee/universita-del-caffe/. Accessed 31.7.09.

Jaffe, D. (2007) *Brewing Justice, Fair Trade Coffee, Sustainability and Survival.* Berkeley, CA: University of California Press.

Jolliffe, L. (2007) Coffee and tourism: A research framework. Presented at the 2nd International Conference on Tourism and Hospitality, Universiti Utara Malaysia and The Department of National Heritage, Ministry of Culture, Arts and Heritage Malaysia, Putrajaya, Malaysia.

Jolliffe, L. and Bui, T.H. (2006) Coffee and tourism in Vietnam: A niche tourism product? Presented at the Travel and Tourism Research Association – Canada Chapter Conference at Montebello, Quebec.

Kivela, J. and Crotts, J.C. (2006) Tourism and gastronomy: Gastronomy's influence on how tourists experience a destination. *Journal of Hospitality and Tourism Research* 30 (3), 354–377.

Knox, K. and Huffaker, J.S. (1997) *Coffee Basics: A Quick and Easy Guide.* New York: John Wiley and Sons Inc.

Montanari, M. (1994) *The Culture of Food.* Oxford: Blackwell.

Novelli, M. (2005) *Niche Tourism Contemporary Issues, Trends and Cases.* London: Butterworth-Heinemann.

Pendergast, M. (1999) *Uncommon Grounds: This History of Coffee and How it Transformed Our World.* New York: Basic Books.

Richards, G. and Hjalager, A. (2002) *Tourism and Gastronomy.* London: Routledge.

Tannahill, R. (1973) *Food in History.* New York: Crown Trade Paperbacks.

Telfer, E. (1996) *Food for Thought: Philosophy and Food.* London: Routledge.

Wallace, H. (2008) Do I Detect a Hint of . . . Joe? *The New York Times*, 29 May.

Wood, R. (2007) The future of food and beverage management research. *Journal of Hospitality and Tourism Management* 14 (1), 6–16.

Index